Big Bucks

Big Bucks

The True, Outrageous Story of the Plymouth Mail Robbery & How They Got Away With It

Ernest Tidyman

W. W. Norton & Company

NEW YORK / LONDON

Published simultaneously in Canada by
George J. McLeod Limited, Toronto.
Printed in the United States of America
First Edition
Library of Congress Cataloging in Publication Data
Tidyman, Ernest. / Big bucks.
I. Title. II. Title: Plymouth mail robbery.
PS3570.I3B5 1982   813'.54   81–22335
                                                AACR2
W. W. Norton & Company, Inc.
500 Fifth Avenue, New York, N.Y. 10110
W. W. Norton & Company Ltd.
37 Great Russell Street, London WC1B 3NU
1 2 3 4 5 6 7 8 9 0

ISBN 0-393-01459-2

Chris
Thee and me.
Ernest

Contents

Author's Note

I was invited to write the true story of the Plymouth mail robbery by a man I believe to have been one of the participants. Up to that time, in 1962, it was the largest cash haul of its kind ever to have been made. I reviewed this astonishing firsthand information in weeks and months of interviewing. This is essentially the story I found, with almost all the names changed, and some reconstruction of conversations. The characters (on both sides of the law) are funny, frightening, brilliant, and evil.

In the course of my research, I contacted all of the investigative agencies involved in the case. The Federal Bureau of Investigation offered to answer "specific" questions to the extent that its records were available. A spokesman for that agency expressed doubt that such records existed, since the over-all control of the investigation rested with the Postal Inspection Service, the statute of limitations on the case had run out, and the agency regularly eliminates what it considers unnecessary and unproductive files. The Massachusetts State Police were cooperative but their information was fragmented and limited. The Boston City Police offered only peripheral data since the robbery took place outside the city limits and their role was to supplement the investigation only when the trail led across the city line.

The Postal Inspection Service has about twenty-five four-drawer filing cabinets filled with material concerning this case. Unfortunately, I was denied access to this rich mine of information in a letter from C. Neil Benson, chief postal inspector of the United States, who gave the following reason:

After careful consideration of your request, I have concluded that I cannot responsibly comply. . . . To allow unrestricted access to the records would involve a violation of personal privacy to a degree I regard as impermissible. I am also concerned with the physical safety of people who furnished information during this investigation.

So this is the story that comes from the other side—the inside—about some very unusual men and women, a bold and spectacular crime, and the fascinating chase that followed. This is the Plymouth mail robbery of August 14, 1962.

Ernest Tidyman
Spring, 1982

Acknowledgments

*The author wishes to acknowledge,
with gratitude, the professional research
assistance of Natalie Jaffe, and the
ongoing help of Richard Chicofsky and
Anthony J. Narekiewicz as guides
through Darkest Boston.*

Big Bucks

The Plot

Boston, Spring, 1962. The most European of American cities primps and paints for the annual influx of tourists looking for as much culture and tradition as a few hundred years can impart. And if the sky is gray, the mood is bright.

Among those Bostonians who found hope and expectations in the season, there walked one man who believed that this was his moment of greatness in a life of middle-class mediocrity. His name was Phil Kalis, and, just past his forty-second birthday, he had been a professional journalist and writer for more than twenty years. Phil Kalis looked like a middle-aged merchant of Mediterranean origin. On this morning late in May, Kalis moved quickly through the clusters of office workers who come to the commercial center of Boston every morning from dozens of such small residential suburbs as Walpole, Falmouth, Braintree, Waverly, Quincy, and Dedham. Kalis's destination was the United States Post Office in Post Office Square, facing Congress Street, a long gray building that is the

center of mail operations for the northeastern United
States. Kalis had ridden an hour and eleven minutes
on a rattling commuter train into the city and deviated
from his daily route to that building only far enough to
pick up a container of coffee. Wearing a rumpled suit
and a bow tie perched on the collar of his white shirt,
Kalis was a familiar figure of familiar habits.

The guard in the lobby of the building nodded to
Kalis, and the ancient who ran the elevator Kalis
boarded remarked on the weather.

Only casual notice was taken of Kalis's arrival in the
offices of the United States Postal Inspection Service,
where the faces of the agents responsible for the internal and external policing of the mails seemed to glow
with a green pallor reflected from the aging paint on
the walls. It was only Phil Kalis again. Kalis had written about them and he was regarded by them as a
friend. An old friend. He came to them every day, sat
on the corner of a desk, and asked what was going on.
If there was something new—if someone had forged a
bundle of postal money orders, if someone had been
apprehended mailing pornography in plain brown
wrappers, if a mail sorter had been unable to resist the
temptation of cash folded into a letter—the inspectors
told him. Kalis would make a few notes, drink his
coffee, and go away to write the story. If there was
nothing, he would simply take part in the small talk of
marital problems and joys, baseball scores, and what
the Kennedy brothers, who were Boston's own and a
constant subject for speculation, were doing in the
seats of power they occupied in Washington. They
might even mention Larry O'Brien, a Kennedy political savant from Boston who had been named special
assistant to the president.

But this morning, Kalis went a step further. Cautiously, casually.

"They going ahead with the Cape run?" he asked.

Frank Olney, cynical and suspicious specialist in mail fraud ranging from Arizona land schemes to blind box diploma mills, seemed amused.

"Yep," he said. "The banks decided they want to give it a try. It's cheaper than an armored car. They got all the money in the world and they want to save nickels."

Kalis nodded and grunted. But sweat seemed to pop out of every pore on his six-foot frame, and a surge of excitement poured through his body like the rising chords of a Beethoven overture. He went pale. Olney noticed.

"You okay, Phil? You look like shit."

"Fucking coffee."

"Yeah. You oughta try Sanka."

Dan Murphy was a full-blooded Armenian. His real name sounded like the label on an imported rug. But this was Boston, and Boston was in the hands of the Irish—the Coughlins, the Curleys, the Devlins, and the O'Doughertys, not to mention the Kennedys. His father died young, and when his mother got married a second time to a man named Murphy in the construction business, Daniel took the name and the protective coloration that went with it. Some of his friends suggested that the name had rubbed off on him and made him look Irish. Murphy was a muscular six-foot-two, with a square, pale, thin-lipped face under light curly hair. There were faces like his passing down every street in Boston. They belonged to men whose ancestors had fled famine and repression in Ireland while Murphy's ancestors were fleeing from Turks in the Balkans.

On that spring day in 1962 Murphy was standing in the serving line of Drew's Cafeteria on Massachusetts

Avenue trying to persuade a cafeteria employee to put an extra portion of french dressing on his salad and an additional dollop of sweet and syrupy raisin sauce on his ham steak. Murphy was offering a ten-cent tip, one nickel for each. Though the steam-table attendant, a recent immigrant from Italy, was unfamiliar with the language, he knew the currency. He regarded the tip with a sneer equal to its denomination.

If the cafeteria attendant felt any satisfaction, it was justified. The big man in a stained sports jacket, shapeless slacks, and frayed, grimy-collared shirt, stalking down the line mumbling curses, was notoriously stingy. But he was more than that, much more. The attendant had just survived a confrontation with the most dangerous, most respected (by criminals and law enforcement officers alike), and most spectacular criminal in America. If Murphy had decreed it, with the smallest gesture and with no cost or effort, he could have sent the impudent waiter to a quick, painful death as the consequence of his insolence.

For at forty-seven (although Murphy claimed then and always had that his age was fifty-three, because he liked the sound of the numbers), he was the country's foremost bank and payroll robber and criminal strategist. The Mastermind. The Brain. A diabolically cunning figure whom Conan Doyle would have regarded as the peer of Moriarty, if not Holmes himself. Murphy was considered the true *consigliore*—the counselor—to the racketeers whose families of crime controlled the six-state New England territory from power bases in Providence and Boston, and they turned to Murphy with problems and questions of great importance. The dons and Capo Mafiosi had received guidance and help with solutions that had earned them millions of dollars, kept them out of prison, and tightened their hold on the organization of crime. For an individual of such standing, the death of an ill-mannered nonentity would mean no more than throwing a penny down a sewer.

Fortunately, Murphy could not be bothered with casual punishments. His mind was immediately flashing in other directions as he shambled across the gray-tiled floor to a wall table where he could watch the door. He ate without manners or pretension, gobbling ham steak and salad in huge bites, turning quickly to dessert. He plunged his fork into the thick mocha cake that would momentarily appease his insatiable hunger for sweets. A gooey chocolate mass with the consistency of drying concrete, it was Murphy's favorite food. When he raised the fork, he also picked up the entire wedge of cake and the plate beneath it. But he knew this predicament well. His thumb held the plate while his forefinger poked at the cake, and he pulled the fork free with a large glob on it. It was a problem and he solved it.

Murphy loved problems. His own, other people's, anything to think out. They were intellectual exercises that had gained him distinction and renown with the ubiquitous "they" of crime. Once they had called him and put to him the following question: How do we take over the gin mills without attracting a lot of attention and heat? Murphy pondered.

"With an ax," he said.

His plan was simple. You pick four of the fanciest and most profitable nightclubs and lounges in the Boston area. On a given night you send eight, maybe ten salamis into those places with axes and destroy them. Everything. Mirrors, bars, bottles, tables, juke boxes ... and the bartender and customers too if they protest.

But what if the operators of these four places are willing to spend two, maybe four hundred dollars a week to protect themselves against such a happenstance? What if they're already paying somebody?

That has nothing to do with it, Murphy explained. You destroy them and that sets an example that everyone can appreciate. Every place you did *not* destroy will give you anything you want and so will the first four places when they get back in business.

That was how Murphy solved one of the problems for the trade association that is called the Mafia. It was so simple, economical, and effective—and only a genius like Murphy could see it.

Naturally they called him again one day and put the following question to him: How do we take over the high-priced call girls who are working out of their homes and apartments but do not have pimps, and are clearing maybe one or two thousand a week? Murphy thought. This was harder because the girls moved around and were not fixed targets like nightclubs. But he figured it out.

"With a glass of water," Murphy said. Nobody smiled. They listened.

He told them to get the names of the call girls by making a date with one of them. Each one knows at least five or six others because they are always being called to supply the entertainment for conventions, business meetings, political gatherings. And once the names are known, you start making the rounds. Give two guys a glass of water. They call up a girl and make a date. They go to her apartment. When she opens the door with her professional smile, they throw the water in her face. They say, "That was a glass of water. The next time it is going to be acid." They tell the girl she can avoid this by simply appearing each Monday morning at a certain address with four $100 bills, which she will hand over, and then depart. And that's how they took over the high-priced call girls in Boston.

As Murphy's eminence as a strategist of corruption

became more widely acknowledged, there was a heightening in the complexity and gravity of the conundrums put to him, which included international power politics and assassination. There were even stars in the tarnished crown Murphy wore for his failures.

"They" came to Murphy once and asked the following question: How do you kill the premier of a Marxist republic in Latin America where major problems are being fomented for the land of the brave, the free, and the mob?

Murphy gave that question more thought than any of the others. His decision, he knew, would reach into the highest level of government.

"You don't," Murphy said finally. Not that he had any objection to blowing away a politician or anyone else. It came down to his conclusion that the circumstances could not be controlled. One, they had to go into the potential victim's territory—and what did they know about that? Two, the target knows he's a likely candidate for murder and you can't get close to him. Three, when he travels to this country, he's being guarded by the agencies run by the same people who want him dead, and you can't keep a set-up in a situation like that as silent as it must be. So forget it.

For the first time since the mid-1950s, when Murphy began to establish himself as an *éminence grise* of crime, his simple but solemn advice was unacceptable. There was too much pressure from sources on a political level beyond the control of even the most powerful among "them." The decision was made to continue with the plotting of the assassination. When Murphy repeated his warning, it was acknowledged almost apologetically. But they continued to move without him.

Ever the pragmatist, Murphy shrugged and went

back to his mocha cake. The assassination was attempted—and failed. The intended victim replied with a contract of his own on the life of the president of the United States. A year and a few months hence from this day in Boston, that contract would be closed on a Dallas street.

Phil Kalis came into Drew's Cafeteria at about one o'clock, looking for Murphy. With a cup of black coffee from the serving line, unable to put anything more on his nervous stomach, Kalis moved to Murphy's table.

"Yeah," Murphy said.

"Yeah," Kalis replied.

Kalis stared for a moment at Murphy's struggle with the cake. As Murphy licked icing off one finger, Kalis wondered how the man had survived on a diet of such crap. He had long known how Murphy had survived the convolutions of crime. The man was brilliant; he knew everything. And as far as Kalis could tell, it all came to Murphy out of the cosmos and he never let go of any of it. Kalis, like several others, could recall walking with Murphy up three blocks of crowded Beacon Street where cars were parked bumper to bumper —maybe 100 vehicles in all—when Murphy had been in a rare capricious mood. He told Kalis to jot down on his reporter's pad the make, color, and license plate number of each of the vehicles they passed. At the end of the third block they turned the corner, where Murphy stood, gazing at the passing traffic. Seeming not to be concentrating, Murphy casually recited the make, model, and color of each car as well as each digit on every license plate without a single error and without more than two or three hesitations to clear his throat. The man knew everything; forgot nothing.

Murphy also survived, Kalis knew, by a certain variable code of honor in the murky world where he existed. For what Kalis was about to tell Murphy, Kalis would receive a substantial reward without any need to bargain, wheedle, or attempt to guarantee it.

On the other side of the table, Murphy was aware that Kalis would not have come to this cafeteria to find him unless this was an opportunity from which both might profit. A Greek bearing gifts—at a price. What was the gift? What was the price?

"There is this thing," Kalis said.

Murphy poured cream and four heaping teaspoons of sugar into his coffee—and waited as he stirred it into syrup.

"Out on the Cape," Kalis went on. "After the big weekends, the little banks are loaded with cash. They have to unload it on the Federal Reserve in the city."

Murphy shrugged with a flicker of his eyes. Of course there was a lot of money out on the Cape after a big weekend. So they stuck it in an armored car and drove it the fifty or sixty miles into the city with state troopers riding shotgun. Murphy liked armored cars— he robbed them regularly—and he had been thinking about going after one of them on the Cape for more than a year. But the conditions were not ideal. He liked to hit them in crowded city streets when they stopped. Open roads were too loose for a controlled situation, armored cars with a police escort too tough to crack.

"Some of these banks have decided to save the price of an armored car. They have made arrangements to mail the money to Boston in a Dodge van with just two guys, postal guys."

"How much?"

Kalis breathed deeply. The excitement pressing against his chest almost stifled him.

"A million at least, maybe two."

Murphy stared into Kalis's eyes for several seconds. Kalis felt the pressure of the mind behind the turquoise agates of Murphy's eyes.

"It's mostly singles, fives, and tens . . . only a few big bills," Kalis said.

"I don't give a shit if it's all in dimes," Murphy grunted, thus declaring that the money was as good as theirs—and signaling the start of what would become the largest cash robbery in history.

Conrad was sitting quietly in the little alcove between the living room and dining room of the old house. It was his library, and stacks of books, magazines, pamphlets, and professional journals of every sort were piled on the window casement, the small table in front of him, and another chair that was opposite him. He was happy, if Conrad ever was happy. This was the only time when Conrad, who thrashed violently even in his fitful, frequently broken sleep, was not leaping up from one chair and moving to another, tugging up his belt, waving his hands, doing a little dance, and getting back up in an instant. Conrad contained such frenetic energy and created such distraction with his constant and fascinating series of spasmodic gestures that he could mesmerize the individuals who watched him. But he never moved a muscle while he was reading.

Information fascinated Conrad, and he would sit for hours like a figure carved in stone, his huge gray eyes flashing across line after line after line. Since he was completely lacking in discrimination as to publication or subject, he was a warehouse of information. He could diagnose better than most internists the illnesses of his friends and could usually prescribe treatments and medication as well—on the basis of reports in medical journals and pharmaceutical bulletins that physicians had no time to study. Conrad also knew how to practice law, repair tractors, clear forests, and operate fish farms, while cultivating orchids. And he knew the works of contemporary and classical novelists more thoroughly than most scholars.

Anything he could get his hands on he read—and that was precisely how he got it. Conrad stole all of his reading material. The assumption among his associates was that he had picked up the habit of reading in prison to fill the solitary hours and control his nervous agitation in a small cell. There, he had become addicted to the magic of language.

Conrad was reading about the jungle Indians of Brazil in the *National Geographic* when the telephone in the bathroom rang. He folded down a corner of the page and moved his short bulky body through the quiet of the house. Conrad had six individual telephone lines running into the house. Some of them had several extensions. But the line into the downstairs bathroom was for one special instrument. Unless it was a wrong number, the caller could be only one person. As the phone continued to ring, Conrad ignored it until he had closed and locked the bathroom door. He picked up the phone and held it to his ear, waiting.

"Yeah," Murphy said. "The Grotto."

Conrad said nothing. He replaced the receiver and prepared to leave the house.

As Murphy sat in the far corner of the dark little bar in Waltham waiting for Conrad, his mind flashed across the logistical problems of robbing a mail truck that would be coming into Boston from the Cape on Route 3. There were advantages and disadvantages. It was a busy highway in the summer and well patrolled by the Massachusetts State Police. But the Kennedy compound was a distraction and the police neglected the highway to maintain the security of it. They were busy supplementing the secret service guards, providing patrol car escorts, or running errands. That was good. But knocking off a mail truck out in the open during the vacation season meant a high level of exposure. That was a disadvantage.

As Kalis could tell Murphy, the postal authorities had a positive record of solution and recovery in mail thefts—99 percent, in fact. But the primary concerns of the agency gave it little experience with mail heists, and other law enforcement agencies (notably the FBI) would become involved and possibly confuse the investigation. Murphy regarded the situation as potentially advantageous.

Well, that would come later. Now he had to plan the job, organize the gang, case it, schedule it, bring it off, and get away with it. So many problems, so many details. A robber's life was a hard one.

Conrad found Murphy in the shadows of the bar, and a rare smile seemed to be touching Murphy's thin lips as Conrad sat down and got rid of the waitress by ordering a Chivas. Murphy, who never drank liquor and frowned on its use by associates, condoned the lapse by Conrad in tribute to their mutual respect and the preliminary nature of this meeting. Later, Conrad, and any others, would abstain or get out.

"We got a thing," Murphy said.

"What do you need?"

"Some equipment. Heavy equipment."

"Cars?"

"Machine guns. Little ones. Those commando guns. Some other pieces."

"How many?"

Murphy paused. The plan was forming itself in his mind but he had not completely worked out the strategy of the strike, nor of the reconnaissance necessary to prepare for it. But in a few moments in a dark little bar on the edge of Boston he did just that.

"Six," he said. "Six of everything."

"How soon?"

"Now."

Gun running is an important small business in any major city, and it is an especially lively one in such ports as Boston, New York, New Orleans, Houston, San Francisco, and Seattle. Colt, Smith and Wesson, Ruger, Remington, Winchester, and several others are shipping guns out, while Walther, Browning, Beretta, Lama, and several others are shipping them in. There is no need for the man who requires guns to break into a gun store or into a home to rummage through a dresser drawer. There are special sources of supply, and Conrad knew exactly where to call to obtain the machine guns and pistols. With a nod, Conrad assured Murphy the calls would be made immediately, and the weapons would be ready whenever Murphy wished Conrad to pick them up, test them, and then distribute them to the team Murphy was beginning to organize. Conrad felt a twist of excitement compounding his normally frantic state: Murphy had declared him into a major caper. With another quick nod, Conrad acknowledged his involvement, pushed back his chair, and left Murphy spooning sugar into another cup of coffee. He wondered, on the basis of his medical knowledge, how Murphy managed to avoid diabetes. But he didn't mention it to him.

Joey and Frank were virtually inseparable. They found this mutual magnetism while growing up in the same neighborhood on the North Side of Boston —the Italian side. When they became friends, the two of them excluded most of their other acquaintances and formed a two-boy gang. They played some street games together, shagged a few of the same girls together.

When they finally got through adolescence, they were typical Italian-based street hoodlums—Joey and Frank, both of them skilled at the delinquencies available to urban youth, strong-arm robbery, petty stickups, car theft and stripping, extortion, and gambling.

As expected, they went into the same lines of business—operating gas stations and auto repair shops. They got married within a couple months of each other to attractive girls who were also friends. They followed the same patterns as adults, went out drinking and chasing girls together while their wives stayed at home, stuck up an occasional grocery store, and eventually went to prison together. Joey, tall, slim, his hooded eyes wide apart over a hooked but not unattractive nose, and Frank, shorter, squarer, more solid but extremely handsome—even though his nose had been broken in a street fight as a teenager—with his hair turning an early silver. Altogether, they were as worthless a pair of punks as ever passed before a judge.

That they had capabilities beyond these early qualities was apparent to Murphy—and perhaps to Murphy alone—when he met them in prison. He saw them as the sort of savages he needed to send into a bank first or to rush an armored car—men who could snarl, "Put the money in the bag or I'll blow your fuckin' head off." The intended victim would know they meant it. That was a special quality, the quality of conveying terror. During the three or four years Murphy was with them in the Massachusetts Correctional Institution (as the consequence of a mistake Murphy made by talking too much about a job, one he would never make again), he cultivated them for future use.

Murphy's style with them was didactic and stern. Did they want to spend their lives in and out of jail for petty bullshit? Did they want to continue fighting the prison system so their time was harder and longer than necessary? Or did they want to learn how to go the easy route, get out and get laid again, live free with plenty of money? They listened. Murphy laid down a program of behavior modification for them—made them quit fighting with the other cons, kept them close to the rules of the slammer, persuaded them to get close to the prison priest and serve at Mass as altar boys. It got them both quick paroles and they were his.

Murphy drove his battered, unwashed white Olds into the Texaco station Joey operated on North Hill Road about an hour after he had left Conrad. He bought a dollar's worth of gas, a parsimonious habit with clear logic behind it: "What the fuck do I need riding around with a lot of dollars in the gas tank?" Joey saw Murphy from the garage, wiped his hands on an oily rag, and came out to check the oil in the Olds. Under the shelter of the hood, the two of them peering at a tangle of wires and greasy engine parts, Murphy said, "We got this thing." They agreed to meet an hour later in a small room at the rear of Frank's muffler repair and body shop.

The two men waited patiently in the dark, gloomy back room at Frank's garage.

"What is it?" Frank asked.

"Who the fuck knows? He'll tell us."

"He won't tell us shit, and you know it."

"So he don't tell us. What do you think the Sox are gonna do tonight?"

"If Runnels stays hot, who knows? This kid Yastrzemski is something else. He oughta change his fuckin' name to something American."

Joey smiled. Frank's impatience was notorious. He

always wanted change, action, movement. Being a kid with him, being in prison with him, Joey had involved himself in a thousand incidents in which he took Frank's arm and said, "Come on . . . the guy don't mean anything . . . let's take a walk."

Frank always wanted to do something or somebody. He wanted action.

Murphy slipped into the room quietly. For a big, hulking man he could move as softly as snowflakes and also very swiftly. Beneath the layer of mocha cake fat on his frame lay the muscles acquired as a youth in the family construction business shoveling sand and gravel.

Frank wasted no greetings.

"What is this thing?" he demanded.

Murphy regarded him for a moment, letting the weight of his authority remind Frank that they would move at Murphy's pace or not at all.

"A mail truck," Murphy said. "Coming into the city from the Cape. We're going to take it."

"A mail truck!" Frank snorted. "What for, fucking postcards of sand dunes?"

"Shut up," Joey said. "We're ready."

Murphy glared at Frank.

"Yeah!" Frank said.

Murphy nodded. "I'll get you the details later," he said and slipped away. As he ambled down the street to his car, he thought it had been a reasonable beginning. He felt even better when he reached the car. There was a fresh bird-dropping splattered across the windshield on the passenger side. Murphy knew from some arcane snatch of Armenian folklore that this signified good luck. He found an old newspaper in the car, ripped off a section and covered the bird-dropping with it. It might rain, and he wanted to protect it as long as he could.

"Must have been a fucking eagle," he thought happily.

Finding Harry was not easy, even though he had left a wide trail of empty glasses and cigar stubs across the city of Boston. His most recent bacchanalian odyssey had begun in the Ritz-Carlton Bar at four o'-clock the previous afternoon. Since then he had consumed three stuffed lobsters, two orders of soft shell crabs, a dozen oysters on the half shell, and great amounts of beer, vodka, and Scotch. He had been in three renowned seafood restaurants on the Boston waterfront, several honky-tonks known as hangouts for prostitutes, and three hotel lounges. His appetite had inspired awe in each place. Harry could remember them hardly at all after the first two or three stops.

He now lay snoring lightly on a large bed in a Dedham motel with two attractive young women who specialized in servicing conventions that came into the larger Boston hotels. One was also the sister of a friend with whom Harry had done time for grand larceny at the Massachusetts Correctional Institution.

Harry, a husky, medium-tall man with round Slavic features, carried his gargantuan appetites from dining room to bedroom, and he satisfied them as frequently as circumstances permitted. As drunk as he got, and as sick as he should have been, Harry was capable of instant arousal and alertness, that enviable facility that frequently marks the man who spends his life on the run, where an instant will make the difference between freedom and prison. His eyes blinked open and his hand reached out at the first murmur of the telephone. His bulky, muscular body crushed the wind out of the dark-haired girl named Margaret as he reached over her to grab the phone. She did not protest.

For all Harry knew, or cared, she was dead.

"Yeah," he said.

"What the fuck are you doing now?" Murphy asked.

"Sleeping."

"I pick you up in five minutes."

Harry hung up. That gave him three minutes to stand under the cold shower, another minute to dress, and a final minute to leave two one-hundred dollar bills on the dresser for the girls and get downstairs.

As he stumbled to the shower, he tried to remember how much fun he had had.

Harry was having some difficulty seeing around the newspaper covering the birdshit on the windshield, but he knew better than to suggest removing it. He had met Murphy ten years earlier and accepted the myriad superstitions swirling in Murphy's mind because they always had some point. Murphy had turned the wheel over to Harry in the parking lot of the motel, an acknowledgment of Harry's reputation as the best wheelman in the business of robbery—or anything else that needed a fast man with a fast car. His perceptions were immediate and his reactions instantaneous, even now with a slight haze of debauchery rising from his body in the combined aromas of perfume and alcohol. His knowledge of what to do and his ability to do it quickly were the reasons for his presence next to Murphy, who seemed to be dozing beside him. Harry thought he would test.

"Where we goin'?" he asked softly, thinking that the roar of the car's air-conditioner would muffle his voice if Murphy was sleeping.

"Waverly," Murphy said.

"Where?"

"One-nineteen North Fenton Street in Waverly. Pull around back by the garage."

For all Harry knew, the garage contained anything from a hijacked armored car to a collection of stolen antique furniture of a period Murphy's wife favored for her parlor. Harry made a tight U-turn and headed for Waverly, hoping for a heavy rain to clear his view. His driving was governed by Murphy's superstitions. If he came to a funeral procession, Harry knew he was to stop, back up, and take another street. Murphy believed a cortege was as bad as birdshit was good. The same rule applied to fire engines. They were bad, and Harry could not drive down the same street as a fire engine. He had long since given up thinking that Murphy was crazy. But occasionally such idiosyncrasies caused him to wonder about his own sanity.

The garage of the small house in Waverly contained a six-month-old gold Pontiac, which had been stolen in Revere on May 12 of that year and placed in the garage at Murphy's instructions. Under the vehicle lay a sheet of plastic to catch the oil drippings and prevent any later connection between this car and this house, which Murphy had rented six months before the theft of the Olds and kept empty just to have the use of the garage. As soon as they entered, Harry knew why they were there. He had been brought there to check the car's reliability for use in a caper. He opened the hood and noted happily that Murphy or someone else had disengaged the battery cables. At least he didn't have to go out and steal a battery. He reattached the cables, tightened the clamps on the terminals with a wrench from the trunk of Murphy's car, checked the oil level, which was clean and full, and then turned the key. The engine groaned at being awakened from its slumber and then came to life. It was a new car. As soon as the oil had completed its cycle through the engine, it purred quietly. Harry listened carefully for warning creaks and coughs. None came.

"Sounds good," Harry said.

"Okay. There's a pickup we're gonna look at."

Harry turned off the engine and closed up the car. God only knew where Murphy had the pickup stashed.

Sam Gilardi was big. His fingers could be described as bananas. The muscles of his shoulders and biceps strained the seams of any off-the-rack suit when he tried to wear one, which wasn't often. He was a hulk, a brute. He was also dumb, but intensely loyal. And he was immensely valuable for robbing banks. Gilardi's size alone struck terror in a bank manager's soul. But if it didn't, Gilardi might pick the man up with one hand and bounce him off the door of the vault to jog his memory of the combination. This was his value to Murphy. This, his loyalty, and the fact that he had never been arrested or suspected of wrongdoing.

Gilardi's family had come to the United States from Canada along the familiar route that passes through Maine, where Sam had worked as a lumberjack. After a few winters in the woods, Massachusetts seemed like Florida, and Gilardi had drifted to Boston, where he was now working for a construction company. Gilardi was the man who crawled into holes and threw out the boulders inaccessible to machines. Gilardi was the man Murphy sent into situations where, if nothing else worked, his phenomenal physical strength could make the difference between success and failure.

Gilardi lived in the quiet suburb of North Weymouth with his wife and two small children. That was where Murphy found him that evening in his organizational tour. It was about ten o'clock and Gilardi was watching television, one brawny arm around the shoulders of his wife Alice, their children asleep in the rear bedroom.

Harry, who was still driving, rang the bell, and when Sam answered, he greeted him with a brief nod of recognition.

"Hi," Sam said, cheerfully. "Come on in." He was a very convivial, friendly man.

"No, you come out. Your friend wants to see you."

It dawned on Sam that this was a business call. With a word to Alice about being right back, he lumbered down the walk to the waiting car and smiled. He was always glad to see Murphy. Murphy had taught him how to rob banks without getting caught. Murphy had always seen that he had gotten a fair share of the loot. Murphy had lectured him on how to keep his mouth shut while being interrogated. Murphy had shown him a hundred and one things about how to have a good life while being dumb. He loved Murphy.

"Yeah," Murphy said, "get in a minute."

As Gilardi climbed into the back seat, Harry turned and strolled slowly down the sidewalk beneath the umbrella of sycamores. He was not bothered by Murphy's reluctance to speak with Sam in front of him. All of Murphy's associates accepted his theory that they could not make mistakes about what they did not hear.

"It's good to see you, Dan," Sam said.

"I didn't come out here to gossip," Murphy said. "There's this thing. A mail truck on the Cape. I'll tell you when. First there's going to be a couple of other things I want you for. You're not going anywhere?"

"No, no. I had a vacation just . . . "

"Shut up. So you'll be around. Go someplace cheap and buy a summer dress that fits you."

"A woman's dress?"

"How many fuckin' kinds of dresses are there? Yes, a woman's dress."

"Jesus, that's a big size."

"Then go to a big store. But get one."

"Okay, Dan. Sure. Anything you say."

"Another thing. You live in the quietest place of anybody. This is the asshole of the universe, you know that? After we do this number, this is where we drop everything. You put it behind a wall or something. You can do that?"

"Sure. Anything you say."

Down the street Harry heard the sound of the car door closing and knew the conference was over. He moved back toward the vehicle and slipped into the driver's seat at about the same time that Sam reentered his living room, sat down in front of the television set, and put his arm back around his wife's shoulders.

"What was that?" Alice asked him.

"Nothin'. Bullshit," Sam said.

In the car, Harry looked to Murphy for instructions. Murphy was looking at his watch. "I'm so fuckin' hungry I could eat a fender," he said. It was 10:38. "Let's go to Drew's."

"They close at eleven," Harry protested. "How're we gonna get there? This ain't an airplane."

"Get there," Murphy said, settling back in the seat as the best wheelman in the East roared away from the quiet little house in North Weymouth, startling the neighbors with a scream of tires, but determined to make the cafeteria before it went dark. He did.

T he dirty Volkswagen that was driven through various towns on the Cape and along its main highway was remembered from among all the other dirty Beetles because it was driven by "this big guy with a hooked nose with the ugliest broad you've ever

seen.... She was a monster." So Sam Gilardi didn't look
so good in a dress and a blonde wig (purloined from the
closet of Joey's dark-haired wife, Gina). That didn't
bother Murphy, who was driving the Volkswagen himself and casing the job. No one noticed the coincidence
that everywhere the Volkswagen appeared, it was
preceded by a red, white, and blue Dodge van belonging to the United States Postal Service, a truck that
stopped at post offices in Hyannis and Buzzard's Bay
and proceeded toward Boston along Route 6, the main
artery of the Cape, until it split off onto Route 3 at
Sagamore and moved toward Plymouth.

With the ugly broad as camouflage, Murphy was
making meticulous mental notes of the truck's movements and the two men who were operating it, Charles
Streeter and David Chaplin. When they had followed
the truck to the South Boston postal annex and seen it
vanish behind the steel gates of the building, Murphy
would call it a day and review his observations. The
"postals" were undeviating in following the same
route. They never stopped for anything but traffic
lights. They never drove faster than forty-five miles an
hour, and they acted like two innocents abroad on a
drive in the country. They wore .38 caliber pistols but
gave no indication that their vehicle contained anything more than mail, routine everyday mail.

Phil Kalis had given them a good one, and they
would all enjoy the spoils of a major score if Murphy
could plan well enough and act fast enough. He was
well prepared. In the previous ten years, since his release from the prison term for the Harvard Trust Company job in Belmont (a bank job he had planned with
his old partner Greek Billy), Murphy had set about
schooling himself in the techniques of bank robbery,
as well as the methods employed to solve them and
bring the robbers to justice. He became a scholar of

crime, reading every factual and fictional crime story he could find on the newsstands, in libraries, and in the Sunday supplements of newspapers. He did not care about the quality of the crimes themselves, no matter how sensational. He only wanted to know how the criminals had been caught, what mistakes they had made, what miscalculations, misjudgments, or misconduct. Murphy drew several conclusions from these studies, primary among them that most criminals were stupid and arrogant and, consequently, did not protect themselves by knowing the enemy. He also concluded that criminals spent too much time in the commission of crimes, that they attracted arrest by immediately changing the pattern of their lives. Further, he found that they failed to take advantage of simple diversionary techniques like false fire alarms or even bank robbery reports in one end of town while pulling a robbery in another area. There was no planning or reasoning. Murphy was a much better general than to let himself suffer failure from false pride, poor intelligence, or blind strategy.

How, he asked himself, would a Feebies' (Federal Bureau of Investigation Agents) surveillance compare with the technique employed by city or state police? And how could he find out? Because he had been questioned by many FBI agents on a number of occasions —and never forgot a face or anything else—it was relatively easy for Murphy to pick up on the movements of FBI agents from their headquarters in the Sheraton Building on Atlantic Avenue and to maintain a surveillance over *them* while they worked on cases that did not involve him. He was most interested in the agents' vehicles and soon determined that they were housed in a parking lot on Beech Street in Boston's Chinatown. He also learned that the security of the parking area was loose because of the natural arrogance of a law enforcement agency which assumed that only a fool would tamper with one of their vehicles and attract suspicion. Murphy was grateful for that arrogance. It made people careless.

Murphy dipped into his compendium of crooks for a specialist in automobile theft and stripping; the man was then boosted surreptitiously into the FBI parking lot. He emerged ten minutes later with one of the mobile radio transmitter-receivers. Within half an hour, an electronics expert who operated a small electrical repair shop had broken down the set, analyzed the communications bands used by the agency, and duplicated them on a receiver that was installed in the glove compartment of Murphy's car. The FBI unit was returned in the same way it had been taken.

Now Murphy had an ear as well as an eye on the private world of the enemy. He found it very educational, and he drove for hours through the city listening to FBI communications about surveillance techniques, search patterns and arrests, as well as the activities of other criminals, many of whom were Murphy's associates. Murphy found himself answering calls with the agents and occasionally going to the scene of a crime before they did. Combining what he saw with what he heard, Murphy learned, for example, how the agency used the "pass-along" technique of automobile and foot surveillance. An agent might drive or walk past a suspect, observing the man as subtly as possible, and move out of the area, while the surveillance was transferred to another federal agent and then to another, and so on. The hope was that the individual would not become aware he was under surveillance. Murphy heard the FBI agents scoff at the technique of one-on-one surveillance—a car trailing another car from behind—employed by the city police and the postal authorities, while the agents admired it when the state police imitated their own technique.

Murphy also learned that the bureau had very liberal attitudes about wiretapping, with or without warrants, which gave him a completely new orientation toward the use of telephones for the communication of his thoughts. He also picked up a great miscellany of information about suspects, informants, law-enforcement priorities, and, of course, weaknesses. All this and much more had been fed into the computer bank of Murphy's memory to help him stay out of prison while he continued to pursue bank and payroll robberies. It was there for the planning of a new project, too.

Murphy estimated that he needed a total of $200,000 to finance the mail truck robbery. His team of six— himself, Conrad, Harry, Joey, Frank, and Sam—had been chosen and were committed to the scheme, although none knew entirely *what* they were going to do nor exactly who else might be involved. Murphy had to protect them as much as possible from intemperate action during the next several weeks or even months, while he dealt with a number of crucial details like having vehicles in the right places at the right times and acquiring special equipment: one state police trooper's uniform (forty-six long), six machine guns, six automatic pistols, rolls of rope and tape, "clean" license plates for stolen vehicles, and several State Highway Department roadblock barriers. Since any or all of this might be connected to the crime during the investigation that would follow, none of the principals could be involved in arranging for it. And good service cost dearly.

If Murphy wished to make a personal investment in the mail truck robbery beyond his own cunning and bravado, the $200,000 was readily available to him. He had more than a million-and-a-half dollars in cash hidden in the walls of his house, cemented behind the tiles of his three bathrooms, and invested in various high-interest loan shark operations. Each time he had staged a bank or payroll robbery, Murphy had torn apart one of the bathrooms, stuffed cash in plastic wrappers between the studs, and resealed the wall. He had retiled his bathrooms about twenty times over a ten-year period and had become a skilled professional in placing wallboard, smearing mastic, setting tiles and grouting, and sealing seams. The money on the street produced a regular flow of payments from the exorbitant profits earned by that system's three-for-two financing charges. And he had several hundred thousand dollars more on deposit in Las Vegas through trusted acquaintances with access to the great and generally uncontrolled river of cash there. But Murphy was also a good businessman. He had no intention of investing his own funds in the heist or drawing attention to himself or his savings plan. If the new scheme failed, he could lose everything, and he preferred to spread the risk.

Murphy had been thinking for several months about two banks that were particularly vulnerable—Essex County Trust in Lynn and City Trust Company on Route 9 in Newton. Small, but choice. He decided that now was the time to knock them off, with the intention of using the proceeds to finance the logistics of the mail truck heist.

Using Harry at the wheel and Sam Gilardi up front, Murphy took the City Trust in May. He counted a take of $112,000. The Essex County Trust yielded $46,000. With approximately $150,000, Murphy felt he needed still more financing. There was too much heat on bank robberies in general, and on people like himself specifically, to attempt a third job. But still he would not turn to his own resources. He chose instead to borrow the money from Alex Tyler, a well-known loan shark.

There was also logic to such a move: If the word got around that Murphy was borrowing large sums of money—and loan sharks advertise their cash balances and customers just like banks or loan companies— then it would serve as additional camouflage for the fact that he and his gang had just scored for $150,000 in two bank holdups.

Why did Murphy need so much operating capital? He had two reasons. First and most important, he wanted to keep the five members of the team completely free of financial pressures during this period of preparation. Any one of them, confronted with an emergency or an opportunity for high-rolling debauchery, was capable of committing a crime to obtain funds and making himself vulnerable to arrest. Second, Murphy needed four additional men, members of a logistical subteam, to make sure that all of the vehicles and weapons would be in exactly the right place at precisely the right time. No ifs, ands, or buts. No excuses. They had to be there.

There were specialists in this work, too. Murphy had used them often. His contact was a short, dark-haired, slender man known as Fast Freddy. He and his three friends (one man for each of three vehicles, one man for guns) received flat fees of $25,000 each—plus expenses—for carrying out their instructions. They would not take part in the robbery, nor would they share in it. They would not even know why the materiel was being gathered. They were aware, of course, that they were taking certain risks for the protection of other unknown individuals who could not later be connected by the police to any of the items which were acquired.

The remaining money went for the guns, the cars, the mechanics to soup them up into racing condition . . . and loose change in various pockets.

There was no time now for amusement in Harry's life. He found himself driving up and down the Cape Cod highways night and day, endlessly, a hundred miles out and a hundred miles back. He began to feel that he was memorizing blades of grass beside the road. He certainly knew the location of every telephone pole, every side road, every café and building, however large or small. For a while Murphy had made the trips to the Cape with Sam in his woman's disguise. Now Murphy sat beside Harry, sometimes dozing, rarely talking. Murphy could sit without moving for as long as six hours (he had been clocked) and without making a sound. Just observing. He was memorizing Cape Cod—and looking for the place, the perfect place.

What he found and settled on was a section of Route 3, northbound to Boston, just beyond the Clark Road exit. It was a section opposite a small state park where the highway is separated by a copse of thickly planted pines. It is impossible at this point to see from the southbound to the northbound lanes for approximately 100 yards. That was the place.

With a great sigh of relief, Harry returned to driving down Commonwealth Avenue to Drew's Cafeteria instead of out the Cape highway. Now Murphy must choose the day.

Having pushed through all of these preparations, Murphy watched and waited. He paid more attention to the comings and goings of the Kennedy family than he did to his own. The site of the projected robbery was only a few miles from the Hyannis compound. Would there be more cops on the road if the family were present, or more distractions from patrol duties? As heat and humidity began their perennial lusty embrace, the influx of tourists seeking relief on the Cape rose—and so did the prospects of heavy loot.

At one point, Murphy could not resist the temptation of the July 4 holiday and the thought of the huge amounts of money that would be spent on the Cape (and shipped to Boston). He alerted his crew to be ready for the strike—then canceled when better judgment told him that the influx of money meant a dangerous heightening of traffic.

During the last days of July and the beginning of August, Murphy was extremely busy—doing nothing. He had to keep a lid on the five that he had chosen, to keep their tension level as low as possible. Murphy had never told any of the others what he expected to find in the mail truck, thus avoiding the risk that they would become bored and strike out on their own. So he spent hours with them doing nothing, listening to Conrad talk about his discoveries in medical journals, lecturing Joey and Frank about the foolishness of gambling, riding aimlessly through Boston and the suburbs with Harry to keep him from women and whisky, even dropping in to see Sam Gilardi every couple of days. Did they have enough money? Was everything all right? He soothed, scolded, lectured, and massaged with the force of his determination and the knowledge of their capabilities.

It carried them through July and into August, unthinking and unfeeling about Marilyn's suicide in Hollywood, the cosmonauts' rendezvous in space, or the triumphs and travails of Pinky Higgins's valiant crew in Fenway Park. There was but one thought: to take the Cape Cod mail truck.

$ II $

The Heist

The signal for the robbery came after more than three months of working and waiting. For Conrad, it was a period of stealing books and reading. For Harry, it was a painful period of abstinence, his tongue parched, his groin aching like an adolescent plunging through puberty. For Frank, it was a time of pacing and cursing, wondering what the hell was going on and why nothing was happening. And for Joey, they were days of placating Frank and teasing him, trying to keep him calm, trying to keep him from getting into brawls just to relieve his tension. Perhaps the waiting period was easiest on Sam Gilardi, who liked the quiet routine and spent the hot muggy days digging cool holes in the ground and the nights tinkering in his basement workshop with a variety of home improvements. For Murphy it was just part of the game he played with consummate skill. He roamed the city with Harry at the wheel, sat and thought for hours on end, read his detective stories, and examined his plan from every conceivable point of view, including his own collection of superstitions. Even the First Family was cooperating unwittingly.

The president was on the West Coast, Jackie Kennedy was in Italy, Bobby was in Aspen, Colorado, Rose Kennedy, the president's mother, was in Southern France, and the president's father was in a wheelchair at Hyannis Port, with the state police and a few secret service men watching over him. It was a distraction, but not enough to clog the highways with motorcades or bring out the surveillance helicopters.

At last, it was time.

Using Conrad as a communications center, Murphy began to pull his men and materiel together for Tuesday, August 14. Fast Freddy and his three associates were the first to move. Freddy was told for the first time about the location of the gold Pontiac that Murphy had stashed. He was told where to find the triptych license plate Murphy invented by chopping plates into three slices and welding the miscellany back together to create a totally realistic looking but uncheckable set of numbers. He was told where to bring the vehicles. Six Sten guns and six 9 mm Lama automatics had been located in New York City and were being held for pickup at an apartment in Brooklyn. Mostly to give Harry something to do, Murphy made the trip to pick them up himself with Conrad in the back seat. Because the commando guns were so easily disassembled into small components, the men were able to carry the armaments out of the Brooklyn building in two reinforced shopping bags, the tops of which were camouflaged with newspaper and bundles of carrots. The trip to Brooklyn took five hours down and five hours back, no stops. It was Conrad's job to take the guns to his cellar and test-fire each of them, sending the slugs into a large log from the supply of firewood at the side of the house. The guns all worked perfectly. After they had been cleaned and stored, Conrad carried the shattered log to his fireplace and burned it (while running the air conditioner full blast). He later collected the puddles of lead from the melted bullets and skipped these into the Charles River. Even if they were recovered, they could never be traced.

Each member of the holdup team was instructed to meet on the morning of the robbery at Conrad's house. The three vehicles—gold Pontiac, blue Oldsmobile sedan, and black Ford pickup—were parked in the alley behind a restaurant a few blocks away, with guns, detour signs, and other materials in place. This would be the first time each and all knew who would be going along on the job. Only three of them had worked together in pulling the bank jobs necessary to finance this venture.

To each, Murphy had repeated instructions he gave in all of his forays. They were not to drink the night before, even at home. They were to go to bed early and get as much sleep as possible with the assurance that everything had been planned and nothing could or would go wrong. They were to get up early, shower and shave, and dress normally so that they would not attract the curiosity of neighbors by a deviation from routine habits. They were to leave their houses at the customary hour. They were not to eat breakfast, only coffee or orange juice. They were to make up their minds that this was all they would have to eat for the remainder of the day until the work was done.

The enforced fast was based on Murphy's experience. He knew—and they all knew—there might be shooting. They were armed; the postal officers in the truck were armed; a stray cop could turn up anywhere at any time. Murphy also knew from experience that the first reaction one of his five men might have if blood were spilled would be shock, followed by nausea.

"You can't run and you can't think if you're throwing your guts up on the grass," Murphy said. "No food." They didn't like it but they all obeyed.

"Relax," Joey told Frank. "It's like you're going on some kind of picnic on the Cape and you don't eat until after the softball game." As usual, they traveled together, leaving Frank's garage at 7:30 A.M. in Joey's car. Harry followed Murphy's instructions implicitly and slept soundly. But having gone to bed early, he woke early, at 4:00 A.M. It was hard not to eat. His job was to collect Sam Gilardi, who had taken a day off in lieu of overtime without telling his wife, and would leave home as usual, with a bag of sandwiches he would discard. After Harry found Sam on a corner near his home at 7:15, they picked up Murphy for the trip to Conrad's house. The two vehicles in front of Conrad's house would be relatively inconspicuous since Conrad had a fleet of vehicles parked there regularly—one each for himself, his wife, and for each of his three children. The two girls and their brother had left for work.

When they gathered, Conrad gave his wife the job of making coffee for them. He had not given her advance notice, but she was not surprised. Twenty-five years of marriage had accustomed her to the comings and goings of silent, fearsome-looking men, including her husband. When she was out of earshot, Murphy went through a ritualistic interrogation of each of the bandits. One by one, they denied having taken food. One by one, he asked if they knew what they were to do. One by one, they repeated the instructions that had been drilled into them for a month. Where was the equipment? he asked Conrad. The guns had been picked up and distributed in the cars that were a few blocks away. Where was the police uniform? Folded neatly into a package on the back seat of the Oldsmobile.

What about the wooden roadblock horses stolen from the state highway department? There were three of them in the back of the pickup under a tarpaulin. And Sam's wig and dress? They were in the Pontiac in a paper bag. Did everybody feel all right? Everybody felt just fine.

They sat and talked about these and several unrelated matters, like the shooting down of a gangster they all knew and the growing tension between the Irish and Italian criminal factions in Boston. But it was a circular conversation that traveled to a number of other areas only to return again to the reason they were all together. They were going to rob a mail truck, and they could not refrain from speculating about what it might contain. Murphy did not join in this talk. He already knew.

At one o'clock Murphy said it was time to move out. They drove to the restaurant, parked, and separated for the drive to the Cape. Murphy was not worried about calls from the restaurant bar complaining about the abuse of its parking privileges. Under a dummy management, he owned the joint as one of several façades which hid his robbery loot.

Conrad and Sam, Joey and Frank, Murphy and Harry—the teams took off at five-minute intervals under dark, threatening skies. The rendezvous for all three vehicles was the picnic grounds at Myles Standish State Forest near Plymouth. It was understood that they were to avoid taking direct routes there, a relatively easy matter since they were now more familiar with the highways and byways of Cape Cod than most of the engineers working for the state highway department. Murphy wanted them to arrive separately at the roadside rest area and give no indication of knowing each other.

The three vehicles drifted into the roadside park

area between 3:00 and 3:30. It had begun to drizzle, traffic was light, and there was no one in the roadside rest area to observe them. As he watched his men, Murphy ruminated on their temperaments and capabilities. Those were always his primary concerns. He had to know what a man would and could do under pressure. Their lives and freedom depended on it, individually and collectively. This group, he felt, had already demonstrated some of their ability to act ruthlessly.

At four o'clock Murphy decided it was time to get to work. He strolled to a picnic table where Sam was sitting and told him it was time to get dressed. Sam got into the back seat of the Pontiac and struggled into the dress and wig. He leaned across the seat to use the rearview mirror to slash red lipstick on thick, unlovely lips. The others smiled when he came out of the car.

"Fuck you," he said, walking unsteadily on modest two-inch heels to the Pontiac with Conrad. They were heading for the Clark Road overpass three miles south. Their job would be to spot the approach of the mail truck and give a signal to Murphy and Harry, who would be watching through binoculars from the Clark Road exit of Route 3.

Then it was Murphy's turn to change, into the gray trousers and shirt of a state police trooper's uniform. He left the tunic and cap for the last minute because they might attract unwanted attention. Then he and Harry left the park to cruise until it was time to take up their position at the Clark Road exit. He had chosen for himself the job of setting up the roadblock markers for diverting traffic from Route 3 while the robbery was in process. That left Joey and Frank fifteen minutes to spare before they would drive off to an interchange, turn around, and take their position on the opposite, southbound side of the highway just where the grove of trees blocked the view from the other side. They stopped, raised the hood, and pretended to be working on the engine—and waited. They were finally ready.

The two men in the red, white, and blue Dodge van were bored. They were bored with the routine of picking up the mail sacks at the small post offices in Hyannis and Buzzards Bay, always traveling the same routes, and always following the instructions of their superiors to make no stops except for red lights. They had run out of conversation. The dull gray weather and the heat could be dealt with in two or three words, and they both knew everything worth knowing about their respective families, which wasn't much.

On August 14, an idea for relieving this boredom occurred to them. One of their friends, another driver, was vacationing on the Cape.

"What the hell," Streeter said. "Let's drop in on old Wally and screw him out of a couple of beers." Chaplin agreed.

Except for its patriotic paint job, the truck had no distinctive markings as a vehicle carrying large amounts of cash, and the state highway patrol escort wasn't around to cause a problem. They locked the rear door of the van and drove out of the parking lot of the Buzzards Bay post office with a degree of enthusiasm and a rising thirst. Wally's cottage retreat was only six miles off the regular route, and they were pulling into the gravel driveway and swinging the truck out of sight behind his one-car white clapboard garage in a matter of minutes. Wally greeted them both in an undershirt stretching tautly over his bulging pot belly and with a can of cold Budweiser in his hand. He grumbled good-naturedly that the next time they came around, they could goddamn well hide a couple of six packs under the mail sacks, and Streeter answered just as good-naturedly that if they had a couple of six packs in the truck, they wouldn't have to bother visiting a pain-in-the-ass like Wally.

The three men sat down on squeaky wicker chairs on the screened porch to drink and belch in easy fraternity.

Where the hell was the truck? The blond wig was heavy and hot and making Sam's scalp itch unbearably underneath it. Conrad was twitching violently. They could not remain too long in this exposed position; some motorist, maybe a truck driver, would spot Sam and stop to help "a woman in distress." A close look at Gilardi would set off an alarm, possibly, or hysterical laughter. They were also afraid of missing the truck and being unable to signal Murphy. They tried to juggle the dilemma by driving back and forth across the overpass, stopping, turning around, and going back in the other direction, keeping their eyes on the northbound lane as well as they could. Every time Sam had tracked the mail truck with Murphy, it had passed this point by now. It had never varied; now it did. Where the fuck was it?

"What the hell are those crazy bastards doing?" Murphy muttered, handing the binoculars to Harry. "Am I nuts or are they driving back and forth across the overpass?"

Harry squinted and said, "There they go again. Maybe something's botherin' them."

"I'll bother them with a kick in the ass if they miss that truck," Murphy said.

Two miles north of the anger rising in Murphy were the most frustrated members of the gang, Joey and Frank. They had no visual or verbal contact with any of the others and only their abiding trust in Murphy's genius to reassure them.

"Maybe they got picked up," Frank said.

"Who'd pick 'em up? There ain't been any cop cars around."

"Maybe some constable or somebody."

"If anybody even looked at Murphy cross-eyed, he'd scratch the whole deal. It's got to be with the truck. The fuckin' thing could be stalled or broke down somewhere."

Streeter and Chaplin were in high good spirits when they left Wally at 7:30. Wally always knew a bunch of funny Irish jokes, and the beer had enhanced their sense of humor. They were still chuckling at 7:43 when Conrad and Sam spotted the familiar colors of the truck rolling toward the overpass at a steady forty-five miles an hour. It was raining lightly and getting dark. Some drivers had already switched on their headlights. When the colors of the truck caught Conrad's eye in the gauze-wrapped evening light, he cried, "Mother of God!" Sam leaped from the Pontiac and stared down the highway to make sure. That was it. Sam ran to the opposite railing, glanced around to make sure there were no other cars around, and waved to Murphy.

"That's it," Murphy snapped at Harry. "Get the trunk

open." Murphy ran to the car, got in. He quickly pulled on the tunic, buttoning the brass buttons and jamming the trooper's cap down on his head, while Harry unlocked the trunk. They waited.

At 7:47 the mail truck rolled past the dark Oldsmobile. As soon as it was past, Murphy was out of his seat, lifting the roadblock markers out of the car and placing them across the highway. As soon as they were in position, he ran back to the Olds, and leaped in beside Harry. The car was already in gear. Harry slipped his foot off the brake and trod down on the accelerator. The powerful car leaped down the highway, going from zero to eighty in a matter of seconds.

"Look at that bastard go," Streeter said as the Oldsmobile screamed past them.

"We'll pass them getting a ticket down the road," Chaplin replied.

Joey laughed with relief when he saw the Oldsmobile racing toward them. Frank sighed. Both of the men reached to the floor of the pickup and put their machine guns on the seat beside them. They were ready. Joey watched the Oldsmobile pull up twenty-five yards behind them. Murphy came out of the car with a Sten gun in his left hand. He held it down and out of sight, nodded to the others in the pickup, and then turned to stand beside the car, looking back up the road to the mail truck.

At 7:51 it came around the long bend in the road and began to approach him. Chaplin saw Murphy in the road and thought he was giving a ticket to the driver of the Oldsmobile. "I told you they'd get the sonofabitch for going that fast," he said.

As the mail truck approached, Murphy stepped away from the car. With his right hand he began flagging down the truck and pointing it to the side of the road between the pickup and the Oldsmobile.

"What the hell does he want?" Streeter asked.

"Maybe a witness," Chaplin said. "At least it's an excuse for being late, if anybody says anything."

As the postal truck slowed and pulled off the road to a stop, both the pickup truck and the Oldsmobile came to life instantly. The pickup backed up to within an inch of the front bumper, the Oldsmobile leaped to within an inch of the rear. Joey and Frank were out of the pickup running toward the doors, machine guns in hand. So was Harry, while Murphy raised his machine gun in a backup position. The startled post office men were staring with disbelief down the barrels of four machine guns. They didn't even try to reach for the .38 caliber pistols in their holsters.

"Unlock that fuckin' door or you're dead," Joey snarled.

Streeter could barely speak. "It's not locked."

Joey and Frank yanked open the doors. They dragged both men out of their seats, took their pistols, and rushed them at gunpoint to the back of the mail truck.

"Open it," Murphy ordered. Chaplin's hands were shaking as he dug the key out of his pocket and tried to fit it into the keyhole. Murphy snatched it from his hand, slipped it in, and opened the door. "Inside," he ordered. "On your faces."

Murphy handed his machine gun to Harry and climbed into the back of the truck after them with a package of adhesive tape and rags for blindfolds and gags. Joey climbed in and held a machine gun on them while Murphy trussed them up, shoving them to one side of the truck then moving the mail sacks to the other side. There were sixteen sacks.

As soon as the postal men were bound, Murphy snatched one of their hats, jumped out, closed the door on Joey and his captives, and ran around to take the wheel of the truck. This was a signal to the others to take off, with Frank at the wheel of the pickup and Harry driving the Oldsmobile.

Murphy had allocated exactly four minutes for the job, from the stopping of the truck to the driving away. It had taken exactly that. And it was done.

Behind them, at the Clark Road turnoff, Conrad and Sam had stopped and quickly tossed the detour markers into the trunk of their vehicle. They had sent approximately thirty cars off the highway for a difficult and meandering ride through the narrow unmarked roads around Buzzards Bay. Now they raced forward to join the others as Sam tore off the hated dress and wig, unaware that the change would confuse the investigation for years to come—a factor Murphy had calculated into his scheme from the start.

Murphy took the first cutoff north of Clark Road off Route 3, and for the next ninety minutes he drove a meandering, aimless trail through uncongested and sparsely populated areas. During this drive Murphy and Joey shouted instructions to each other using the names "Buster" and "Tony," and the postal men remembered that Buster ordered Tony to make three separate stops to unload the leather-and-canvas mail sacks. Both the long ride and the stops were camouflage in the form of false clues. Joey also snarled loudly from time to time, and the postal guards later said there was an attack dog in the truck covering their movements.

The pickup trailed them for the first twenty-five minutes of the ride, or until the first stop. There, a few blocks from the freeway, all of the sacks were unloaded into the back of the pickup as were all the machine guns and most of the other weapons and disguises including Murphy's state police uniform and Frank's dress and wig. Gilardi took over the pickup, and drove off with all of it. Conrad and Frank also left in the Pontiac. Harry trailed the postal truck for another hour, until it was abandoned with the guards inside. Then Murphy and Joey sped off with Harry.

As Sam Gilardi drove off in the blue pickup with the mail sacks and guns covered with a tarpaulin, he fought his own excitement and tried to drive carefully and cautiously. Murphy had done it again. It had been perfect. It was only 8:30 and he would be home by 9:00, 9:15. He had sent his wife and children to a movie with his mother-in-law. They would not be home until 11:00, maybe later. There was plenty of time to stash all the equipment and mail sacks behind the wallboard he had put up loosely in the new basement recreation room he was adding to the house. He would get out of there by 10:00, dump the pickup, and be home again by 10:45, sitting in front of the TV with a beer, ready to help carry in the sleeping kids and tuck them into bed. The drizzle turned into a heavier rain and he switched the windshield wipers higher. They beat a rhythm that matched the pounding of satisfaction he felt from his groin to the top of his head.

It had been a hell of a day, and if Alice wasn't too tired, he was going to make it a hell of a night.

"The goddamn wig was driving him crazy," Conrad laughed. "I'll never go on a caper again with that broad."

Frank laughed with him—for the first time in weeks. Both nervous, temperamental men, they let it out now as high spirits bubbled through them. They were going to take the Pontiac to a quiet street in Dorchester.

There was a two-gallon can of gasoline in the trunk. They would douse the car, the road signs with it, toss in a couple of matches, and walk swiftly but calmly to Frank's car parked three blocks away. Conrad thought he would read all night and be calm enough to sleep by dawn. Frank was thinking of taking the odds on the next day's ball game and going for a bundle.

Greek Billy was a short, squat man who seemed wider than he was high, particularly when he wore a garish plaid blazer, which he often did. He was celebrating his forty-fifth birthday at the small bar he managed in Watertown, complaining without bitterness that his dark wavy hair was falling out by the handfuls. Maureen, the twenty-five-year-old resident hooker and occasional waitress, assured him that he didn't have anything to worry about until his balls dropped off, and Greek Billy was laughing when the astonishing news was broadcast as a bulletin on the television set above the bar.

"Sonofabitch," he shouted. "Quiet!"

The bar fell silent as the newscaster told of the robbery earlier in the evening of a mail truck on Route 3 near Plymouth, and that the truck may have been carrying two or three million dollars in small bills from the Cape Cod banks. The Federal Bureau of Investigation, the Postal Inspection Service, and the state police had scores of investigators involved in the search for the bandits, and sources close to the investigation said that arrests were expected momentarily.

"Sweet Jesus, what a beautiful score!"

Greek Billy knew about such matters. Fifteen years earlier he had been in the business of payroll robberies with Danny Murphy, until a passing patrol car had interrupted one of their jobs in Quincy. Because Greek Billy didn't run as fast as them, he had gotten separated from the others, who managed to get away by car, and he ended up traveling by foot over the fourth green of the golf course that adjoined the bank. He was a short, wide target, and one of the cops put two bullets in his back, sending Greek Billy rolling into the bushes and into the lap of a fourteen-year-old high school truant who screamed, "Jesus Christ, don't shoot me! I'm only playin' hookey!"

Billy's heart was the last place to look for sympathy; it was the day of his mother's funeral, which he regarded as the perfect alibi to cover the robbery, and now this, bullets in the back. After his recovery, Billy did six years of a ten-year sentence and more or less ended his association with Murphy, although they were still acquaintances if not friends. He wondered if Murphy had had anything to do with the Cape Cod heist, but he couldn't make an educated guess on such sketchy information. It depended on the planning and the technique. There were two men, maybe three, who could plan a job the way Murphy might, and Murphy was the best among them. So unless it was a freak thing where a couple of guys just happened to score big (and would probably get caught because they were inexperienced and dumb), then it would all narrow down. Billy suddenly felt the excitement of the chase, vicarious now, but a tremor he had frequently known in his own escapades.

"Listen—everybody have a drink on me!" Greek Billy said to the cluster of men around Maureen. "I gotta run an errand."

They hated to see him go, but a free drink would ease the pain.

It was about two hours after the robbery before Chaplin and Streeter struggled free of the tape and rope. They were so frightened, they were shaking and could barely speak. Outside the truck, they started to laugh hysterically as they fumbled with trembling fingers at zippers and relieved themselves in the road. But where were they? It was a major thoroughfare, but they were so disoriented it took them a few minutes to recognize it as Route 128, the Boston beltway, at the Randolph exit.

Drivers on the freeway at that hour were in no mood to stop for two disheveled men standing at the side of the highway waving their arms at the raindrops. Chaplin said that as many as fifty cars whizzed past before someone stopped. Even then, he wasn't much help.

Carlos Guitterez, a twenty-two-year-old premedical student, happened past on a motor scooter and stopped, he would say later, out of "duty," although his "heart was full of suspicion." The postal officers yelled at him, "Robbery. . . . Call the police!" After they calmed down and explained, he buzzed away at top speed, found a telephone booth, and called the police. The officer on the other end of the line seemed "incredulous," to use Carlos's indignant expression. "He broke in on me. He made me spell my name and tell him where I am from. Then he said, 'Now what's all this about a robbery?' Then he made me spell my name again." Rebuffed but not yet fully stripped of his ideals, Carlos mounted his scooter again, drove frantically into nearby Stoughton, and accosted a cop on the street. The cop took him to the station house. The chief of police was summoned. The chief asked Carlos to spell his name, demanded to know where he lived, and asked him why he was in the United States in the first place. And finally the alarm was sounded.

When Murphy reached home about 9:30, his slender, sparrow-quick wife was mending one of their son's shirts while watching television. He grunted a greeting, fed his two pet cats, and departed—this time by his own car. About 10:45, Murphy drifted into the Fairfax Hotel Bar on Fenwick Street. Although he never drank, Murphy used the tavern as a hangout because of his long-standing friendship with the hotel owner—tiny, talkative, and nervous Abe Shapiro—and the accessibility of its rooms. No matter how crowded Boston might be with tourists, Abe could always find a room for his pals. Murphy, for example, needed a room about once a week for an assignation with a hooker and, less frequently, for a private meeting with his partners in crime. Years ago, when Murphy was just getting started as a stickup man and was working with people like Greek Billy, he would also use the rooms of the hotel for high-stakes crap games in which Abe occasionally took part. Because Abe displayed a permissive attitude bordering on blindness toward the moral imperfections of his guests, most of Boston's underworld figures also dropped in from time to time. A man like Murphy, a plotter and leader, could stroll into the bar any hour of any day or night and find the talent he needed for any caper up to and possibly including Fort Knox. It was a good place to be seen on the night of a big robbery because everybody in the joint would remember his presence—and everybody there, with the possible exception of the bartender, would be questioned about the job Murphy had just pulled.

Harry had gotten to the bar ten minutes before Murphy and was leaning against the mahogany talking over a drink with Johnny Luccidi, a hitman from Providence. Luccidi's purpose, they all knew, could be something as minor as delivering a message or paying his respects to the Boston branch of the family. If it was business—the business of killing—no one would have known he was in town until the intended victim had been removed.

As Murphy walked up to the bar, Harry smiled and extended a hand in an effusive greeting.

"Hi, Danny! Long time no see. How ya doing?"

"Yeah," Murphy said, smiling. Then, turning to Luccidi, "Good to see you, Johnny."

Luccidi nodded. All three noticed, because they lived on the edge of danger and always noticed everything that happened in the range of their vision, that Joey and Frank had come into the bar and taken side-by-side seats at the other end of the establishment, closer to the door.

"The Bobbsey Twins," Murphy said.

It brought a small smile to Luccidi, who gave away smiles as if they were emeralds.

Murphy wanted them all together in a public place, accessible for questioning if anyone wanted to ask them questions—all except Sam Gilardi, who had no record and was seldom seen in a place like this. With the four of them on hand, he wondered about Conrad, who had stopped at home to tell his wife, in his customarily considerate manner, that he would be out for the evening.

Conrad was at that moment nearing the entrance of the hotel, when he heard his name shouted and turned to see a short box of a man tumbling toward him across the sidewalk on tiny feet.

"Jesus Christ!" Greek Billy exclaimed. "Did you hear about the score on the Cape?"

Conrad tried to look puzzled and shrugged. "What's to steal—dead fish?"

"Somebody took down a mail truck at Plymouth for two, three million. It's on the news."

"No shit!" Conrad's astonishment was honest. Not about the robbery, of course, but that the score had been so big.

Greek Billy was babbling with excitement. "They

banged off this truck almost on Kennedy's fuckin'
lawn. What a score."

Greek Billy may have been exuberant, but he was
also studying Conrad carefully for a hint. If somebody
had scored for two or three million, it was worth knowing who that somebody might be. It was an edge and
an advantage, and that could often be turned into a
profit. All Greek Billy got from Conrad was his real
state of surprise. Greek Billy spun away from Conrad
and hurried into the bar. "Come on," he said. "I'll buy
you a drink."

When Murphy saw Greek Billy hurrying into the bar,
eyes bright with excitement, he knew that Billy had
heard about the heist. Greek Billy was there to find out
as much as he could about who had pulled it. It would
be very dangerous knowledge—for all of them. Greek
Billy was a ruthless opportunist. Would any but the
most ruthless of them use his mother's funeral as an
alibi for a robbery?

Murphy, who could run faster than Greek Billy,
could also think faster. "There's a story going around,"
Murphy said as Billy was about to speak, "that you're
really not a Greek at all. You're a fuckin' Puerto Rican.
You know, you really look like a spic."

"Oh, fuck you, you Armenian asshole," Billy said.
"Where you been all night?"

"Lookin' for you. I wanted to buy you a drink for your
birthday. Where *you* been?"

There was a moment's pause. Greek Billy felt that
Murphy had outsmarted him again. The sonofabitch
never forgot anything, not even a birthday, and now
Murphy had put the question of where Greek Billy had
been during the Cape Cod robbery before the meeting.
Billy was just as good a suspect as Murphy might be,
and he was glad he had an abandoned birthday party
as an alibi. He would be on the first-flash list of sus-

pects along with Murphy and maybe 80 to 100 other guys. The Greek glanced at Harry and Luccidi. Their eyes were question marks, too.

"I wasn't out on the Cape if that's where you were lookin'," he said. "A mail truck got knocked off out near Hyannis Port for maybe two million, three million dollars—they don't know, they ain't counted it up yet."

Murphy whistled softly, impressed. But Harry almost swallowed the cigar he was puffing. He choked and was wracked by a spasm of coughing. Like Conrad, he had no idea that they had made that size score. And as Conrad stepped forward from behind Greek Billy and began to pound Harry's back, the stocky wheelman exchanged a glance with Conrad that acknowledged their mutual awe of Murphy the mastermind. They'd drink to that—and they did, while Murphy's bland expression masked it all.

The largest single cash robbery in the history of the country had gone down without a flaw—just as Murphy had promised them.

"I think I'll go get a paper," Murphy said with a nod at Greek Billy, "and see what this asshole is talking about."

Tally Ho!

For the past week, many people have been admitting a secret admiration for the Massachusetts highwaymen who taught us that the mail needn't always go through. The Massachusetts special delivery was a work of art. Its splendid imagination, its flawless execution and its $1,551,277 have inspired the downtrodden. . . . I've received countless letters like this one from a Bronx mother: "I've lost $3,000 in the stock market. Now I think I'll try to get it back from Kennedy's post office." A Stuyvesant Town man writes: "For years I've done part-time work in the post office. Now I'm going to do some work *on* it." And a Bayside teenager proudly tells me: "I'm through with stealing stocks. I'm going Federal. Neither rain nor snow nor stoolies can stop me." . . . From a Staten Island butcher: "Can I get detour signs at Korvette?" From a Riverdale housewife: "Do I tip the drivers if they've been polite?" And from an Astoria mother of four: "Is postal robbery a Federal offense even if the truck has only local mail?"

—Ralph Shoenstein
New York Journal American, August 21, 1962

This is a disaster.

—William F. White
Chief Postal Inspector for New England

Clarence Humboldt's wrinkled, moon-round face, which made him look like a road map without route numbers, turned a slightly brighter shade of crimson with each memorandum he read in the first few days after the Plymouth job. A heavily built, white-haired man just past his fiftieth birthday, Humboldt was considered the Postal Inspection Service's top investigator, and he sat fuming with frustration in his office in Portland, Oregon, over what was happening in and around Boston. Nobody seemed to know who the hell was in charge of the humiliating case. The Boston newspapers were having a field day with a variety of conflicting statements from his own agency, as well as with the FBI's traditional attempt to capture as many headlines as possible, if not the robbers. Then there were the leaks by the state and city police, and possibly by postal inspectors as well, to old friends on the papers.

The most recent report had made him so angry that he could no longer sit at his desk. He got up and began to pace the small office like a prisoner walking his cell while the parole board meets. Two "mad dog" gunmen —of the several in Boston—had been seen on Cape Cod and were prime suspects who would be picked up immediately if not sooner. It was embarrassing. From that piece of information, the investigators in Boston seemed to have found two hundred—or maybe it was four hundred, what the hell was the difference, Humboldt grumbled—potential suspects roaming around Boston in very little danger of going to jail except to visit friends.

According to the bulletins that had been accumulating like dust on Humboldt's desk, all of the one thousand postal inspectors had been alerted to contribute whatever they could to the investigation—facts, rumors, tips, ideas, anything. They were tripping over each other in Boston trying to get a handle on the case. The Feebies, on the other hand, were being as mysterious as ever about what they were doing, taking as much information as they could from the Postals but giving up very little in return— if they had any to give. And the state police, with sixty-five men assigned to the case, were traffic cops who weren't going to find these bandits doing seventy-five in a school zone.

Humboldt's thoughts went to the two clues that had been found—the stolen vehicles that had been torched (one with highway department detour barriers in the trunk) and the motorist who thought he saw an ugly blond woman built like a wrestler waving hysterically on the overpass near the robbery scene. Humboldt discounted the blond for the moment. He expected every nut in Boston to call with a tip like that. It had to be checked, but thinking about the cars was more to the point.

They had been very carefully cared for and undoubtedly parked in some secret place until the robbers needed them. That took brains and professional skill as well as patience. Those qualities alone would seem to narrow the search to the experts, the true professionals of armored car robbery and the kind of men who could finance waiting and watching for just the right moment to take a stolen car out of storage and put it to work. He made a note to determine just who those people were—in and around Boston first, then regionally—god, he sighed, New England was a nest of thieves—and then nationally. The counterattack had to be just as methodical as the planning for the robbery had been.

Then he considered the woman on the overpass and wondered if she had really been there. Her presence in the crime was not impossible but very unusual. Certainly there were women around who would and could take part in a job of that magnitude and precision, some of them capable of functioning far more carefully and ruthlessly than most men. But very few major criminals would trust a woman to that extent. They were a very old-fashioned, conservative bunch. He cautioned himself not to be caught in that trap of narrow thinking.

Humboldt believed that there were cops in Boston who could see the same things he could, but he didn't know if any of them had the authority or the muscle to demand a proper pursuit along the painstaking lines he would follow. The entire leadership of the Boston Postal Inspection Service had its authority cut off at the knees by the robbery. Damn fools! Merchants mail million-dollar diamonds without insurance or taking special precautions and they arrive without incident, but it was foolishness bordering on madness to do that with a large bundle of small bills that could be moved without difficulty. It was stupid on the part of the Postal Service and it was more foolish on the part of the banks to try to save money on armored cars. The work records of those two men, Chaplin and Streeter, showed that they were less than prepared to deal with a robbery; it was lucky they hadn't shot themselves. Humboldt chewed anxiously on one of his knuckles and glanced again at his desk where there was a memo among all the others that said the two men in the mail truck had only had two opportunities to practice with their pistols. And stopping to drink beer with a friend! The tall, white-haired man started thinking of all the people of influence who owed him favors. He had to get into this case. Finally, he found a simple answer: make the chief look good.

Humboldt was simply going to suggest that they move swiftly on this one with an offer of a $200,000 reward. That would do it. It was direct enough to give the chief something flamboyant to do and oblique enough to get Humboldt into the action.

Every Friday night Murphy managed to be home at six o'clock to give his wife her weekly allowance of $75 so that she could go shopping Saturday morning. Marlene also had to pay the utility bills out of that and she would invariably complain that it was getting impossible to feed the four of them and cover such things as the gas, the phone, and electricity as well. Their two sons were eating like starved jackals and prices for everything were rising. Murphy tried to allocate as little time as possible for this ceremony.

"You think I stand on the corner of Comm. Ave. all day and people throw fuckin' money at me?" he would shout and walk very swiftly out of the house.

On the Friday evening following the robbery, Harry was waiting outside Murphy's house behind the wheel of Murphy's car, noting that the floor was covered with a variety of debris—orange peels, an apple core, the wrappings from several packs of Rolaids, crumpled newspapers, and three used cardboard coffee containers. A man of almost antiseptic habits except when he was drinking and whoring, Harry felt a customary twinge of discomfort in the debris, but he knew that if he attempted to clean it up, Murphy would be in a snarling rage for days. The debris might even be one of his superstitions. The car was covered with bird shit even though it had been raining. Harry glanced up at the unpretentious gray house, knowing to the second how long it would take Murphy to complete his ritual with the $75, knowing also that Murphy would want to get the hell away from the place as quickly as possible. And here he came.

Harry was confused. For three days the newspapers and the television and radio reports had spoken of all the money those bags in Sam Gilardi's house were supposed to contain. Murphy hadn't said a goddamned word, and nobody had the nerve to ask what he was thinking or intending. They were all going bananas wondering. Harry guessed that Frank was about to punch holes in the cinderblock wall of his garage in frustration. Even Joey wasn't smiling or teasing any more. Was Conrad able to sit quietly reading? And what about Sam Gilardi, looking at the television news and thinking that he had all those millions of dollars down in the basement with the Sten guns and the rest of it? Sam must be a basket case by now.

Harry also questioned himself. He wondered if he wouldn't lose his own self-control while Murphy did this to them.

Murphy came loping down the steps and hit the door of the car in a few long-legged strides.

"Go," he ordered. Harry slipped the car easily into gear and let it roll with a surge of power. He liked the power of cars.

"You want to go to Drew's?"

"I'll tell ya when I want to go to fuckin' Drew's. Sam's house. We're gonna have a count."

Conrad wasn't reading. As Harry suspected, the tension had been too much. He could barely get through a newspaper article about the Plymouth mail robbery. The news accounts on television also failed to hold him. His wife worried that he would wear furrows in the thick beige carpeting as he darted from one room to another, staring out a window for a moment and then fluttering off in another direction. She had never seen him this bad and she was concerned about his health. Like the wives of many men with Conrad's professional habits, she wasn't sure after almost twenty years of marriage what he did for a living. There were times he seemed to be selling used cars, promoting real estate, turning over investments in restaurants and bars. But how could she know? Conrad never said; it was always "just business," and all of it was conducted outside of the house or over the private communications system in his bathroom. She had accepted this weird aspect of his behavior long ago; why not accept the rest of it?

Conrad had disappeared into his small soundproof cubicle the day before.

"Yeah," a familiar voice had said. "Let's count. Tomorrow. Eight o'clock."

Conrad stayed in the bathroom for an hour, calling, trying to locate Frank, Joey, and Sam, confident that Murphy himself would prepare Harry. Sam followed a pattern tied tightly to his work and home, and Conrad was able to get word to him without difficulty. Frank and Joey were problems with their aberrant behavior. Joey had decided to take Frank deep sea fishing. If the salt spray and bobbing boat were not calming to Frank, Joey thought he might drown him. Frank had become absolutely impossible.

But find them Conrad did, through information supplied by Jimmy Gondoulis. Jimmy operated a forty-foot Chris-Craft sports cruiser that was maintained for private meetings of criminal groups. It was a convenient way to avoid electronic eavesdropping or to dispose of members of those groups who had become disposable.

The news that there was going to be a count brought a degree of self-control to Frank and saved him from the sea.

"Why don't you go see your mother?" Sam suggested.

"I seen her enough lately," Alice replied.

"Go see your mother, and I want you to take the kids."

Murphy and Harry watched Alice Gilardi leave the house, through the stained windshield of Murphy's car. They had already noticed Joey and Frank drive past the house and turn the corner at the next intersection, looking for an inconspicuous parking place. Conrad drove past and placed his car three or four blocks away. Murphy sat in silence for ten minutes after Alice Gilardi had stuffed the kids in their car and driven off. They began one by one to move toward Gilardi's house, each man as casual as the other, friends gathering to play poker perhaps, or drink beer and watch a night game on television. Murphy first, then Conrad out of the shadows, Harry next, then Frank, and finally Joey. As each member of the gang arrived, they stood silently with Sam in the kitchen near the door to the basement of his single-level ranch style home. They exchanged nods but their throats were too dry for talk, and there was really nothing to say. As soon as Joey entered the house, Murphy nodded and Gilardi led them down the stairway into the basement, which was lighted clearly by three seventy-five-watt bulbs. Murphy glanced around. The others were waiting for a signal from him. He nodded toward the three or four ground-level basement windows. Wordlessly, Gilardi took towels from a laundry basket near the yellow Maytag in the corner and affixed them over the windows with thumbtacks. They were now private and alone. They had shut and locked the basement door behind them and could not very well be surprised. "Okay," Murphy said. Gilardi took a small claw-nosed pinch bar from the tools on his workbench and began applying it to a section of the wallboard. He was an excellent workman. The short wide-headed nails came out without a mark on the surface.

Murphy felt a renewed sense of confidence about his choices and his assignments as Gilardi carefully lifted the wallboard away from the studs and leaned it against the panel to the right. Gilardi did things precisely. He was the perfect man to hide the loot and the equipment; and it all lay there in neat stacks. A strange sensation crept over the conclave: For the first time they all felt—standing there looking at the bags—that the job was completed, had been successful. They looked at each other and smiled. Even Murphy smiled. He nodded again and the count began. One by one, the sacks were spilled onto the waist-high workbench, each large mail sack containing individual money sacks of bills or change. They divided the denominations automatically. Murphy took the hundreds and fifties—and allowed himself a whistle at the sight of two $1,000 bills. Harry and Conrad counted twenties, tens, and fives while Frank and Joey gathered up the singles with Sam Gilardi. They all pushed the change aside. Since this had been the spending money of tourists, some of it was sticky with ice cream, soft drinks and chocolate smears. A small amount of it was counterfeit.

"Would you look at that, for chrissake," Conrad said, tossing a twenty in the middle of the workbench. It was funny money so badly made that they were offended by the lack of craftsmanship. Harry used it to light a cigar. The others laughed until Murphy made him put the ashes in his pocket so there would be no telltale residue left in Gilardi's basement.

Two hours and twenty minutes after the count began, all of the money had been sorted. They began to add it, without writing down any of the numbers, but leaving the final calculation to Murphy's infallible memory. When they had given him the totals of the huge stacks of singles and a couple of stacks of two-dollar bills, great piles of fives, tens, and twenties, and a relatively small number of fifties and hundreds, Murphy gave them the total of their take instantly: $1,551,277 (if you included the counterfeit bills). This is how it broke down: $2,000 in $1,000 bills; $12,000 in $100 bills; $24,000 in $50 bills; $452,000 in $20 bills; $792,000 in $10 bills; $139,000 in $5 bills; $4,100 in $2 bills; and $42,700 in $1 bills. The remainder was in change.

While it wasn't the two or three million dollars the newspapers had speculated about, it was one hell of a haul, still the largest single cash robbery that had ever been pulled off in the United States, and, so far at least, they were getting away with it.

Murphy would have preferred to wait for any division of the loot. But he had obligations beyond the now smokey basement as well as to the condition of the men there with him. These five, himself included, had been under iron discipline for several weeks. They had followed orders implicitly. They were entitled to some reward.

"Everybody take fifty large," he said. "Take as many singles as you can handle. That's going to be the pain in the ass, moving all that little shit."

When $250,000 had been cut out of the pie and each man had stuffed his pockets with bundles of bills, Murphy asked Gilardi for a sack of some sort—anything

but one of the mail or money bags. There was a stack
of brown Shopwell bags in the far corner of the basement, kept there for eventual use as trash bags. Gilardi
got two and created a double-strength bag by opening
one inside the other.

"Ten percent for George," Murphy said. They
quickly counted out an additional $150,000 and stacked
it inside the shopping bag, folded over the top of the
bag, and sealed it with masking tape. This was the levy
that Murphy would send to Providence for the boss of
bosses for New England. Murphy would keep the package with him on the rear floor of his old car until he
got word from Providence. Then he would hand it to
some salami driving from Boston to Providence for
delivery. Murphy had paid such homage before
through the drivers of fish trucks or buses, once or
twice personally, and occasionally by turning the
money over to a third party who had a payment coming. That left more than a million, and they looked
from the piles of currency to Murphy with expectation.

"I got to pay the shylock sixty large," Murphy said.
That was the $50,000 Murphy had borrowed from the
loan shark to prepare the robbery, repayable now at
the special six-to-five rate given to favored and reliable
clients. They cut $60,000 more out of the pile and
wrapped it separately, understanding that Murphy
would not make the payment immediately because by
so doing, he would attract gossip and subsequent police
attention. He had to poor-mouth his condition for the
time being and expected the others to do the same.

"The rest goes back in the wall for now," he said.
Without hesitation, they began stuffing approximately
$1,000,000 in bills and change back into eight mail
sacks. Any one of them, that close to a million dollars,
might well suppose he would never see any or all of it
ever again. Yet they knew that Murphy's counsel had

been good and true, that they would not be here in wealth and comparative safety without him. There was no cause to doubt, as Gilardi tapped the tacks of the wall back in place and sealed their contentment.

It was time to get the hell out of there and go have a little quiet fun.

$ IV $

And in the Other Corner

The biggest and most splendidly negotiable haul in the whole, wistful history of stickups was consummated in Massachusetts only a fortnight ago, and consummated with an ease, an audacity, and a quiet thoughtfulness which no citizen who ever dreamed of stealing $1,551,277 himself could help but admire.... They would quite probably ... be envied and even applauded by millions who savor crime in thrillers. On the evidence they had committed that rarity—a pleasant crime and one with literary overtones. They had behaved with imagination and intelligence, they had spilled no blood, they have enlivened the dreary lives of multitudes and had, in one sense, contrived to steal an enormous sum of money without really costing anyone a nickel.... Is there really a chance that the Great Bank Robbers can, in fact, escape unscathed? A more selfish question now suggests itself—if they do not get caught, how in the name of Alcatraz are any of us ever going to find out what really happened?
—*Life Magazine,* August 31, 1962

At the time of the Plymouth mail robbery, Jim Reno was perhaps the most feared man in Boston. He was six feet tall, three feet wide, and all hate. He hated crooks large and small. He hated corrupt cops and politicians who permitted criminals to function. He hated the pockets of power their activities created in the city, and he even seemed to hate himself for not being able to rip them from the fabric of society and destroy them. In the expression of that hatred, he had committed severe brutalities, violated most of the covenants of the Bill of Rights, and left a trail of broken limbs in his path.

He was, all in all, a very good cop, forty-five years old, almost bald, constantly dour and snarling. He was the lieutenant in charge of the undercover intelligence squad of the police department, although there was very little inconspicuous or undercover about his activities. Reno seethed now with a volcanic rage at the effrontery of the Plymouth mail robbers. Although they had struck outside his jurisdiction, he was certain that he knew each and every man and woman who had any connection with the robbery. He knew he had seen their faces and studied their dossiers in his files. He knew he was going to catch them, and he hoped he would get a chance to kill them.

Reno was a pariah in the department, feared by both his superiors and subordinates. He came to the department after a childhood as a loveless orphan and a high school athlete whose exceptional physical strength and prowess had to be controlled by his Jesuit teachers for the safety of his opponents. In boxing or wrestling, Reno would bludgeon or strangle. In football or baseball, he would crush and smash. His coach directed him to gold medals in javelin, discus, swimming, and weights.

"If there was a competition for running through brick walls, Reno would be champion of the world," his school coach would say. He might have been a champion professional fighter too, but his sharp, incisive mind pointed him away from an occupation he considered corrupt. He was inherently honest and he also felt, having been abandoned in a church in South Boston, that something in life had been stolen from him by an unknown force or group of persons who lacked honesty and courage. He wanted to apprehend that unknown corruption. That was the motivation that put him on the path to the police department.

As a rookie, Reno smashed the face of the first man who offered him a bribe and left him lying in a puddle of blood and broken teeth beside his automobile in the middle of Commonwealth Avenue. His first partner to suggest that they share a box of pound-and-a-half lobsters from a fish dealer who wanted them to extend parking privileges for his trucks ended up sharing a semi-private room in Deaconess Hospital with the fish monger and the foreman of his loading dock. Reno would not explain these encounters in his reports, but the word got around. Attempts were made to isolate Reno, but his enemies were not able to isolate him from the exams for promotion to sergeant and lieutenant. Nor were they able to keep Reno's exploits from the press, where his efficiency and stainless steel honesty were extolled to such a degree that his appointment to squad commander was impossible to avoid. There was hope that he'd get himself killed by leaning too hard on the wrong psychotic, but it always worked the other way.

On the night of Murphy's count, Reno sat at his desk in police headquarters on Berkley Street looking through the files that he had compiled with contributions from the ten detectives who worked for him as undercover specialists. Reno was looking for the specialist of the enemy criminal force, trying to put together portraits like terrazzo. Among them, he thought, would be the best of the stick-up artists in the Boston area.

While he made no mention of his prescience, Reno had not been surprised by the Plymouth mail robbery. He had expected it—or a caper very much like it—without knowing who the culprits would be or where they would strike. Because he extracted a penance of information from the felons he terrorized, Reno had been privy to a flurry of rumors about the disappearance and movement of automatic weapons. From the indication of two or three sources, six Sten guns had been moved to New York from the Baltimore-Washington area to fill a specific purchase order from New England. He had heard only that. But he had concluded that there were only three groups possibly requiring such armaments: Blacks who wanted them for their terrorist acts against cops, some nuts who were organizing a private army to stop the Chinese invasion of the eastern seaboard, or a holdup gang that was preparing for a major number. He hadn't heard any rumbles of activities by blacks or crazies, but the bank jobs and armored car stickups were another story. They were coming off every other day. And hijackers, armored car and bank robbers with a specific haul in mind—those were the people who put in an order for six Sten guns. Try as he might, Reno had been unable to squeeze a hint of who that might be out of his informants. Then came Plymouth.

Now Reno organized the stacks of files on his desk into three categories. The first deck covered criminals capable of organizing a job like Plymouth. Murphy's file was third in a stack of eight. First was Paul Goodmaster, who lived across the Massachusetts line in New Hampshire, where he was technically out of reach and hopefully out of surveillance, but known to put together jobs in the Boston area. Second was Arthur Schultz, sometimes known as the Crazy Dutchman, who lived in Somerset and was better known as a specialist at blowing or ripping open supposedly impregnable vaults, but who also had the capacity to organize a group of robbers and would not pass up an easy one like the Plymouth mail truck if he knew about it. Then there was Dan Murphy, who was smart—very, very smart—and one of the regulars on the list for questioning every time a smooth and well-planned bank or payroll job was pulled.

Reno worked his way carefully through the files, looking for indications of recent activity or even rumors of a desperate need for money. He was refreshing his memory with details about them, a lot of little things that might pull together as the Plymouth investigation progressed. Then he turned to the second stack.

The second stack consisted of files of the fixers, the Fast Freddies of the underworld—and Fast Freddy himself was about fifth in the stack. They might be the soft underbelly of the caper through which Reno could slash to get to the men he wanted. One of them probably handled the guns and cars. The third stack, the group least likely to be involved but certainly capable of aberrant criminal behavior, dealt with the organized crime figures who were active in the six-state New England region. They would certainly know on one level or another about the job and who had done it, and there might be some among them who would finance it and even some who were suffering an economic crisis of such degree that they had committed the robbery. Most were too fat on gambling, extortion, loan-sharking, and prostitution even to bother, Reno thought, but you could never be sure.

Goddammit, they were somewhere in these stacks of files. All he had to do was squeeze hard enough.

Among the first to know that the United States Post Office would pay $200,000 for information leading to the bandits was the man who made it all possible, Phil Kalis. He had not deviated a hair's breadth from his normal schedule while Murphy was putting together the strategy for the robbery, nor had he communicated with Murphy about his intentions. Thus Kalis was just as surprised as anybody by the broadcast and headline announcements of the event and its enormous success. He was able to express real astonishment when he hurried to the postal inspector's office—now with a cluster of other journalists, who normally ignored the Postals—to get the official version. As much as Kalis respected Murphy, he found the alacrity and speed with which the caper had been managed incredible, and the fact that there was not so much as a single viable clue was staggering.

Kalis took notes with the rest of the newsmen, and observed that his old friends in the service seemed haggard and harrassed. They were catching hell in large order from Washington, as well as from their own bosses who were, of course, responsible for making such a debacle possible by permitting the unchaperoned truck to carry all that cash. He offered commiseration to a couple of old friends about the pressure they were feeling, folded his notes, and prepared to depart. He was stopped on his way out by John Dunphy, a grizzled old-timer whose arthritis had reduced him from fraud investigations to filing. Dunphy nodded to Kalis and stepped aside to chat with him. Dunphy liked the feeling that he was still active in the service and got that feeling by supplying Kalis with odds and ends of information that he might not get through normal channels.

"Did ya hear? Humboldt's coming in from Portland to run the investigation," Dunphy offered.

"Nobody said anything."

"He'll just be coming in with a bunch of other guys to beef things up but he is really gonna be in charge. Bet he'll burn some tails. He's a ballbreaker." Kalis nodded. He would remember Dunphy at Christmas with a bottle.

The news of Humboldt's arrival to take charge of the investigation concerned Kalis. Humboldt was a real investigator, the best, and a bulldog who never let go of a case. He had directed the solution of hundreds of them. He was as capable as anybody the FBI could put in the field.

Kalis paused as he left the building and felt the wave of August air wash over him with the consistency of steam. He wondered if Murphy knew about Humboldt and if Murphy would be worried about having such a formidable investigator working on the case. But that was another problem. He could not and would not go anywhere near Murphy or his regular haunts for the time being. Kalis decided that he would communicate with Murphy through the press. He knew that Murphy would be reading every line in every newspaper about the investigation into the Plymouth mail robbery. Kalis decided that he would include in his report a veiled paragraph about rumors that a top postal investigator was being put in charge of the investigation. Murphy would notice it and if he wanted to know more, would find a way to get to Kalis and elicit the details. That question resolved, Kalis speculated on how his deal with Murphy would improve his fortunes over the years to come, if Murphy stayed out of jail. It was a simple but elegant arrangement. Kalis was to get 10 percent of every job Murphy pulled for the next five years but nothing from the Plymouth job itself. Kalis's guarantee was that he alone was the only outsider who knew for sure who had done it. Curiously, it would not occur to Kalis that the information he regarded as a guarantee might place his own life in jeopardy. He strolled over to a newsstand to pick up a paper to see if J. Edgar Hoover had issued another announcement that his intrepid agents were closing in on the perpetrators. Announcements were still coming out of Washington along those lines about twice a week.

Tony Castle looked like a gangster trying to look like a graduate of an Ivy League college, in a conservative summer-weight suit and a discreetly striped poplin tie tacked precisely to the front of his white short-sleeved shirt with a small gold pin. The hair on his chest pushed against the thin fabric of the shirt and gave the momentary impression that he was a manicured gorilla who took his lunch at the Harvard Club. This was a very good camouflage for a special agent assigned to the Boston office of the Federal Bureau of Investigation in the Sheraton Building, which had been Castle's official home for three years. He had been in the Bureau eleven years, and at thirty-four, was considered one of the more competent major crime street agents in the Bureau. Although he did not meet Hoover's peculiar standards for WASPS in high places, if it came to Hoover's making a choice between him and the two or three blacks in the Bureau, Castle would become the agent-in-charge; the other guys would get to run into the burning buildings. A few generations back, the name was Castelani.

After Cleveland, Salt Lake City, and Denver (each transfer related to notoriety Castle had achieved through success in solving major crimes), Castle found himself immediately at ease in Boston. Because of the city's long-standing political corruption, there was an entrenched criminal element that thrived on law enforcement laxity and provided a consistent flow of action. Because that criminal element was divided on ethnic and racial grounds—the Irish, Italians, and blacks—there was a constant struggle for territorial preeminence. Somebody was always shooting somebody. And Castle was sitting right there behind home plate catching all the fast ones. The Plymouth mail robbery was the fastest one of all, not just because of its size and the obvious deftness of the criminals, but because of the jurisdictional dispute that went with it. The pressure was in the air, even in the men's room. There wasn't the usual kidding around or casual conversation. Guys would run in, take a leak, splash their hands in the sink, and run out clutching a paper towel without bothering to see if their ties were straight or their hair was combed. The Director wasn't letting any moss grow in his scrapbook either. Ten additional men had been flown in from the New York office, and Hoover had announced that sixty special agents had been assigned to the case. Castle thought that was funny. What the hell would they do, wash and wax all the cars in the motor pool? Maybe they could get up a golf tournament with the sixty-five Massachusetts state police detectives who were announced as working on the case. Or maybe the special agents and the state guys could go in together and issue a challenge to the one thousand postal inspectors, the entire contingent, who were said to be available to contribute to the investigation. Castle thought privately that one good man with one piece of information would solve this crime, and he might very well be the man.

Castle wasn't sure what all the others were doing, but his assignment was on major offenders. There were a lot of them in the files. Half of them would turn out to be in prison someplace, the others out on the street. Some junior agent, a nice kid who had come into the agency from law school in Georgetown, was now digging through the files for him. This morning Castle was thinking about the loot: over $1.5 million. Old bills, small bills, no marks, no numbers. It was a dream. Most gangs would *pay* half a million for an opportunity to steal a bundle like that. They wouldn't have to sell it at a discount or take any great risks in using it so long as they didn't attract attention with crude displays of sudden affluence. Were these guys too smart for that?

Castle began by sending flyers to Washington and the individual bureaus asking for accounts of unusual activity by known criminals with records of major robberies. That was part of the Bureau's drill. It would look good in the files but it didn't mean anything. He was convinced that it was a Boston job, work of one of the locals. The stupid business of hauling all that cash around in a Dodge van could not have been going on long enough for an outsider from, say, Chicago or Dallas, to be tipped off to it, get it organized, and pull it off with such attention to detail. He felt that it all had begun right here in Boston and would end right here. He got out the preliminary interrogation transcript with Postal guards Chaplin and Streeter. Those poor dumb bastards. It was difficult for Castle to believe that the postal officials were that dumb. Two relatively inexperienced and untrained men transporting $1.5 million. The invitation to robbery could not have been more clearly given. Now the media seemed to be making heroes out of the bandits, and Castle was both angered and shocked by the reaction. Did the press think the machine guns the robbers were waving were toys? They might better speculate on how it feels to get hit with a handful of .45 caliber slugs just for doing a lousy nine-to-five guard job—which is exactly what would have happened to those postal guys if they had drawn their guns and resisted.

For Castle, like virtually every officer, there was no romance in robbery. How, Castle wondered, did the hoods learn about it? That was so easy for heist artists, so difficult to determine later. A casual remark anywhere along the course of any tipsy evening could have set the plan for the robbery in motion. A bartender hears everything. Or somebody hanging around a bowling alley, or a postal employee's relative with shady friends. If there was any indication that Streeter and Chaplin had figured it out and tried to set up the robbery themselves, Castle was certain he would find it in the interrogation report. After that, he would have conversations with the two non-Bureau cops he respected—Captain Bill Shaney of the state police and a tough old lieutenant, Reno, who was mean and crazy but still the best street cop anywhere in the country. Castle had to go to those meetings prepared to trade information. His problem now was to gather up information worth trading, because the FBI did not seem to have any other than what was appearing in the newspapers. This trading was not acceptable under the director's standards of unilateral procedure, but it solved crimes and made life easier, if you didn't get burned.

The Plymouth mail robbery attracted a lot of attention in Washington, for obvious reasons, among them the fact that it had occurred in the home state of the president and his attorney general, within a stone's throw of their touch football field. Also, it brought up the many areas of disagreement between the Kennedys and the one great conservative bureaucrat whom they could neither control nor bend to their will: J. Edgar Hoover. They thought he was in many ways dishonest about his statistical evaluations of criminal activities and the bureau's effectiveness in dealing with them. The disrespect was mutual. Hoover considered the Kennedys rich young punks whose family fortune had been built through unsavory associations during Prohibition and had eventually bought them their fragments of power, the way some rich men supply their sons with convertibles. He had dossiers on all of them, and they knew that he knew. He was, nonetheless, outraged in late August when Attorney General Robert Kennedy directed through a meeting of top level federal and state law enforcement officers that the Postal Inspection Service take charge of the inquiry as the primary police agency.

Dan Murphy, on the other hand, was pleased, even happy. He didn't think the Postals could solve crimes any better than they could deliver mail.

Who's in Charge Here?

The United States Post Office was transporting money as if it were something from the five-and-ten-cent store.

—Frank S. Giles
Massachusetts Public Safety Commissioner

For many years the Post Office Department has been urging the public to avoid sending cash by mail yet the federal government has continued to use the mail to send billions of dollars in cash every year.

—J. Edward Day
Postmaster General

Just for once when something stupendously stupid or careless happens in a department of the Federal Government, we'd like to hear its head man say, "It was a king-size goof-off. Hardly anybody ever got so much egg on his face before."

—Detroit *Free Press* August 30, 1962

The man in the middle, William F. White, chief postal inspector in New England, in whose jurisdiction the $1,551,277 robbery took place, was asked if the Postal Department considered it was taking a chance in transporting huge sums of money over back roads without escorts.

"That's hard to say," he answered. "If we say 'yes,' we look stupid. If we say 'no,' we still look stupid."

—Boston *Herald,* August 17, 1962

There was an Admiral television set in Pirov's small shop near the raggle-taggle Boston University complex along Commonwealth Avenue near Kenmore Square, a display of radio tubes, and a couple of small generators. The sign over the window promised repairs of such things—if the customer could find Charlie in the shop and accept his casual promises to get them working again maybe in ten days or three or four weeks. Charlie Pirov guaranteed his work but he was not fast, and consequently, he didn't get much of the neighborhood trade. Even the students who were looking for cheap service with their small radios and record players were leery of Pirov because they couldn't be sure of getting their things back before the term ended. That was all right with Pirov; he was the electronics expert used by Murphy as a specialist in anti-surveillance and very busy with such clandestine pursuits.

Pirov came by his skills honestly. He joined the army to learn a career skill during the Korean War, believing what he saw in a recruiting poster that showed a man with a crew-cut working in electronics. Pirov's parents, who were World War II refugees from Eastern Europe, had not been able to provide him with any educational refinements beyond public school and there weren't many available to a slim, shy Latvian kid who seemed to have continuing troubles with English and no special abilities to compensate. While some men can darken an entire neighborhood by plugging in a lamp, Pirov took to electronics like second nature. He was forever grateful to the army for having thrust him into the mysterious world of electronics, where he seemed to understand instantly how and why everything worked. He became a communications specialist, First Class in the Fourteenth Ranger Battalion. Pirov had never met a woman as interesting as the inside of a television or radio set, so he spent hours in the back room of his small shop planning, theorizing, and building. That's where Murphy found him five years before the Plymouth mail robbery.

"Anybody in this fuckin' joint?" Murphy bellowed as he stood at the counter gazing around at the dust-gathering television sets, toasters, steam irons, clock radios, and small generators. Pirov ambled out to discover that Murphy had come looking for the cheapest television set in Boston. It was for his wife, who had been complaining. Apparently it was impossible for her to sit in the living room and watch television in the evenings when he was out prowling the city because the old wood frame house was so drafty and cold at the temperature she had to maintain on their austerity budget. She wanted a set in the basement recreation room, where the oil burner gave a certain amount of heat in its immediate vicinity and the underground walls admitted no frigid drafts. There were times when she was a stubborn woman. She turned aside his suggestion that they move the television set from the living room to the basement, and she ignored his querulous demands: "Why the fuck did I buy you a fur coat? Why don't you put that on when you're sitting around?" No, she insisted on a second television set, and Murphy had gone out to find her one. A cheap one.

That was at a time when Harry, who had just completed a twenty-eight-month prison confinement for strong-arm robbery, extortion, conspiracy to commit extortion, and second degree burglary, was looking around for a score, a getaway car to drive, anything to keep body and parole together. Because he was so adept behind the wheel of any vehicle, Harry found himself being cultivated by Murphy, and it was Harry who had to drive Murphy to every out-of-the-way, run-down, dust-covered appliance shop in Boston in search of a cheap television set to go in the basement of Murphy's house.

"Jesus Christ, how many of these fuckin' places do you have to go to?" Harry groaned after fifteen or twenty of them. Since he never forgot anything he ever saw, Murphy knew of at least fifty or sixty more. He knew that in one of them, he would find a man who wanted desperately to get rid of a television set and that he would be able to pick it up at a price almost equal to the amount of money he was spending on gas.

"There's a little place over near Boston University," Murphy grumbled.

It was Pirov's. "That television set in the window work?"

"I guess so," Pirov said. "I haven't turned it on for about three years. You want to try it?"

"How much as is?"

"I don't know, two hundred dollars maybe."

"I'll give you fifty."

"I'll take a hundred. I want to put a vacuum cleaner in the window anyhow."

"Seventy."

"Take it."

"How much to fix it if it don't work?"

"You said, 'as is.' "

" 'As is' means I can watch a fuckin' basketball game on it."

Harry carried the television out to the trunk of Murphy's car while Murphy counted out seven $10 bills. "That's cash, no tax," he said.

Pirov shrugged, stuffed the money in his pocket and turned away. But something about him attracted Murphy, who followed him back into his shop and watched him climb up onto the high stool in front of his well-lighted workbench that was blanketed with an assortment of wires and tubes as well as testing devices.

"You know a lot about that stuff?" Murphy asked.

"If I didn't, I'd get electrocuted," Pirov said. Murphy invited him out for coffee and cake—and a whole new career opportunity.

Humboldt arrived in Boston just after the Postals took charge of the investigation. He felt like a man trying to step into a leaky rowboat with a cast iron stove in his arms. He thought he was going to drown in all the reports that were flooding the office. Tips, rumors, and theories, but hardly any substantive information. Yet supposedly there were more men working on this crime than any event since the Lindbergh kidnapping.

Pranksters were having a marvelous time with all of them. One man with four dimes could get on the phone and whisper to the four agencies involved in the investigation, "There's a guy with some information about the Plymouth mail job at 121 Boylston," and have forty cars containing nearly one hundred men descend on the address in a matter of minutes. It was a great joke to play on a newlywed couple or an old lady who had been complaining about the noise in the next apartment. But Humboldt wasn't laughing.

His first job, he felt, was to bring some order into the investigative procedure. His second was to open communications between his own agency and the others by attempting to circumvent the traditional rivalries and even jealousies among them. He was sadly aware that his own office contained a limited number of professional detectives familiar with this variety of crime and proven techniques for apprehending its perpetrators. That methodology was based on a combination of detail, leg work, and squeezing informants—the sort of things street cops did by constantly circulating among known holdup men and by pressing the stoolies they had developed over the years with favors or fear or threat of exposure.

It was no problem to list the premier robbers operating in Boston. You could dig that information out of the files in an hour. But you had to put it together with what you had learned on the street. His people really didn't know anybody on the street. They were specialists in specialized crime. This was ordinary crime, made spectacular by the numbers, and the obvious capabilities of the individuals who brought it off. There was one man in the Boston office, Arthur Clappin, who might qualify in both areas. Clappin had been with the Boston Police Department for ten years. He was a decently educated, soft-spoken, and honest young fellow who had found the door-crashing, head-busting routine of basic police work as it was practiced in Boston offensive to such an extent that he had quit and qualified for the Postal Service. Life there was quieter, cleaner, and certainly less bloody. Clappin's file told Humboldt that he was a good man, still full of the decent citizen's sense of outrage that motivated a good cop, but free of the flaws of easy compromise and corruption. In two or three things that he had handled, Clappin had distinguished himself by demonstrating a patience and perseverance beyond what was reasonable to expect for achieving success in catching a crook. Clappin had broken one mailbox theft ring with eighty-seven consecutive days of surveillance, which had gotten him a set of frost-bitten toes, the identities of four women using stolen mailbox master keys, and a punch in the mouth when he arrested one of the females. She proceeded to beat him up until uniformed police came to the rescue.

As soon as he unpacked the cigars from his attaché case and got comfortable, Humboldt called Clappin into the small, sparsely furnished room.

"I want advice," Humboldt said with calculated flattery for a man who got little of it out of the civil service system.

"Anything at all," said Clappin, who knew when he was being conned and rather liked it, because just three weeks short of his fiftieth birthday and without any advancement foreseeable in his career, he felt there might be an advantage to be had here.

"You know the situation better than I do," Humboldt mused. "It's a goddamn mess. Somebody is probably gonna catch these bastards as soon as they start spending the money—I want that somebody to be one of us and not J. fucking Edgar Hoover. You know why."

Clappin shrugged. "Politics," he said. Humboldt nodded and went on.

"You know the story. I don't need to spell it out for an experienced man like you. Well, there's no way we can compete with those spooks. Not because they're any better than we are, but they sure as hell have a better public relations department."

Clappin permitted himself a grin.

"But here we have the attorney general telling us to take charge of the investigation, which is spread all over town like cowshit on a cornfield. Now I don't know Boston that well or the people here. I want you to tell me what you think we should do to get this thing under control."

Clappin thought a moment and glanced out of the window at Boston's changing skyline. There were a lot of new buildings going up. Humboldt had a nice view. He turned back to Humboldt. "Chief," he said, capable of his own flattery, "I think the best thing to do is to get everybody together and form some kind of central place to exchange information, with one guy from each agency reporting for his particular group, like a war council."

"Exactly what I wanted, and I want you to be our man in such a setup. We'll find somebody who will take over your active files. If you have any trouble with any of the other agencies, I want you to refer it back to me, but I don't think you will. Issue a memo saying all reports on this case are to come to your desk. Is there anyone out there you'd like to work with you on this?"

"Maurice Leibowitz," Clappin said without hesitation, thinking of the one other postal inspector who didn't bore him with never-ending repetitive conversations about sporting events.

"You got him," Humboldt said. "But you're in over-all charge of this thing and you report only to me—you understand?"

"Right, Chief."

"Try to set up your meeting with the people from the other agencies tomorrow morning. I want to be there." Humboldt smiled grimly. "Good luck. Let's get these bastards."

Clappin nodded and walked out of the office toward his desk. He ignored the questions and glances from his fellow inspectors. He noticed that Phil Kalis was not hanging around the office at the moment and thought of tipping Kalis off to what was going on and letting these pricks find out when they read about it in the newspapers. That would jar them out of their complacency. Oh, the hell with it, they would be insulted enough that Humboldt had chosen him, an ex-cop, to do the job. It would be enough to run their asses off over the sloppy reports they turned in. He was looking forward to that.

Lieutenant Reno woke at 5:00 A.M. and went through a series of stretching exercises at the side of his bed to limber up his heavy muscles. He padded through the dark apartment in bare feet without bothering to turn on the light. There was hardly any furniture to bump into even if he had forgotten where it was placed. Wriggling his toes against the cool asphalt tiles, he squeezed several swallows of orange juice out of a cardboard container. That was breakfast. Back in the bedroom, Reno pulled on the baggy gray training flannels that hung from the hook on the inner side of his closet door and stuck a .38 caliber pistol into a chamois leather holster with a strap that held it against the flat muscles of his belly and concealed it from view under his sweatshirt. Reno tucked a single key under his doormat and moved as soundlessly as dandelion fluff down three flights of stairs into the dawn murk that still cloaked the street. Then he began to run, part of his training for the fight he expected would come somewhere, somehow during the day. Run and think. He tried to remember if he had ever met this Postal guy Clappin who said he was an ex-cop and knew Reno from someplace. Maybe he had. Reno could remember the face and specific description of almost every wise-guy and punk in and around Boston, but he never paid much attention to the cops unless they did something special or worked with him directly on the intelligence squad. At any rate, Reno was pleased that they had chosen an ex-cop to set up the central desk for the exchange of information among police agencies about the Plymouth mail job.

Reno was neither a health nut nor a sports enthusiast. He considered his body, like the pistol at his waist, one of his tools of the trade of being a cop, and he took care of it the same way he took care of his guns. He wore heavy rings on the index fingers of both hands for the same reason. When he swung, as circumstances often required, it was metal that tore into the flesh of his hoodlum prey. There was hardly a week in his fourteen years on the force that this had not occurred at least once. Whatever was required, he felt prepared. Reno was still running when he returned to his building and headed up the three flights of stairs to his apartment, where he stripped down, showered, shaved, and got into one of the four conservatively cut dark blue suits that were hanging in his closet. He called his office to ask Kaminsky, the night man, if anything had happened to alter his thinking and planning for the day. It was quiet to the point of dullness. Reno told Kaminsky he was leaving his apartment momentarily, that he'd be at a meeting at the Statler Hilton Coffee Shop at 10:00 A.M., and until then he'd be at the intersection of Saratoga and Meridian.

Reno selected a new corner every morning; frequently he returned to an intersection to confuse his enemies, but all the corners were on the fringes of areas dominated by the gangsters. His premise was that every crook, stick-up artist, mob wise-guy or generally unsavory character would at one time or another, on one day or another, on one illegal mission or another, cross those intersections. Quite frequently they ran into Reno, to the hoodlum's discomfort and Reno's great pleasure. The performance was usually the same. Already word was being circulated throughout the underworld by phone or foot to stay away from the intersection of Saratoga and Meridian as Reno would be standing on the corner watching each pedestrian and automobile pass. On the morning he was to meet Clappin, Reno's attention was attracted three separate times.

Charlie Bontempo and Bernie Machete, a couple of low-ranking runners (or salamis, as they were known) who collected extortion money from bookmakers and bar operators in the area, were talking about the ass on a hooker named Jenny who had been sitting at the bar they had just visited on a standard business call. Their ruminations distracted them from being alert to the danger of the streets.

That was when Reno saw them, and they felt immediate pain. They were looking at each other when he ran toward them, kicked Charlie's feet from under him, and sent him sprawling, while almost simultaneously hurling Bernie across the sidewalk against a building. Before any of the morning pedestrians or shop owners could perceive what was happening, he had yanked Charlie to his feet and was pushing both their noses into the red brick wall and shouting his standard morning greeting:

"Assume the position, you little cocksuckers."

As collectors well suited for their jobs, both were mean, brawny men who knew the ways of street brawls, but they stood docile, unresisting, groaning their pains and protests of innocence: "Leave us alone, we didn't do nothing. What do you want with us . . . we're clean."

Reno's hands were frisking roughly. Neither had a weapon, but Reno found the money they had been collecting in Bontempo's pocket—$5,000 in $100 bills, half-folded in a large wad. Reno ripped it out of his pocket and whirled Charlie around with a hand that felt like a steel claw. Reno held the wad under Charlie's bleeding nose. "What's this, scumbag?"

"My mother loaned it to me to buy a car," Charlie tried to explain. He had just about finished the sentence when Reno stuffed the wad of money in Charlie's mouth. "He'll strangle," said Bernie, who had turned his head from the wall to watch. Reno pushed Bernie's nose back into the wall.

Reno glared at them, hating the fact that they were unarmed and unresisting.

"You're garbage," he said. "Get off the street. Move!"

They scrambled away, ignoring the loss of three or four bills that fluttered away as Charlie removed the wad from his teeth.

Over the years, a number of plans had been devised for dealing with Reno by eliminating him. It was possible at any time to find a foolhardy assassin to take the assignment. But it was impossible to find anyone to face the consequences of failure. They were certain that Reno would take an attempt on his life as a license to retaliate and simply kill them all. He would do it so abruptly, they were certain, that it would be over before anyone could impede the slaughter. Reno wore that fear, real or imagined, like bullet-proof armor.

Within ten minutes, Reno was racing into the intersection toward a red Cadillac stopped at the light. The driver, Dennis Delahanty, a 300-pound loan shark, bookmaker, and fence of stolen goods, heard the car horns honk at Reno and the screech of tires as drivers braked for him. Delahanty regarded the noises as none of his concern since his car was stationary and not blocking the intersection. It was too late for flight when he realized the noises concerned Reno. The heavy door of the Cadillac flew open and Reno reached in with both hands—one grabbing the red curls on the top of Delahanty's head, the other the front of the lime green silk shirt that bulged with Delahanty's corpulence. For a moment Delahanty thought he was being robbed, until he heard Reno shout, "Out of there, you fat tub of shit!" and felt himself hurtling out of his cocoon of luxury. He was jammed up against the fender and hood of the car, his feet kicked apart, and he was roughly searched. When he glanced up, Delahanty saw Reno ripping apart the interior of his car, smashing open the locked glove compartment with a kick, and scattering the contents on the floor. The alligator-bound attaché case on the back seat went into the street where Reno jumped on it and broke the lock and hinges. Under other circumstances, Delahanty would have been screaming for witnesses and the intervention of other officers. But he hugged the car and gritted his teeth in silence, trying desperately to remember if there was anything in the car to annoy Reno.

"Where is it?" Reno demanded.

"Where's what?"

"The gun! I heard from two people you're carrying a gun now."

"I got a permit."

"You need a permit from me to live, you blood-sucking bastard. If I find a gun on you, I'm gonna stick it up your ass as far as my elbow and pull the trigger."

"I'm not carrying anything. Honest to God! On my mother!"

As Reno looked at him, Delahanty felt his body begin to tremble with shock and fear and he tried desperately to control it.

"You got a felony record, you miserable fuck. I don't care where you bought the permit, don't even think of carrying it where I can find you." Reno whirled away and Delahanty waited until Reno reached the other side of the street. Then he scooped up as much as he could into the attaché case and climbed into the car. His shirt was shredded and his suit was filthy. He was gasping and sobbing in relief as he put the car in gear and drove away from the intersection.

Reno, on the other hand, felt just fine, like an athlete after a good workout, and proceeded serenely toward the meeting with Clappin and the others.

The robbery was an ongoing embarrassment for the state police and Capt. Thomas Manning, who was in charge of their role in the investigation. When he permitted himself a moment to relax from the strain of the inquiry, Manning had a couple of drinks with a friend and remarked, "I feel like the host at a big party and the neighbor's cat has wandered in to take a shit under the dining room table. We can clean it up, but the smell won't go away no matter what we spray on it. I want to hide. I'll have another drink. In fact, I'll have several."

His problem was not just to find the crooks who did it, but also to avoid becoming the scapegoat for having let it happen. Postal authorities were not helping.

The Hyannis postmaster, for example, said he called the Yarmouth State Police barracks at 6:30 P.M. on August 14, to advise that the mail truck would leave in one half-hour and to request the upper Cape patrol to be on the lookout for it. But the Yarmouth barracks log listed the call as having come in at 6:55.

The state police maintained that they had removed a trooper escort from the mail van runs in July when postal authorities indicated that they would no longer require that service. Postal office officials, however, said the escort was withdrawn at the request of the state police who pleaded a manpower shortage. Middleboro Barracks State Police said they had a heavy summer load on the Cape with tourists and the Kennedys, which would make it difficult to continue the mail truck convoy.

Even Postmaster General J. Edward Day had declared that special arrangements had been made with the Massachusetts State Police to convoy the shipments, while Massachusetts Public Safety Commissioner Giles denied such arrangements existed and stated that the state police were to be advised only as to the route of the shipments. Referring to a meeting on July 16 between state police and a postal inspector, Giles said, "It was then that both agencies agreed to the termination of the escort. . . . We then agreed to the alert system. . . . At no time did we agree to check the run at predetermined locations."

There it was—confusion—and Captain Manning had to live with it along with the words of the naïve lieutenant who said, "This is the biggest thing that's happened around here since two people were killed in the fireworks explosion of a couple of years ago."

The problem, in Manning's eyes, was to shake off all this confusion, contradiction, and embarrassment—and get down to the job of solving the crime, rather than replaying the circumstances of blame like an old movie looking for a place to die on late-night television.

The only explanation his department could give was that the men who might have been escorting the mail truck and its load of money had been "occupied elsewhere." Now it was time to shut up and get on with the job for the about sixty men assigned to the case from various barracks and headquarters in Boston.

Manning had begun by personally driving with Chaplin and Streeter, the postal guards, over what they guessed to be the route taken by the bandits while they were unloading the mail sacks from the commandeered van. They tried it fifteen times, using the same sort of truck, with the two guards in the rear cargo area calling out instructions on when to turn, and when to stop. Each attempted reconstruction brought them to another destination but never to the location where the bandits had abandoned the vehicle.

If he could get the route, Manning felt he could come up with the witnesses. Somebody had to have seen the van and the man who was operating it. Manning sent fifty detectives from his office into a canvassing operation of Cape Cod and the little towns north and south of Plymouth. They had composite sketches made from descriptions given by the Postals, but the response was limited. It had been raining, about dinner time, the streets had been empty. There were two or three reports from angry motorists who had been detoured off Route 3 by the detour signs. They had seen a state trooper there—but only with his back to them. As usual, he had been short or tall, slim or stout. It really was an easier life giving speeding tickets to the cowboys racing out of Provincetown in their convertibles, and he yearned for it. He really didn't want to go to the meeting with Clappin and the others in this mood. But there was no choice.

Castle lived in Cambridge because of the girls. They were all over the place. Unfortunately, he was forced to live a romantic masquerade. He couldn't tell any of them that he was an FBI agent. That was much worse than being a cop, who were merely pigs. He was part of the fascist elite guard.

So he told them he was a lawyer, which was sort of true. He had a law degree; it had been an important factor in his appointment to the Bureau. Lawyers and accountants, lawyers and accountants. Give J. Edgar

Hoover all the lawyers and accountants he wanted and the Director would probably clean up the world on legal technicalities. The girl in Castle's bed that morning played folk songs on a guitar, blew clouds of marijuana smoke at him, and told him he should grow a beard. Growing a beard would be worse than getting busted with a bag of weed in each pocket. So he lied and lied.

As he dressed for the meeting with Clappin and the others, Castle felt some amusement at the bureau's reaction to the postal service's claim of preeminence among the investigative agencies. The Director was obviously fuming. Castle's supervisor, a nervous, worried southerner who had a tendency to throw up in periods of stress, and consequently took the onerous desk job of keeping track of street agents, tried to tell Castle to cooperate without really cooperating, without really telling him not to cooperate.

"You know what I mean?" the supervisor kept asking during their conversations about the case.

Castle knew, but he thought it was bullshit. He was going to give all the information he had, and it was very little, and take as much as he could from the others, and try to break this thing. It would look very good in his file. This exchange of information between them could also put the inquiry on some level of efficiency that might work. Manning would understand. Reno wouldn't unless he could grasp the idea by the throat, smash it to the ground and kick it. Castle determined to make full use of the situation. He was reaching for his revolver, the bulky heavy .357 magnum hidden behind the extra rolls of toilet paper in the small bathroom utility closet, when he was startled as the door was pushed open against him.

" 'Scuse me," the girl said sleepily as she sat down on the toilet. He had his hand on the butt of his pistol but he couldn't move. When she finished, she pulled the flush handle and made her way back to the door.

"You okay?" she asked.

"Sure," Castle said.

"Wanna ball?"

"Later."

The girl continued back to the bed without asking for an explanation. Maybe she was still asleep. It was a close one. The incident might have wiped out Castle's entire social standing.

Rita, who worked the tables in the rear of the Statler Hilton Coffee Shop, knew immediately that they were cops, these cold and mean looking men who took a table in the rear while better ones were available in front near the window. She considered cops rotten tippers who always tried to get by with a nod and a grim smile as if they were giving approval to your morals instead of thanking you for your attention and service. They would sit there and drink three to four thermal jugs of coffee and look pained if she gave them a check for more than one. Rita preferred gangsters, crooks in general. They were not only polite and flirtatious but lavish with gratuities which frequently exceeded the bill for the meal.

Rita filled the cups for these four, and asked if there would be anything else. Only one of them, the cute one who looked Italian, said, "No, thank you." The others just shook their heads. That's cops for you, she thought. She screwed around with the condiments on the table and delayed her departure just to annoy them. They stopped speaking as soon as she approached the table and they didn't talk until she left.

"I don't guess there's any question we should pool

our information," Clappin said as soon as the waitress trudged away.

"What information?" Reno asked.

"Well," Manning said. "We have got statements from those three motorists who saw the perpetrator in the trooper's uniform. Have you all seen those statements?"

"I think," Castle said, "Clappin means we ought to have a central collection and sorting station, one place where all the information goes. Am I right?" Clappin nodded and Castle could sense the resentment provoked by his brusque manner. He did not want Clappin hiding information from him. "That's probably the best idea we have had yet," Castle added. "And the postal inspectors will certainly be a central point for that information since this is essentially your case."

Now Clappin was happy and he would stay happy. "The Bureau will maintain its own files, of course, but I will see that a copy of all the pertinent information is hand delivered to your office everyday." He turned to Reno, who looked as if he wanted to bite his coffee cup in half. "Can you handle that drill, lieutenant? I know you're short on clerks to do paperwork."

"What? Oh sure. It's only another sheet of carbon paper. You may not get them everyday but you will get them."

Manning volunteered, "We can do that without any problem. I would like to take Inspector Clappin's thoughts a step further along the same line. I think we ought to get on the same radio band so we can communicate with each other and coordinate street activities. The radio technicians can put this into operation in a day or so." Castle did not know for sure but guessed that everyone would bust his ass to get it done. He said, "We can use the bureau's communications setup as the dispatcher receiver. I think it's one of the best around."

The others glanced at each other. It was a novel idea but it seemed to rob each of them of individual freedom and put them under controls.

"That agreed," Castle went on, "I would like to begin work on another joint project that will help us all—compilation of a directory of hoods, with photos, descriptions, MOs. All of the pertinent and professional details on habits, weaknesses, even their family activities. Everything about them we can get out of our files, personnel reports, and whatever we can pick up from wires and informants."

They were startled by the audacity of the idea. Reno spoke their thoughts, "Jesus Christ, a social register for the scum of the earth."

"We can call it the Blue Book," Castle added.

Rita wondered what they were laughing at, the sour bunch of bastards. They were probably going to put somebody's grandmother in jail for double parking. She ignored the gesture one of them was making with his coffee cup indicating that it was empty and hurried off to the table of an elderly couple who would probably want to talk about all the tourist attractions in Boston while they were ordering pancakes. Old people, like kids, ate a lot of pancakes.

Murphy was on the move the morning the coalition of law enforcement agencies was formed—moving as he had in the days since the robbery and as he would for most of the days to come. It was all part of his logic, a frenetic coming and going through Boston, into the suburbs, down to Providence, even out on the Cape, once as far as Maine, and then into New Hampshire as well. In addition to assuaging his restless spirit, Murphy was keeping an eye on what the enemy was doing while also confusing them—if they were watching—about what the hell he was up to. The pattern was normal for Murphy although now he seemed to accelerate it.

Four of the others had places of occupation that limited their movement and, in fact, required their presence to avoid raising questions. They were under instructions from Murphy to maintain all their regular schedules and habits with as little variation as possible. Joey and Frank, their garages; Sam Gilardi, the holes to climb into for the construction company; and Conrad, a used car lot where he was on the records as a salesman. Harry, who had occassionally operated gourmet food shops stocked with delicacies he liked to eat, had been consistently unemployed in recent years. Working would attract attention to him. Anyhow, he was at the wheel for Murphy's perambulations. That was torture for him.

Murphy did not sleep in the manner of the normal individual who goes home to the same bed most evenings. Murphy only visited his house from time to time and never for more than fifteen or twenty minutes, then only to feed his pet cats or to deliver his wife's allowance.

As they approached the house, he would dig a small collection of crumpled bills out of various pockets until he had a total of $75, and hand it to Harry. "Count it," Murphy would order. Harry would flip through the bills, glancing back and forth from the street to the money.

"You got seventy-five dollars here," Harry would say.

"Count it again."

The ritual would be repeated perhaps four or five times. Murphy never explained why he made Harry count the money repeatedly; the amount was always the same.

Harry asked why only once, and the answer was a snarl: "Just fuckin' count it."

As Harry eased the car into a space on the street as close as possible to Murphy's gray clapboard house, Murphy would snatch the money and leap out the door, plunging toward his home. That's when Harry would sleep. His eyes would be closed and he would be gone in the instant that the door slammed behind Murphy and his own fingers turned off the ignition. He slept then, and when Murphy dashed in and out of all the other strange places he visited, including the establishments of four loan sharks who kept several hundred thousand dollars of Murphy's money working on the street—at pay-or-pray interest rates.

While Murphy generally rode in silence with the air conditioner roaring at top power and all the windows wide open "or you'd catch a cold," he would occasionally ruminate on matters that were important to him.

"You never see a dead bird," he would say, "unless it has been knocked down by a truck or caught by a cat. Where do all the little birds go when they die? You never see them lying around."

Harry was too weary to ponder the question, passing it off as somehow related to Murphy's deep roots in Armenian folklore and superstition, which had been passed along by his grandmother and then his mother. Each time they saw a fire truck or a hearse, Harry would change direction without waiting to be told, and it never seemed to matter because they never had a direction or a destination. Even when they traveled out of state, the journey seemed mindless. One afternoon, Murphy told him to "get on the Pike and take 95 South."

"Where are we going?"

"Connecticut. A little place just across the border."

Harry believed that some urgency was being communicated by Murphy, so he pressed the stained and dusty car for its maximum performance along the main East Coast highway that connects Boston and New York.

"Get off at the first exit in Connecticut and head east," Murphy ordered as soon as they crossed the state line. Murphy directed him through a half-deserted New England town of antique shops, mortuaries, and gas stations in equal number, to the old Boston Post Road, then south again for a few blocks. When they approached a small diner, a structure made to look like an old railroad car and called Bill's Diner, Murphy directed Harry into the gravel parking lot beside it. The building was old and dilapidated, a stranger to fresh paint or even a garden hose, probably because most of its commerce had been drawn away by the parallel superhighway.

"What's in this dump?" Harry asked, thinking that it was an inconspicuous, out-of-the-way place for a meeting or even a hideout. No self-respecting cop would eat there. He assumed a meeting was about to take place, perhaps with some influential crime boss in the area or even with someone out of New York.

"Best fuckin' beef stew I ever ate," Murphy said, getting out of the car. Although Harry knew he should have been fully adjusted to Murphy's idiosyncrasies, he felt like ripping the steering wheel from the column and hurling it at Murphy's head, which was disappearing into the side door of the diner. Instead, he followed, to appease his curiosity. Murphy was already perched on a stool hunched over the cracked white glass counter spooning chunks of beef, potato, onion, carrot, and celery out of dark sludge that looked like it had been drained from the crankcase of a truck. To Harry, the interior of the restaurant was as unappetizing as the exterior—unswept, grease-stained, fly-specked, and permeated with a faint odor of garbage. The counter attendant, a red-eyed man Harry guessed to be somewhere between 70 and 125 years old, appeared to have come directly to work from the drunk tank of the local police station and was dressed accordingly. Harry did not so much as sit down in the establishment and risk contamination by what he assumed to be hordes of bacteria.

"Have some," Murphy grunted with a full mouth.

"I'm gonna grab a little nap in the car," Harry excused himself.

Harry managed to get about half-an-hour's sleep. He estimated that, based on the usual speed with which Murphy devoured his food, the man had gotten through three bowls of the stuff in that period, and he seemed content and relaxed.

But Harry had been so appalled by the condition of the restaurant that he was compelled to ask Murphy about the point of the journey.

"You know, this is about a three-hour trip, this little picnic we went on in Connecticut," he said. "Was it worth it?"

Murphy popped a couple of digestive mints into his mouth and sucked on them for a moment.

"Yesterday is gone," he said. "Tomorrow is too late. Today I felt like having beef stew."

For all of his seeming aimlessness, Murphy was working, looking for the pattern that was being shaped at the breakfast at the Statler Hilton, and he couldn't see it—because it had not yet been put into operation. He made himself take small side trips out of town to clear his vision and freshen his perspective. Each time he returned from Maine, New Hampshire, or beef stew in Connecticut, he expected to sense or see a different scene and figure out what the police were doing to apprehend him. His technique failed. They didn't seem to be doing anything except picking up bums and half-wits, while announcing that the case would be solved momentarily.

Not knowing what the police were doing bothered Murphy more than having them sit on his front porch. Like any good general facing a major campaign, Murphy needed battlefield intelligence.

"Let's go over to that little old TV place near the university," he said. Harry wondered if the set they had carried out of there had broken down.

Even without the announcement from Washington that the postal inspectors were to be the dominant law enforcement officers in the investigation, Phil Kalis could tell just by looking at Art Clappin, who was so full of himself that he seemed to have grown two inches. Among other things, Clappin had obviously purchased a new suit of more conservative tailoring and shade and a new tie as well. Kalis surmised quickly that Clappin was trying to look like an FBI agent. He was also trying to be secretive, Kalis thought, which was probably Clappin's idea of how an FBI agent conducted himself.

"What's going on?" Kalis asked as he leaned on a corner of Clappin's desk and noted that the Postal seemed to be shuffling papers under cover so that they could not be read.

"All the information comes from Humboldt," Clappin said.

"I know it's difficult for you, but try not to be an asshole. If I wanted the information about the Plymouth mail robbery, I would go to the FBI anyhow. I just came over to say hello."

The insult relaxed Clappin as Kalis had hoped it would. It was a reminder that they were friends and had known each other for a long time. Clappin smiled. "The usual bullshit," he said. "Somebody had the bright idea of pulling together a list of all the people around here who could have done this thing."

"That's half the people in Boston. What do you do with it after you get it?"

"Same old thing. Check them out, narrow it down. The Feebies will tap everybody's phone—including yours and mine."

Kalis's laugh was more nervous than hearty. "Keep them off my phone. I don't want them to get the number of my bookie." He strolled away, speculating on ways to get the information to Murphy that the investigators were putting together a catalog of potential suspects—and that there would not be a safe phone in the city in about a week. His stomach grumbled in a twist of protest as he decided to have lunch for the next two or three days in the milling, anonymous swarm at Drew's Cafeteria.

W hen the meeting at the Statler Hilton Coffee Shop ended and the four law enforcement officers set off for their vehicles, Castle found himself walking with Lieutenant Reno and assumed that they had parked in the same area. When Clappin and Manning were out of sight, Reno stopped him with a light touch on the arm.

"What's on your schedule?" There really wasn't anything on his schedule. Castle's supervisor had cleared his caseload for concentration on the Plymouth mail robbery by reassigning his cases to other agents and by eliminating routine matters.

"There's a lot to do to set this thing in motion—pulling files, getting clearance for the taps everybody will want, setting up this radio operation," Castle said. "No schedule but a lot to do."

"Fuck that. Way to go is to crack open one of these little punks and see what's inside."

"Who?"

"You know Greek Billy Stanoupolis?"

"I know him. Banks and payroll. He hasn't been up for anything for three or four years. Do you have information about him?"

"I don't have to hear anything about the little prick. He'd steal the pennies off a dead man's eyes and he gets around. One way or another Billy'll get himself close to that mill-and-a-half just to see what kind of change drops into his pocket."

Castle nodded, and they set out for Watertown in Reno's car because the lieutenant knew how to get there with minimal traffic problems and it was his idea—he was leading the way. They rode in silence—Reno had no capacity for small talk—while Castle thought about Greek Billy. He remembered three or four cases in which the Greek had been involved, the shooting on the golf course, and the arrest and conviction that followed. It occurred to him why Reno wanted him along, and he was cynically amused. Greek Billy was on parole, federal parole, and the presence of an FBI agent would add weight to whatever threats Reno might use to obtain information. Castle was also somewhat concerned about Reno's well-known interrogation techniques. Being involved in police brutality might be as dangerous as getting caught with a Cambridge antiwar pothead. On the other hand, Greek Billy was a gutter rat with a long record of criminality and more sources of information in a single afternoon than any police agency could develop in a month. Crooks talk to crooks, the way cops talk to cops and doctors talk to doctors. Castle also conjectured that his own presence meant that Reno intended to use psychological pressure rather than brute force to extract information from Greek Billy.

Before they got out of the car near the small drab tavern that looked like a sleeping bum in the harsh sunlight, Reno used his radio, as any good cop would, to transmit the information that he would be out of the car at such and such an address in Watertown. If he disappeared, at least they'd know where to start looking.

The radio operator repeated the information, confirming the call.

Driving down Wilson Street, Murphy heard the call on the receiver Pirov had installed in his glove compartment. His memory clicked immediately with the address of the bar and the image of Greek Billy. He grunted; they wouldn't get anything out of the Greek by kicking his nuts up around his ears because Billy didn't have anything to give, anyhow. Then he thought that if Billy was sufficiently frightened, he was capable of making something up to appease Reno—and that was dangerous to everybody Billy knew.

"Drew's," he said.

"What the fuck?" Harry said, braking the car, slicing to the right across two crowded lanes and turning a corner. He had not expected to turn two seconds earlier, but now they were on the path to Drew's Cafeteria.

"You said that we were going to Philadelphia."

"I'm hungry."

$ VI $

Last of the Big Spenders

Marlene Murphy loved antiques, and despite her husband's grumbling, she managed to put together an estimable collection of French period pieces that glowed with the patina of age and her attention. As one of Murphy's friends put it, "There wasn't a fucking chair in the place you could sit on without figuring to fall on your ass." But the walls of the three bathrooms in the house were all new and completely modern, covered from floor to ceiling with tile, which Murphy had installed himself. Those walls were among his banks, and one or the other of them was in the constant process of reconstruction as he distributed the Plymouth mail robbery loot and put his own share away for safekeeping.

After adding $25,000 to the money he had on the street with loan sharks, Murphy felt he had reached the saturation point. More deposits would have indicated to his gossiping acquaintances that he had made a very large score, precisely what he was attempting to avoid. He wanted the rest of the world to believe that he was impoverished. In many ways, he acted as if he actually were.

Murphy's tailor was the discount garment racks and tables of Filene's basement, where he bought short-sleeved sports shirts made of woven plastic for $1.50 each. If the long-sleeved shirts on sale were less, Murphy would buy those and rip the sleeves off at the biceps. Here also in the underground chamber of bargains, Murphy found trousers that had been reduced to the point of abandonment by the clothing department and jumbled in piles on the counters. A few feet away were the sports jackets hanging like clusters of wrinkled confederate battle flags. He would snatch off a size too large or a size too small if his own wasn't available. Occasionally, he also bought a necktie here—the clip-on type with small metal wings on the knot that slip on under the collar of the shirt. Every three months or so, Murphy would notice that the tie could be read like a menu at Drew's Cafeteria and he would snatch it off and throw it out the window of his car. Murphy bought one pair of shoes a year from the Regal Shoes outlet, a plain-toed black oxford from one of their most economical lines. And he expected them to last an entire year without any additional attention beyond tying and untying. But when it occurred that Murphy had to move across hard pavements at an excessive rate, the shoes would wear through in October or November at the onset of Boston's rain and slush season. Since he only had one pair of shoes, Murphy could not leave them for repair. He would return to Filene's basement (it was cheaper than going back to Regal's) to get a pair of rubber overshoes. Once he slipped those on, they remained in place, rain or shine, until the following March, which was his traditional month for purchasing a new pair of shoes.

Murphy's shoes were wearing thin early after the Plymouth job. His pinch-penny habits were the cause. While most bank, store, or payroll robbers grab only the big bills and run, because they are easier to handle, Murphy never left so much as a penny behind. In the Plymouth job, as in all others, he insisted that they take along several thousand dollars in loose change as well as $42,700 in single dollar bills. Both the change and the singles took up a good deal of room in the special cache in Sam Gilardi's walls. Every two or three days, he would summon those of his cohorts who could spare the time to gather for a dime rolling session, during which they would spend endless boring hours counting, stacking, and sliding coins into cylindrical bank wrappers. When the sessions ended, their eyes glazed and fingers aching, they would be dispatched with pockets sagging with coin rolls to make the rounds of bars, restaurants, small shops—any form of commercial enterprise that required change for its transactions. The job of getting rid of it all took about a month. Hardly a bank in Boston experienced a call for change from any of its usual customers. Murphy's men were also required to stuff their pockets to the bursting with wads of singles. Night after night, they would canvass bars where large bills are tendered for large checks, offering to take all the hundreds, fifties, and twenties they could get in exchange. When they complained, Murphy snarled, "It's fuckin' money, ain't it?" He went back to retiling another bathroom wall, replenishing his own private bank.

Even from so much evidence, Murphy's men failed to reach the obvious conclusion that Murphy did not steal for the love of money and the acquisition of material possessions, but simply for the love of stealing.

Joey Marcetti was extremely jealous of his wife. He had good reason although she never really let him know it. Gina was a tall, slender, full-breasted woman with delicate features and a translucent complexion. Sexually, she had the appetite and discrimination of a flea in a crowded kennel.

While Joey's interests were focused on his garage, gambling (at which he was very bad and very bold and thus a consistent loser), and crime, Gina floated like a lascivious butterfly swept by the winds of passion from one blossom to another. It was a pastime she had developed out of physical necessity and boredom during the early years of the marriage when Joey was doing eighteen months of a four-year sentence for armed robbery —a necessity that turned into a hobby and eventually a compulsion.

During the day when her two small children were in the care of her mother or Joey's—and later when they were old enough to be occupied by school—she would organize a routine around dalliance. After Joey left at 6:30 or 7:00 A.M. for the garage, which opened early in the tradition of repair shops and gave him legitimate cover for his criminal activities, she would lope through the house on long slender legs, putting it into order and dealing with the telephone calls that began with her husband's departure as if by signal. The callers were almost exclusively male. Was she doing anything at 10:00 A.M. for about half an hour? Could she be in Brookline at noon, the place near the Howard Johnson's Motel? Could she get over to Somerset about 3:00 P.M. and would she like to have a drink about five before going home to prepare dinner for Joey? Sweet-natured as well as sensual, Gina was remarkably cheery about the demands of such a frenetic schedule. She always said yes.

In the brief periods between assignations, she would shop with eclectic good taste and an eye for durability, considering the wear and tear on her wardrobe, which required regular replacement of shredded lingerie. Some of her friends were more frenzied than others. They were also dangerous.

It was Joey's habit to leave the garage between six and seven o'clock and return to the two-story wood frame house to find his children bathed and fed, Gina refreshed and loving. The evening would commence after a quick shower and an attempt to dig the grease from under his fingernails. There were any number of possibilities for dinner—all the good restaurants on the North End and the pier, Joey's, Charlie's, Vinnie's, Charter, the Trocadero, the Casa Loma, the Via Appia. Then they might settle in one favorite place for drinks and talk, possibly to be joined by Joey's best friend, Frank, and Frank's wife, Kay. Because she was both attractive and well turned out (and preceded by her reputation), Gina drew admiring glances and furtive inspections but rarely an overt approach. When that happened, as it did one night in an illicit gambling club above a waterfront bar, Joey's teasing, relaxed good nature vanished and the urge to maim and kill emerged. A blackjack dealer suggested foolishly to Gina that there was a way she could guarantee good cards. Joey went across the half-mooned table for the dealer's throat and left him unconscious and unfit for employment. Others were more subtle, if just as lustful. At some point in the months immediately following the Plymouth mail robbery, these included Rocky Gallagher, the tall, red-haired, flat-faced sociopath with dead-blue eyes who controlled the Irish elements of the Boston underworld with the savagery of Attila the Hun. Gallagher had killed at least a dozen men personally and ordered the execution of several others, principally through his two associates, Duke and Sean O'Brien.

Gallagher and the O'Briens were in a small club called the Lido one night when Joey and Gina stopped for a drink before heading home. They knew of Joey only vaguely as a small-time robber who was ethnically and geographically identified with the rival Italians, but they had never seen Gina. She leaned over the bar to reach for a book of matches and exposed a plump breast to Gallagher's flat stare.

"Get her," he said to the O'Briens, who had managed to survive ten years with a functional psychotic by doing exactly as they were told, whatever and whenever. So they did. The next day, Gina went to bed with all three of them in reasonable sequence—Gallagher first and the O'Briens later—and in the heat of passion, or whatever it was, murmured that her husband had been involved "in something big" recently. Maybe she did it to give her lovers a sense that they were achieving something of real value in this casual conquest. But she was also opening the lid on the truth about the Plymouth mail robbery, and the day after that Joey demonstrated that he had made a major score by handing the kids over to their grandmother and taking Gina to Las Vegas. He lost $38,000 shooting craps, an event that was duly noted by an Internal Revenue Service snoop prowling the casino to keep an eye on big winners and big losers for obvious reasons.

The losses almost dissipated Gina's tingling memories of her experiences at the hands of Gallagher and then the O'Briens, but as Joey told her on their way to McCarren Field and the flight back to Boston, "There's more where that came from, baby."

One of the big problems at Sam Gilardi's house had nothing to do with its day-to-day operation. He was so good with his hands and so mechanically oriented that he could fix anything and make what he couldn't buy, up to and including all of his electrical appliances. There is a man like Sam Gilardi in almost every neighborhood, the one who installs his own electronic garage doors, raises his own television antenna, repairs his own plumbing, remodels and panels his recreation room. The problem in Sam Gilardi's household was his brother-in-law, who worked for the Internal Revenue Service in New Hampshire as an agent, and was a snob about his white-collar achievement as compared to Sam's status as a skilled laborer. Sam's diminutive sweet-natured wife, Alice, was caught between them, like a kernel of wheat between two grinding stones. Because Alice's father had died when she was still a young girl, her brother George had taken a more rigid masculine role of protector and guardian toward her than might be allowed to most siblings. As a man of limited authority, he felt a great need for it. He was unwilling to abdicate that position after Alice met Sam Gilardi. After their marriage, it was George's habit to appear at the Gilardi home at least once a month with the air of an inspector general reviewing the condition of the troops. Sam's preoccupation with his hobbies spared him for the most part from confrontations with the visitor. If he didn't have anything specific, Sam could always think of something to take apart, clean, oil, and put back together again.

"What kind of life is this? You sit around up here with the kids, while he's always in the basement."

"Please, George. Sam's busy. He works hard."

"Do you ever go out? Does he ever come upstairs?"

"George, mind your own business. He's happy. I'm happy. Why aren't you happy?"

"Why don't you go over to Ma's house more often? She's lonely."

"I see her too much already. She's sick of looking at me."

"What's he building down there now? An airplane?"

"He's putting in a new patio with awnings above it, George, leave him alone."

Sam Gilardi would face some of these same questions when George stayed for dinner, but he responded to them with grunts and shrugs. He felt only contempt for George's lack of mechanical aptitude. But Sam would suffer some bruises to his pride, especially in the image he hoped to maintain in the eyes of his wife, who gave him a kind of love and constancy he had never known. Those bruises occasionally showed in their quiet moments alone, as they did one night when George had been particularly sour about the working man's lot because it did not contain the benefits attached to his own civil service status.

"You got everything you want, don't you?" Sam asked as he held Alice's small frame in his great muscular arms.

"Of course I do. Don't pay any attention to George. He's a pain in the ass."

"I don't need no pension from the government. We've got enough money."

"A pension is nice but I know you'll always take care of us, Sam."

Sam breathed deeply, kissed her, and thought about the distant future.

"I mean, we got a lot more money than you think we got. I'm gonna put in a whole new room in the house, so the kids will have their own place to play when the weather is rotten. We can afford everything we need and more."

"You give me enough already, really, I don't need any more, and you do everything around here. Who else has got a house where everything works?"

"I can't tell you about it but I got friends with a lot of money who trust me and take care of me. There's big numbers involved. Really big."

Sensing that his need for reassurance was overwhelming, Alice moved her hands down the strong body beside her to the one area of Sam Gilardi's anatomy that was totally disproportionate, a startling contradiction to his great size. She had a slight difficulty finding the object of her quest but having done so, paid him the ultimate flattery.

"Promise not to hurt me," she said unaware that Sam had almost revealed to her that the Plymouth mail robbery loot was hidden in the basement below them.

After eighteen years of marriage, Conrad's tall, slender, immaculately neat wife Grace could not recall having had more than a five-minute conversation with her husband since his proposal, which had been brief. He did not sit still long enough for extended talk, only for reading. Nevertheless, he was always polite, always provided her with sufficient funds to operate the household, and made sure she had a new car to drive each year.

However, she wasn't quite sure what he did for a living. He seemed to come and go at very odd times, maintained a strange communications center in his private toilet (which she cleaned but was not permitted to use), would frequently be gone for extended periods, and would be home for equally lengthy periods. Grace couldn't figure it out. Early on, when she thought there was some point in inquiring into what he did and why he did it and possibly where he did it, his reply was a mumble and a shrug.

"I got business," he would say and bounce out of the house. She speculated that "business" might be selling cars or real estate, that he might be an investor who lived off the profits of his ingenuity. She was remarkably prescient without knowing that Conrad made his deposits and withdrawals with a gun or a fraudulent scheme. It remained the case that she had a great deal of time on her hands since he seemed to want no social life whatsoever and discouraged visits to the house by neighbors or friends when she suggested them. Since she was somewhat shy, Grace accepted the situation and found other pursuits. One was cleaning and polishing her house, another was praying, and the last was vodka.

She discovered that a small glass of vodka on a cold day gave her warmth, quieted whatever uneasiness she might feel about the mysteries of her husband's activities, and freed her energies to push a vacuum cleaner through the house while softly reciting prayers. If one glass achieved such positive results, it was only logical that two would make greater improvements. She surrendered herself to the joy of this mathematical logic—and by the fourth year of her marriage, she was consuming a quart of Wolfschmidt vodka for each twenty-four-hour period, vacuuming and dusting the house at least once, scrubbing down all three bathrooms, and waxing the kitchen tiles every other day. She had also begged forgiveness for most of the sins known to organized religion, none of which she had the temerity to commit.

Conrad, meanwhile, continued to function as one of the most selfish of men, and it was his compulsive greed that provided Grace with the first inkling that there might be something wrong with the structure of their domestic tranquility. The portly man with bulging gray eyes was incapable of passing up a situation where he might turn a profit, even if it might endanger larger schemes and greater gains. Shortly after the Plymouth mail robbery, when he received his initial share, Conrad decided to turn the mystery of the missing loot into a private fund-raising scam. He permitted himself a reasonable allowance for the operation of the house and cars and other personal needs and then invested the rest of it—about $40,000—as a bank loan to a Walpole bookmaker named Shorty Weiss. The bookie had failed to pay the required bribes two or three years earlier, had gotten arrested and jailed, and was now in the process of reestablishing his operations. Conrad and Shorty were splitting fifty-fifty with an override of several thousand dollars per month until the original $40,000 was repaid. From this amount, Conrad was again taking limited living expenses and turning the remainder back into the street with loansharks he considered reliable.

Still it was not enough. As the news media speculated on the whereabouts of the $1.5 million taken from the mail truck, Conrad speculated on a scheme to put the magic of money to work. He had noticed over the years the successful operation of the Gordon brothers, wholesale produce suppliers to several retail outlets throughout the South Shore area. The Gordons were considered to be highly successful businessmen. The brothers, Joe and Dave, were big hearty men of the sort seen around loading docks and warehouses. Although the profit margins in their business were relatively small and the industry itself was highly competitive, the Gordons had managed to accumulate considerable personal holdings through shrewd but honest practices. While they also paid small fees to passing police for the privilege of double and triple parking their delivery trucks, they had no connections with criminal elements in the city and little knowledge of how they operated. Conrad considered them ripe plums ready for picking.

He began stopping at the produce market to buy an occasional box of avocados or a case of oranges. What he could not use, he distributed to his friends or simply threw away. There was a period when crates of produce could be found on unlikely corners throughout the city, all abandoned by Conrad. As he made his small purchases, he put himself in the path of the Gordon brothers, who quite naturally wondered about the resources and the demands of this new customer. They were surprised that Conrad did not operate a small restaurant or store that would require the limited amounts of produce he was purchasing. They were equally surprised by Conrad's disclosure that he was motivated by a momentary need for economy while he fed his large family. He suggested that there were eight hungry children at home waiting impatiently for the next dinner of cabbage soup. Conrad had also chosen to play the role of a tough, shady character, with allusions to even more dangerous associates. They also were in difficult circumstances at the moment. But, he also suggested—with the air of a conspirator—their poverty was not a situation that they would have to endure forever. With winks and nods and quick movements that were his natural style, Conrad imparted hints and suggestions that a great deal of money would be available to him in the near future.

"As soon as we cut up the melon," he said, conjuring an image the Gordons could understand.

He also hinted that the other participants in the melon were prepared to wait until a certain statute of limitations ran out, while he was not, because of the constant and immediate demands on his resources.

"Melon? Statute of limitations? What the hell is he talking about?" the Gordons asked themselves. Each morning the Boston newspapers, several national publications, and the broadcast media suggested to them that it was probably the loot from the Plymouth mail robbery and that this unlikely customer of theirs had access to it.

But when they suggested that this might be the case, Conrad went silent, smiled knowingly with a trace of bitterness, picked up his cabbages, and departed. He managed to put the Gordons in a position of assuming that he had a share of loot coming, and sympathizing with his financial problems. They saw Conrad's situation as an opportunity to profit. And no taxes! Between them, having deduced all of these circumstances, they formulated a plan to swindle themselves by suggesting a deal to Conrad.

They put it together one morning, somewhat earlier than Conrad had expected. First, the Gordons said they wanted to know how much money Conrad had coming, and, second, if he would be interested in selling his future share for cash in hand at a considerable discount. Conrad hemmed and hawed for a week and said he was worried that they could see through him so quickly.

Then he suggested that his share—and, mind you, he was not saying that he had a share of the Plymouth mail robbery—could come to more than $400,000. At the same time, since he was dealing with honorable men, solid and trustworthy businessmen, he was prepared to discount his share by 50 percent and take $200,000 in cash for it. The Gordons could hardly wait to come up with $100,000 each since it meant at best doubling their money. At worst, all they had to wait for was the split.

Grace never knew about the $200,000 her husband collected, since he put it in a safety deposit box under an assumed name and attached the key to a ring he carried with three others just like it representing three other depositories of such funds. What she did get was an inkling that something unusual was going on, when she was cleaning her husband's bathroom one afternoon and one of the telephones began to ring. It startled her. This had never happened before. In the confusion of her vodka she decided that somehow the call must be for her and she answered it.

"Is Conrad there?" David Gordon asked.

"No."

"Oh. When do you expect to hear from him?"

"I don't know."

"Who is this?"

"His wife."

"Oh."

Now Gordon was embarrassed and didn't know what to say or how to hang up.

"Sorry to disturb you. I hope the kids are feeling better."

"The kids?"

"The twins."

"The twins?"

Gordon, feeling the first touch of anxiety tip-toe across the pit of his stomach, put the phone in its cradle and shouted for his brother. Grace hung up and went out to the kitchen to find the Wolfschmidt. She felt she had made a terrible mistake. Or somebody had.

Harry's wife did not get along with Harry's mother. Since he loved them both, it was a constant annoyance getting caught between their competitive personalities. Like any good Eastern European mom,

Harry's mother was devoted to seeing that he was clean, neat, well-dressed, well-fed, and rested, no matter how much personal strain and pain this demanded of her. Like many young women who have married out of the dizzying swirl of playing and partying that seems to be the off-duty routine of successful criminals, Harry's wife wanted very much to continue the sybaritic chase and escape the boredom of domesticity. Conflict was the natural consequence of keeping them both under the same roof, which was Harry's major mistake. Murphy did not help. He was moving constantly, apparently without need to sleep, and Harry was his wheelman. Go here, go there, go everywhere.

In the rare instances when Murphy decided to pursue an interest by himself, Harry would stagger numbly into his home in Jamaica Plain—not far from the residence of Boston's corrupt and colorful mayor, James Michael Curley—and leave a trail of clothes from the doorway to the bed, where he collapsed. As far as his wife Mildred was concerned, the scattered garments could stay there until they disintegrated into dust. But, of course, his mother would scoop them up, empty the pockets of hundred dollar bills (which had been acquired in exchange for singles and fives), put the money aside in some secret crevice, plunge the shirt into the laundry, and then spot and press his suit at an ironing board set up in the kitchen. She could simultaneously prepare some heavy Eastern European meal to be ready at whatever moment the snoring hulk of her son stirred again. Along with the stuffed cabbage, pirogi, and babka, she would give Harry an honest count of the cash his garments had disgorged. Frequently, he told her to keep it or stash it, pay the household bills or get herself something nice to wear to church.

From Mildred, however, there were only demands,

which grew angrier as his presence became more fleeting. She would track him from the front door to their bedroom with questions like, "Where have you been? What are you up to? Can we go out tonight? What the hell good are you if I never see you?" Harry was usually sound asleep by the time the last question bounced off the shield of his fatigue. Mildred would sweep out of the house in anger, taking such cash as Harry had provided—and the amounts were not small —leap into her car, and begin a round of shopping, drinking, and film going, leaving mother and son to their own just deserts. She would return to find Harry sleeping, eating, or missing. On the rare occasions when he was eating or dressing to leave, she would berate him savagely for his wayward lifestyle and demand remedial action.

"I don't have time" was not a satisfactory response, but that was all Mildred got. He had time to run around, he had time to go out, he had time to disappear for twenty-four and forty-eight hours at a stretch. He had time to come home smelling of cigars and Scotch, and perfume.

The fact was that Harry had not even had time to dispose of more than a few thousand of his share of the loot. In fact, there were four packets of one-hundred dollar bills, each totaling $10,000, stashed in the closet about eight feet from the bed, each packet stuffed into the toe of a shoe.

Mildred discovered them there one afternoon after an ascerbic exchange with her mother-in-law, who voiced a frugal protest at Mildred's discarding of several hardly worn dresses. Mildred told the older woman to mind her own Lithuanian business, and seeking justification (or at least ammunition), went to Harry's closet to make a survey of his spending habits on new clothes. The money was in some new shoes

Harry had not worn and a packet of bills fell out as she was examining them. One good packet led to another. She replaced them carefully, but Mildred began to make plans of her own for the division of the Plymouth mail robbery loot.

Kay D'Amato would never believe that her Frank had taken part in the Plymouth mail robbery or shared in any of its loot. He was too sweet and gentle toward her in their private life. She knew that this was the real Frank D'Amato, the hard-working operator of a tire sales company and auto repair garage, whose sole interests were their home, his work, an occasional evening out with their best friends, Joey and Gina, and the sporting events that fascinated him. He had even convinced her that his conviction and imprisonment for armed robbery early in their acquaintance had been the work of corrupt police attempting to shield the real bandit for a price. That Frank was bad-tempered seemed to her a natural part of his protective personality. He only blew up at people who were trying to screw him, take advantage of him, or question his integrity.

In the ten years of their marriage, she had grown quite interested in the one luxury that Frank allowed himself, tickets to sporting events. He seldom seemed to miss a game while the Celtics or the Red Sox or any other team were within driving distance, and if he did not go with his friend Joey, he would take her. She was unaware that every dime he had above the operating expenses of his business and their home was riding on the outcome of those games—as well as on horses in every race at every major Eastern track, as well as on the turn of cards in a long-standing poker game in the back of his garage, as well as on dice wherever he could find them being rattled and rolled.

"You'd handicap a fucking chipmunk if they put a saddle on him," Joey teased him.

That was true.

"Yeah? I would probably make a bundle on it."

That was false.

Frank D'Amato had the worst luck of anybody in town. He was happily known as "Louie the Loser" among the bookmakers who took his action. His bad temper was exacerbated by the constant demands that he pay his gambling debts. These ranged upwards of $150,000 at the time of the Plymouth mail robbery, and he made no attempt to reduce them when Murphy began distributing the cash.

Instead, Frank embarked on a foolhardy program of doubling and tripling his normal wagers, using cash only when necessary to reinstate his credit rating when certain books were reluctant to risk the probability that he would be slow in paying. He also decided to add a cinderblock section to his garage—where business was good—and install in it a concrete vault to which only Joey and he would have access.

He told Kay that business looked good, the future bright; and she was content. He told no one of a very big gamble he was planning with the Plymouth loot and Murphy's wrath.

Greek Billy decided to cooperate with the inquiry while Reno was chasing him around the bar screaming that Billy was going back to the can with a broken leg to serve out his parole. Greek Billy was a tower of fear under the onslaught of Reno's legendary wrath. He was ready to give anybody anything they wanted to save himself.

"I want the names of the people on the Plymouth

mail job," Reno said when Greek Billy was backed into a corner.

"How do I know?" Greek Billy whined. Reno stabbed at Billy's chest with a stubby finger. Billy tried to climb the wall behind him. Castle controlled a stray impulse to laugh at the melodrama.

"You know because you're the nosiest little cunt around," Reno said. "Tell me!"

Billy's mind raced over rumors he had heard, all of the faces he remembered. The truth was, he didn't know anything. But this was survival time. Reno was merciless, and the Feebie who looked like a gorilla with a good barber could really step on his parole.

"Please," he begged.

"Talk!"

Greek Billy could only think of two or three men capable of organizing and executing the Plymouth mail robbery. The problem with throwing suspicion on any of them was that it would qualify him for an underworld execution if anyone found out. Reno might send him to jail; the others would send him to hell in a basket. Of the three men he considered, one was inactive with a very touchy heart condition. The second was in prison, and the third was Murphy. Because they had worked together years ago and he knew the potential of the man, Murphy was his first guess—except that they had met in a bar only an hour or so after the robbery report was broadcast. Murphy had to be clean. Greek Billy seized the golden opportunity: He would give them Murphy, knowing that Murphy would certainly have an alibi. Besides, because of his record, Murphy had to be high on their list of suspects anyhow.

"Dan Murphy," Greek Billy said. "I heard some talk about Murphy."

"Who was with him?" Castle said.

"Honest to God, I don't know."

Castle had been looking at Greek Billy's face searching for a clue to the truth of what the little gangster had been forced to divulge. Reno was acting like the recreation director at a concentration camp, and the Greek was in a panic. All he had given them was Murphy, and Castle already knew about the big redhead.

But Reno was not through.

"You are gonna work for me, scumbag," Reno said. "You're gonna find out who Murphy had with him and what he did with the money. You call this afternoon for instructions." And then to Castle, "Let's go."

In the car Castle was silent until after Reno had found a small clean cafe where he went in to wash his hands. For whatever reason, the cleansing seemed to relax Reno. The FBI agent noted that Reno's style of driving had changed from barely controlled fury to impatience. As they threaded their way back to the area where Castle had parked his car, the FBI agent decided that they might as well discuss the case.

"What do you think about Billy?" Castle asked.

"Greek Billy never said an honest word in his life," Reno said. "It don't matter who he said done it or heard done it or thinks done it. It's why he said it."

"He was afraid you'd kill him."

"He had good reason but that wasn't why he said Murphy. If you know Greek Billy, you know he tried to find out who did the PMR the minute he heard about it."

"Why would he finger Murphy?"

Castle did not have all the information about Boston crime and its perpetrators that filled Reno's mind. The detective sensed this and felt generous about it.

"Billy had to give me somebody I know could have done it. Murphy. To cover his ass, he had to give me somebody he maybe thought really did it. But he had to give me somebody he knew he could get close to, when I kept the pressure on him, which I was gonna do, or I was gonna kill him."

"Are you going after Murphy?"

"Greek Billy is going after Murphy," Reno said. "If Murphy's the man, he may have the little prick killed. If he's not, he could feed us the one who is because Murphy knows everybody who did everything in Boston for the last fifty years. That's what he knows."

"Then why not go directly for Murphy and squeeze him?"

Reno laughed an ugly little snort of derision.

"Try it sometime," Reno said. "It's like squeezing a handful of sludge out of your crankcase. It oozes through your fingers and all you got is shit all over your hand. So we go up against that motherfucker through the back door."

"There's my car," Castle said. Reno pulled to a stop.

"Tell me something, Jimmy," Castle asked. "Why did you take me along to see Greek Billy?"

Reno had planned to spare him the humiliation but he saw no reason to lie since the FBI man asked for it.

"If I killed the sonofabitch, I wanted a nice, upstanding witness to the gun he pulled on me before I shot him."

"Billy didn't have a gun."

"Yeah? They woulda found one on his body."

Castle got out of the car without a comment, flaming with rage and embarrassment. He slammed the car door hard on Reno.

"You make me want to puke."

Reno laughed. "Be careful of your nice clothes."

$ VII $

Enter the Actor

Murphy decided to give himself a new automobile. His old white Chevrolet was beyond resurrection and winter was approaching. His tires were balding, all the fenders were dented, torn, and flapping in the wind like weary seagulls. The interior was stained and littered with trash. There was also a gaping hole in the passenger's side of the vehicle, a token from a passing truck. Noting in the surveillance communications on his police band radio receiver that he was being watched (and confirming it simply by turning to look behind him every now and then), Murphy traded caution for mischief and acquired the biggest, flashiest car he could: a new black Cadillac Coupe de Ville. It was a vehicle that even the most inept surveillance team would be able to spot in a traffic jam.

After Murphy had Pirov transfer his special radio receiver console from the Chevrolet to the Cadillac, he consigned the old vehicle to a pair of professional auto thieves with instructions to take it somewhere and burn it (which they did), waited twenty-four hours,

and reported it stolen to the police while he simultaneously filed an insurance claim to cover most of the cost
of the new car.

The change was gratifying to Harry, who found the
new vehicle much easier to drive, a great deal more
comfortable, and certainly a cleaner place to spend so
much of his time as they roamed the city. It occurred
to Harry that Murphy was being somewhat obvious
and could not have picked a more visible vehicle if he
wanted the police to be aware of his movements. As
usual the same thought had occurred to Murphy several days earlier. He did want to be obvious. He did
want to be seen.

With a reward of $200,000 hanging over the investi-
gation, Murphy knew that somebody would try to collect it by putting his name at the head of the list of
likely suspects. But he was already formulating plans
to use this apparent visibility as a kind of camouflage
for his activities. The Plymouth mail robbery may
have been spectacular, but it wasn't the end of the
world. There were many other places and people to
rob, many more bathroom walls to tear down and
retile.

Within a couple of weeks after Reno's initial inter-
view with Greek Billy, each of the law enforcement
agencies involved had been notified that an underworld informer was working for them and that the
prime target was Daniel Murphy of Watertown. After
the drudgery of searching through the files, checking
out countless bits of information without result, and
interrogating almost everyone in the Boston area with
a tainted past, the police were relieved to have their
suspicions focused on one real honest-to-god suspect.
Clappin and Leibowitz coauthored a long memorandum to Humboldt about Murphy, his record, and his
reputation. Castle did a long memo that he knew would

find its way to J. Edgar Hoover's desk. Manning put together his own report for the commissioner of public safety, and it went to the governor as well. Lieutenant Reno alone did not seem to care much about impressing his superiors but he did make a brief note for the files and also for the inspector in charge of the detective division to the effect that Murphy looked likely as the mastermind of the Plymouth mail robbery. And everybody got down to watching the big hulking man in the black Cadillac while Murphy got down to letting himself be watched.

That was a lot of watching. In eight months, Murphy and Harry put 50,000 miles on a car (the average driver does between 12,000 and 18,000 a year), and they moved so quickly the police teams had difficulty keeping up. To play such sophisticated hide-and-seek, the authorities eventually equipped a light plane with advanced electronics equipment and sent it out at daybreak each morning to circle Murphy's residential area. When the fliers saw the Cadillac—or any other car—leave Murphy's house, they alerted the hounds in the unmarked police cars that the fox was out of his lair and in the field.

But now the days had turned into weeks and the weeks into months, and the pressure for a solution to the case was high as it could get. The day-to-day newspaper accounts of the mystery became retrospective magazine articles and the city editors and broadcast news editors glanced at their calendar and instructed their crime experts to begin preparing anniversary stories.

Reno had formalized his arrangement with Greek Billy by calling the frightened informer to a suburban motel parking lot. There in the shadows Reno informed Billy that he would receive $75 a week, made Billy take off his shirt, and planted a small tape recorder in the middle of Billy's back with adhesive tape. The speaker cord ran under his arm into a microphone which was attached to the front of his shirt just below the second button. Although Greek Billy complained that the whirring of the tape recorder spools sounded like a cement mixer and would certainly be detected by anyone within ten feet, Reno told him to shut the fuck up and get on with his work; the only thing he had to worry about was making contact with Murphy.

Greek Billy lived in fear. He couldn't see how he could survive a confrontation with Murphy. The man was too smart and had too many connections. Trying to outflank Reno was just as dangerous. If he tried to run away, his loan-sharking operations would be quickly snapped up by some barracuda and he would be yanked off the streets as a parole violator and sent back to prison.

He would punctuate his own terror by slipping into a cubicle of the men's room of his bar and turning on the little tape recorder. Even with the juke box blaring on the other side of the wall just outside the toilet, he could still hear the reels turning. They sounded to him like a freight train rolling down a rough track to hell.

He needed help. He needed it desperately.

Hardly anyone knew the truth about Jerome "Actor" Sternweiss. Those who did treated him with the utmost respect, preferably at a distance. At thirty-two, he was a big handsome man with a trim athletic body, dark curly hair, and a face that gave him a remarkable resemblance to Rock Hudson. Hence the nickname, which Sternweiss regarded with what seemed to be diffident good humor and a soft ingenuous smile.

He was married to a gentle, sweet, and extremely

attractive girl from a middle-class North Shore community, where Sternweiss also grew up. He was known during his youth as a "good boy" from a nice family, although his father was a bookie and had some unsavory associates, not in the neighborhood, of course, but in his business—a circumstance that was forgiven of anyone who kept a neat yard and provided for his family.

Jerry's friends began calling him Actor when he reached mature height and weight at about seventeen and his boyish good looks took on a more masculine edge. He carried the name with him into the army for two years in Korea and then back into civilian life, where he seemed to shun the gray areas of his father's occupation by seeking employment as a rug and carpeting salesman. Since he was very attractive to women of all ages and his sales manner was easy and charming, Sternweiss was quite successful. That was the surface personality of Jerome Actor Sternweiss. Beneath it lurked at least one other personality, sociopathic, psychotic, homicidal.

He was believed to have murdered two or three men in each of his adult years. He was efficient, imaginative, audacious—and successful to such an extent that he moved in only the highest circles of crime. With a modest grin he once told a friend that an attempt had been made to recruit him into the hunt for Nazi war criminals in South America. Not bring them to trial, of course, but to cold-blooded justice.

It was one of the few assignments Actor Sternweiss turned down—although he gave it careful consideration as both a Jew and a patriotic American, which he considered himself to be. He also liked the challenges it represented. But there were other considerations.

Sternweiss wasn't the clichéd machine-tooled murderer who starts out as a decent young man and is

taught to kill by the army, tastes blood on the battlefield, and cannot control his lust for homicide when
he returns to civilian life. Sternweiss always enjoyed
the idea of killing, even before he became a soldier. He
enjoyed the act itself as a soldier and decided without
equivocation or guilt—the same way he murdered—to
make it a career.

It was easy enough for Jerome Sternweiss to find
work as a killer. There was always someone among the
men who circulated in the gambling world surround-
ing his father's profession who desired the termination of someone else's life. This desire, usually motivated by money, was the traditional settlement for a
bad debt, for example. Or the elimination of a witness.
Or the dissolution of a partnership. Or the retaliation
for a betrayal. Or the response to an insult. Or the
extinguishing of a passion. Or the culmination of a
hatred. Or merely a business maneuver.

The act of murder is quite simple. It can be performed with a sewing needle or a small pillow or, of
course, bare hands. The challenge to Sternweiss—or
more accurately, the fascination—was the preparation
for the act and the avoidance of prosecution or repri-
sal. He trained for his work with religious dedication.
In the charming cedar shake four-bedroom ranch
house in which he lived with his small family, Sternweiss maintained a special room for himself in the
basement. Its walls were cinderblock, its entrance a
heavy metal door with double locks. Actor called it his
den, carried the key for one of the locks with him, but
hid the other in the basement, constantly moving it
from one dark corner to another. In this room, he gathered several life-size store manikins which he used as
practice targets. While his wife watched television or
read, and his children slept, he practiced hour after
hour, night after night, the proficiency of his profes-

sion. He could, from a distance of twenty feet, hurl an object with absolute accuracy from any position he happened to be in—walking, standing, sitting, crouching or lying prone—into any portion he chose on the anatomy of the manikins. He practiced with hatchets, ice picks, large and small knives, Ninja stars, and dollar-sized metal washers with their outer edges honed to razor sharpness.

He could snap the head off a manikin with a garrotte of picture wire, waxed twine, or clothesline or—as he came to prefer—old piano strings.

His body was one of his weapons and he sharpened his reactions and polished his timing with a series of exercises that gave him strength, speed, and stamina.

He also studied anatomy.

That was how he developed such techniques as the one he reserved for special situations in small communities that lacked competent practitioners of forensic medicine. If his victim should be in such a place, Sternweiss approached the victim during sleep or some other comatose condition, as a result, say, of having been lightly drugged or heavily plied with alcohol. Sternweiss would lift the victim's eyelid with one steady hand and drive a needle-sharp ice pick through the soft flesh of the eyeball into the man's brain. There was little loss of blood. Death was instantaneous. A cursory examination would result in a death certificate of death by cerebral hemorrhage.

A killer with such skill is worth protecting. Sternweiss had proven himself two or three times and had the confidence, as well as the patronage, of a few of the most powerful men in organized crime. They didn't talk about him, build his reputation, or in any way advertise him and make him vulnerable. Sternweiss was much too valuable for that.

Thus, a hood like Greek Billy knew none of this. Billy

met Sternweiss in a bar and thought he was merely a big, good-looking guy who would be nice to have along for company if not protection when he confronted Murphy at the behest of the law enforcement agencies.

Billy consequently found reasons to stay in Sternweiss's good-natured company, talking ballgames, betting on them together, chasing a few broads.

Clappin assigned himself to street duty the night Greek Billy planned to make his initial contact with Murphy in search of salvation from that hound of hell, Reno, as well as a clue to the solution of the Plymouth job. But as fraught with drama as the night might be, the whole thing annoyed Clappin. He tried to concentrate on the crackling of the radio about the movements of Murphy's big Cadillac as Leibowitz drove their government-issue Chevrolet through the tight old streets of the North End, but annoyance nagged at him. His distraction was Reno.

The target of his anger was Reno's decision to set up a private informer without consulting the department running the investigation—and right on the heels of a meeting in which they had all agreed to work together. Here they were, chasing Murphy all over town because this punk of Reno's had decided it was time to make a move.

"He's going out to the pier," Leibowitz said. Their car was one of about twenty-five involved in the massive surveillance and tracking operation, and Murphy's choice of the mile-long wharf jutting into the Boston Harbor was a problem for all of them. There would be a massive traffic jam at the narrow, single-lane bridge that led to the wharf and nobody, including Greek Billy, was quite sure what to do.

Once again, it was Reno who made a unilateral decision. "Drop him, drop him," his angry voice snarled over the radio. We can't lose him out there. . . . Stop where you are and wait."

All twenty-five cars stopped. So did Greek Billy's sedan, which had been trailing Reno, until the detective poked an arm out the window and waved Billy forward, pointing toward the bridge. It was clear enough. Greek Billy accelerated, pulled around Reno, and headed for the pier, where Murphy was probably going to have dinner at one of the four or five good restaurants that had been built on the pilings, hard by the source of some of the best seafood on the northeastern coast.

As Greek Billy's car passed him, Reno was surprised to see some big guy who looked like a movie actor riding along to the meet with Murphy.

"Jesus Christ," Reno said. "I'm going to kill him."

Murphy chose the largest, most ostentatious, and certainly the busiest of the restaurants on the pier. He was an infrequent but special visitor to the place, remembered for the notoriety of the men with whom he dined. Powerful, important men. Though Murphy was accompanied only by Harry this cold spring evening, he was given the best table in the quietest area of the cavernous dining room. There was room for six or eight.

The waiter looked startled when Murphy asked for sliced tomatoes on a bed of plain lettuce and a few sliced oranges to follow. He would drink coffee. It was an insult to the menu, which had been netted, hooked, or trapped out of the Atlantic only a few hours earlier. Harry tried to make amends. He ordered from the top of the list—soft-shell crabs—a dinner order as an appetizer, followed by baked lobster stuffed with lobster chunks and a large Greek salad with roquefort dressing.

"That stuff will fuckin' kill you," Murphy said. "Those shellfish live on dead people. They eat garbage at the bottom of the ocean."

Harry's hunger overrode his caution. "It's better than living on fuckin' nothing, running around with you."

Murphy was distracted from responding by the approach of the maître d', followed closely by Greek Billy and Jerome Sternweiss. The first two were of no significance, but as he regarded Sternweiss, Murphy felt as though someone had unlocked the cage of a great savage beast. This was a killer, and the man who knew everything did not know who he was. The maître d' stepped aside and gestured.

"Hello, Billy," Murphy said. "Sit down and have a drink. Who's your friend?"

Greek Billy was shaking so hard he appeared to be suffering an onset of incipient palsy. With his hand in the flap of his suitcoat, he walked to a position a few inches from Murphy. Sternweiss, with a genial smile, circled the table and chose a seat near Harry, who had frozen in movement between a large crust of sour dough bread and the butter plate, his eyes locked on the flap of Billy's coat.

"I want . . ." Billy said in a voice that was forced and choked, "I want to borrow $50,000 of that dough you got in the Plymouth job." With the barest movement Billy's hand came out from the flap of his jacket clutching a short-barreled .38 caliber revolver and he pointed it at the center of Murphy's forehead. The distance between them was only a matter of inches. Billy's hand was trembling. Harry's first thought was whether he could get under the table and out of the line of fire just before or just after Billy shot Murphy in the forehead. His second thought was to wonder if the smiling stranger who had come with Billy was part of the assassination team.

He was astonished to see Murphy smile—and then carefully and quickly reach up from the table and take the gun from Billy's trembling hand and drop it into his own pocket with a movement as smooth as the drop of sweat rolling down his own forehead.

"Billy," Murphy said, "If I knew where there was fifty thousand dollars, I'd take this gun and go steal it with you."

Jerome Sternweiss was the first to laugh, a rollicking guffaw that turned glances toward them from the occupants of other tables. Harry found the strength to continue buttering the bread and Billy stood staring into the depths of his own fear.

"Sit down, Billy. I'll get you a drink—hey, waiter, give this gentleman a double Chivas."

Billy sat. When the drink came, he gulped it and ordered another, and for the next hour and a half Greek Billy remained almost completely silent while Murphy and Jerome Sternweiss became acquainted with small talk about sports events, the foolishness of gambling, the quality of automobiles (Sternweiss had a new Thunderbird he liked very much and Murphy extolled the comforts of his Cadillac), and Harry ate his way through a second lobster stuffed with lobster but passed on the suggestion of another salad. At one point, Sternweiss identified himself as a rug salesman and the son of a bookmaker. Now Murphy remembered Actor and knew who he was. His mental picture of Sternweiss, however, had been of a gangling school kid, before Sternweiss had filled out and gone into the army. At another moment Sternweiss decided that Harry, who had always been called Harold, was Jewish.

"You're Jewish, too, aren't you?" Sternweiss said.

"I'm Catholic when I'm anything."

"You shouldn't be ashamed of being Jewish. A lot of great people are Jewish."

"I've always been Catholic."

"Listen, Harry, you should be proud of it. I can tell a Jew when I see one. Everybody in my family is Jewish except one of my aunts by marriage."

"Listen, goddammit," Harry started to say. Murphy cut him off.

"What are you doing besides rugs?" Murphy asked Sternweiss. The tone of his question told Harry to shut up.

"Oh, a thing or two," Sternweiss said.

Greek Billy sat silently between them and sweated profusely. He seemed to be almost forgotten except when Murphy turned to him and said, "You ought to see a doctor, Billy."

Billy was so startled he almost leaped from the chair and ran into the street. His paranoia pounded in his skull. What did Murphy mean?

"Why? Why do you say something like that?"

Murphy stared at him. "You're making a funny noise when you breathe," Murphy said. "It's like wheezing. I bet it's those goddamn ten-cent cigars you smoke."

It was the goddamn tape recorder Reno had strapped to his back. The reels were scraping. These men would soon figure it out and shoot him dead on the spot. He wished he were anywhere else in the world except there with them. Even prison was better. It was safer. Greek Billy seized the suggestion of bronchial problems as an excuse, faked a cough and said, "You're probably right. I'd better get an X ray."

"Everybody should throw away the fuckin' cigarettes and cigars," Murphy said. He ended the conversation with that gem of advice and lumbered to his feet. "Good to meet you," he said to Jerome Sternweiss. "You got a number where I can get in touch?"

Sternweiss produced a small engraved card from the lapel pocket of his well-cut gray suit. The card identified Sternweiss as president of the Revere Craft Company and gave two phone numbers.

"Yeah, give me a call," Sternweiss said. Harry nodded to Sternweiss; he wasn't certain that he cared for this big smiling man who had impugned his Catholicism and given him the benediction of a new religion so casually. "See you, Billy. Take care of that cough," Murphy said.

Murphy was already moving away from the table, moving quickly for such a big man, and Harry hurried to keep up with him. They were soon outside the restaurant collecting Murphy's Cadillac from one of the teenage attendants, feeling the soft damp air of the harbor on their faces. Harry could no longer contain his resentment.

"Why does that sonofabitch keep saying I'm Jewish? I've been a Catholic all my life."

"With this guy Sternweiss," Murphy said, "You're better off not complaining if he calls you a fuckin' Chinaman. He's got real capabilities."

"But I'm not Jewish, goddammit."

"Real capabilities," Murphy repeated. "So my advice is to forget about it. And watch your driving. I counted at least eighteen cars so far full of Feebies, Postals, and cops. They'll all be waiting at the other end of the bridge."

Harry was slightly surprised by the information, more so than Murphy had been by the discovery. To Murphy, it led to the conclusion that he had been fingered for the Plymouth mail robbery by Greek Billy.

He wondered why and thought upon the question as the black Cadillac rolled off the pier and back into the mainstream of Boston's traffic.

The argument between Sam Gilardi's wife and her brother began on the telephone. The brother had called from his office at the Internal Revenue Service because he was momentarily bored and felt a need to exercise his frustration. The quarrel came out of his reference to Sam Gilardi as "that big jerk." The remark touched the fuse of Alice's anger and she exploded. Her reaction was probably based on her awareness of how hard Sam had been working each night when he came home to install a new game room and patio and the fact that he had reassured her that they had plenty of money to meet whatever needs might arise in this small happy family. She was not aware that Sam Gilardi's assurances were backed by about $2 million in cash hidden around the house—the remainder of the Plymouth mail robbery loot (about $900,000 now), and Sam's share of the loot from bank and armored car robberies he had participated in over the last ten years. Alice never knew anything about it nor that he had been hiding anything in their house. What she had on deposit with Sam Gilardi was an accrual of love, years of good-natured affection, gentleness, devotion, and security. Her brother had maligned it for the last time.

Alice screamed at him. She denounced his criticism, parsimony, suspicion, and general all-around attitude. She declared that Sam could buy and sell people like him every day of the week. She meant in his richness of spirit, of course.

The brother bridled under the onslaught and was stunned to his own fury. "How did he get to be such a big shot—with a gun and a mask?"

"I don't give a damn," Alice cried and slammed down the phone.

After the first ten or fifteen minutes of fulminating resentment, Alice's brother did what anyone might do in his position—he requested copies of Sam Gilardi's four or five most recent income tax returns to see just what the bastard had and where he got it.

The report that Joey Marcetti, that simple hard-working mechanic from Boston, had dropped a bundle on the crap tables at a Las Vegas strip casino, came across Castle's desk at the FBI offices in the form of a memo from one of the anonymous observers who watch the high rollers in the casinos and count their losses and winnings just as carefully as the pit bosses. It was an estimable indication that Marcetti had struck gold in the greasepit. These were big numbers. He had scored somewhere, somehow. He needed looking into.

Castle was still resentful about the way he had been used by Reno in setting up Greek Billy as an informer, but Castle needed Reno's street-level expertise in going after Marcetti. A good deal of what Marcetti had done or was suspected of doing would not be on the record but in Reno's head, that great storehouse of criminal data. But was this a time for foolish pride? He wrote a memorandum about Marcetti's possible involvement in major robberies in the New England area, basing his speculation on the man's previous record and the big spending. He made an insightful note that Marcetti's freedom from involvement with the police over the last several years would suggest that he was either guiltless—highly unlikely—or working for a much smarter individual; that is, a gang boss who had the power to control a Marcetti and keep him out of the eye of suspicion. The FBI agent went on to suggest that this would be the sort of person, this gang leader, who could put together a group that would include a Marcetti and others like him to pull off a job like the Plymouth mail robbery.

Castle thought it was elegant ratiocination on his part, swallowed his pride, and put in a call to Reno. He needed to know what Reno knew about this little creep who was a grease monkey one day and a high roller the next.

Reno was very disappointed with Greek Billy. The lieutenant had received three telephone calls from his informant expressing terror at having attempted to tape a conversation with Murphy. He was so terrified, in fact, that Billy didn't want to meet Reno and play the tape. Nothing Reno threatened would shake Billy from his fear. Reno knew Billy's habits better than the Greek himself, but Billy was so filled with panic he could have gone to ground anywhere, including the sewers. Reno ran his mind down the recollection of bars, broads, whorehouses, friends, and assorted backrooms where Billy might be hiding. What the hell had Murphy said to Greek Billy to fill him with such terror? A threat? Had he tumbled to the wire Billy was wearing? Or was it just Murphy's reputation for omniscience and his ability to erase a smudge on the face of humanity like Greek Billy? Reno did not care whether Billy lived or died—although he would show a marked preference for the latter if he got the tape. Where *was* the sonofabitch? The intercom buzzed and interrupted his theory with the information that Agent Castle of the FBI was on the telephone.

"Go ahead," Reno said.

"Joey Marcetti," Castle said.

"Punk asshole. Couldn't get wet if you threw him in the Charles River."

"Joey just dropped forty thousand in Vegas."

"Not Marcetti."

"My information is that he dropped a bundle and still had more."

"Marcetti? The one who owns a gas station, got a wife who'd hump a gopher?"

"Gina. She was with him in Vegas."

"Jesus Christ, it *is* Marcetti. Frank D'Amato. Was he there?"

"Who's Frank D'Amato?"

"Another asshole. They hang together."

"He wasn't mentioned."

"Forty grand, huh?"

"That's what it says."

There was a wheezing chuckle from somewhere deep in Reno's throat. It startled Castle. Reno had several curious traits; laughter was not among them.

"This little motherfucker and D'Amato were in the slammer together eight, maybe ten years ago," Reno said. "Meet me at Donovan's Bar near the Quincy Market in fifteen minutes, and I'll tell you about these guys so you can put both of them on the shit list for a wiretap."

"Okay."

$ VIII $

The Antisocial Register

After Harry put 50,000 hard miles on the black Cadillac in six months, Murphy bought a new Cadillac (burgundy), then another (white), and then another (gold). As fast as he bought them, Harry wore them out. Each time the postal authorities looked into Murphy's bank account, they discovered that the funds had come from a relative (his mother or sister) through the legitimate sale of real estate.

Beyond that annoying and frustrating display of ostentatiousness by a notorious pinch-penny suspect, there wasn't much the investigators had to point to as evidence of anything. The press noted that there were five hundred of them working on the case, with costs of the inquiry having doubled the $1.5 million loss in the robbery. The outlook was grim.

An unreliable and frightened informer's suggestion that Murphy could have operated such a holdup gang ... a thread connecting Murphy with Joey Marcetti and Frank D'Amato that was stretched very thinly over the decade since they had been in prison together ... Mar-

cetti's unusual spending sprees against a moderate income . . . incomplete profiles of five men and one
woman who were thought to have pulled the job . . .
more than a thousand tips that were virtually worthless . . . more than a hundred phone taps on homes and
known hangouts throughout Boston . . . a compendium
of criminals in the New England area that would have
been terrifying had it gone into general circulation,
the Blue Book.

What Murphy had was a sophisticated communications system that enabled him to keep track of the surveillance teams that were keeping track of him . . . an
insider at the center of the investigation in the almost
daily presence of Phil Kalis . . . more than half of the
loot (about $900,000) still undistributed . . . one of the
finest holdup gangs ever assembled (particularly with
the addition of the deadly Jerome Sternweiss) . . . an
audacity beyond compare, and a lust for adventure.

Murphy also had his own copy of the Blue Book,
which was stolen, copied, and returned on the same
day. Only two copies were run off for law enforcement
agencies, under the tightest of security conditions, but
one of the participants saw that it had wider circulation. It was rich reading material for Murphy, since
every member of his group except Conrad, Sam, and
Sternweiss was mentioned, along with details of their
records, their visible activities, and personal proclivities. Only one area of the book really disturbed him. It
was the transcript of a telephone conversation between Gina Marcetti and a friend that went as follows:

"Hi, Gina."

"Hi, Sally. What can I do you for?"

"You going into town today?"

"Maybe, I don't know. I'm half-expecting company."

"Just don't get caught."

They both laugh.

"Sal, do you take bread from the Drake's guy, Angelo?"

"Sure, every other day."

"I got news for you. He delivers more than cakes and jelly donuts."

"Angelo? The bread man? You're crazy."

"The hell I am. He don't look it, but he's got a shlong on him the size of a ball bat and he sure knows how to use it."

Sally gasps, Gina chuckles.

"Oh my God, Gina, I don't believe it."

"You'd better believe it."

"I can't believe you're saying this."

"All it took was a cup of coffee."

Giggle. "What did he do, stir the sugar with it?"

More laughter.

"Two big lumps."

More laughter.

"Gina, are you putting me on?"

"Honest to God, he's fantastic. Give him a try the next time he comes around."

"I couldn't do that."

"Why not? You only live once. Get it while it's hot."

This insight into Gina Marcetti's activities came as little surprise to Murphy. Her activities were common knowledge to everyone except her husband, but it meant that Murphy could not show the Blue Book to his associates. He hid it away and decided that if its contents represented the total knowledge of their activities, the gang was safe and it was time to strike again.

Sam Gilardi's brother-in-law felt unwelcome at the neat, comfortable Gilardi home where he had taken so many meals.

What did Alice mean, he worried, that Sam could buy and sell him? He was too goddamned dumb to do anything but work with his hands. Anything beyond that, and Sam would have to steal it.

Steal it . . . the light dawned. Would Sam, *could* Sam be leading a double life that provided an unlikely source of income? Was there a thief behind the taciturn blankness of his expression? There could be.

Before the morose day was over, Alice's brother addressed that thought a hundred times over. But where? He couldn't steal anything from work except buckets of dirt. Did he rob smoke shops and delis on the way home? He wasn't smart enough for anything else. Sam Gilardi couldn't organize a robbery.

But could he be organized into one by somebody smarter and more experienced? Where did that thought come from? Of course, Alice's brother remembered, the papers were always full of stories about gangs. The Irish gang, the Italian gang, and that gang that pulled off the big robbery and never got caught. What was it? The Plymouth mail robbery. That gang.

Sam? It couldn't be. . . .

Reno and Castle neglected to inform the other investigating agencies that they were putting a special surveillance on Joey Marcetti and Frank D'Amato because the pair had been in prison with Murphy a decade ago. It was too tenuous a connection, that delicate thread a good investigator tries to weave into his case with the knowledge that it may break or dissolve at any moment. It was such a small thing, involving a couple of men from Reno's squad and a couple of agents from the FBI, that there was no need to spread the embarrassment if the idea turned out as badly as all the other

leads they had been following. They also did not want
to alarm either Marcetti or D'Amato. A full-scale surveillance would not have gone unnoticed. A cop named
Higgins and a black agent named Jordan were the first
to report unusual activity. They said D'Amato had
brought in a construction crew to dig the foundation
for expansion of his garage building by three and a
half car stalls.

"What's this half stall bullshit?" Reno demanded of
Higgins. "It's either three stalls or four stalls."

"One of the guys on the dig was having a couple of
drinks and he said there's a half stall extra and it's
gonna be like a room."

"So it's a tool room."

"Yeah, but there's no tools. It's gonna be sealed up
like a vault to hide something, which is why this guy
was talking about it. You could see it from the street.
It's just blank walls made of cinder blocks."

"Who's the contractor? Talk to him quietly."

"That's the trouble. He's got his cousin doing the job
and is paying him 25 to 30 percent more than anybody
else would get."

"Shit. Keep watching."

Within twenty-four hours there was news from the
second front for Castle and Reno. As a matter of courtesy, this report came to Castle from an FBI agent
named Fowler.

"At 9:32 this morning," Fowler reported, "a large van
from the Krantz Furniture Company of 1201 Inglenook
Avenue arrived at the premises occupied by Joey and
Gina Marcetti to deliver a large amount of new furniture. Four other men were observed carrying the following items into the house: a brown three-cushion
couch, modern in design, two beige club chairs, a dining room table of dark wood, presumably mahogany,
plus twelve matching chairs, a complete set of . . ."

"Will you stop the fuckin' inventory and tell me what happened, Fowler?"

"Don't get so feisty."

"Just give me the goddamned information. I don't want to know how many hairs you've got around your belly button."

"Okay, they carried in a houseful of crap and carried out the old stuff at the same time."

"What was it worth?"

"I proceeded to the Krantz Furniture Company and . . ."

Castle was shouting in frustration. "I know where the fuck you went to find out. Tell me *what* you found out."

"You're in a rotten mood, Castle."

"If you don't give me the information, I'm gonna come out there and shoot you in the fuckin' head and plead insanity."

"Marcetti paid $27,381.52 for it. Cash."

"Jesus Christ, are you sure?"

"I got a copy of the receipt from the bookkeeper."

"Great. Good job. Stay on Marcetti."

"Hey, Castle—before you hang up . . ."

"Yeah?"

"Go fuck yourself."

The Gordon brothers were becoming a nuisance to Conrad. Enraptured by his myth of great hidden treasure that would be forthcoming "as soon as the coast is clear," they had depleted all of their personal savings and part of the operating capital of their produce operation. They turned their eyes from the fantasy of riches to the realities of account books one day and discovered that they were flat broke. Conrad had taken them for nearly $400,000. After months of almost daily visits to wink and whisper about the great stash of loot that would one day be his, now Conrad had also taken his leave of them. There was no more money to advance him so there was no more Conrad to ask for it.

"I think we have been taken," Joe said one morning with a startling burst of acuity. There was no need for Dave to speak his agreement through the forlorn mask that covered his ebullient features; he felt sick and looked it.

"What the hell are we going to do?"

They agreed to ask Conrad to begin returning the money, and it was relatively easy for them to locate him—the first time—since his home was only a mile from their office. They approached him coming out of a corner smoke shop with two purloined paperbacks in his pocket. Conrad knew they would eventually be coming, for he had no intention of giving back any of the money when he collected his full share of the Plymouth loot or at any other time.

"I've been looking for you," Conrad said before they had a chance to greet him. "I was just using the phone in there to call your office." The Gordon brothers were surprised by the ploy; they expected him to ask for more money, which, as a matter of fact, was a technique Conrad considered and discarded upon reading the desperation in their eyes. "The money's coming through. I will make arrangements to give you guys your share along with a little bonus for each of you."

"You don't have to do that," Bob Gordon said. "All we . . ."

"What kind of bonus?" Dave interrupted.

"If each of you guys had a choice of any car you wanted to drive, what would it be?" Conrad asked. "Caddy, Lincoln, Chrysler, maybe one of those German cars, a Mercedes? How 'bout it?"

The Gordons both drove Fords, occasionally with crates of cabbages stuffed in the back seats and trunks. Luxury cars represented comfort and class to them and an escape from the aroma of decaying vegetation that attached itself to their vehicles (and to them). Was Conrad going to buy each of them a new car? It wasn't quite clear, but what was? He seemed to be saying that he was ready to pay off—maybe.

"I guess I'd go for a Caddy," Dave said.

"Yeah, a Caddy would probably do it," Joe agreed.

Conrad went on to ask them about their preferences in colors and models and the availability of garage space at their separate domiciles. The brothers could feel the keys of the new vehicles jingling in their pockets before he finished. Their anticipation reached a level that turned their thoughts from the purpose of this confrontation. Dave, the more pragmatic of the pair, remembered, as Conrad was about to turn and scurry down the street.

"When are you going to pay us?" he demanded. His tone was cold and his voice strong. All Conrad had provided with his strategy was temporary relief. He had to come up with something definite, if only a promise.

"A week from Friday . . . or a couple of days. . . ."

"We'll expect you a week from Friday," Joe said, "or we'll come find you."

They turned and walked away. Next Friday never came. Nor did Conrad, nor did the money. The Gordons stayed close to their office through the appointed morning, then tried calling Conrad at the number he'd given them. It had been disconnected. By the end of the day, they were convinced of their own gullibility. They decided to run him down.

"He knows we'll be looking for him," Joe said.

"Yeah, and he knows we know he knows," Dave said.

"But there's two of us and only one of him. You want days or nights?"

Joe said, "I'll take nights. I guess we should start with his house and work from there."

"Do you want to tell the guys on the trucks we're looking for him?"

"I'm going to tell everybody I know we're looking for him—and maybe the one who finds him gets a little bonus, like a new Caddy."

"Don't rub it in. We got into this together, we'll get out of it the same way."

They chased Conrad for two weeks but it was like chasing a raindrop. Conrad was here and there and then nowhere, a peripatetic ghost. To get home, he occasionally climbed over fences and wandered across back lots in the middle of the night, tripping on rose bushes, hissing at snarling animals, entering the house in darkness, and leaving in the same surreptitious manner. It was one of the neighbors whose yard he violated, the manager of a small store supplied by the Gordons and contacted by them for information, who eventually spoiled the game. The man was annoyed with Conrad's furtive invasion of the backyard, since it stirred up all the dogs in the area and they in turn disturbed the storeman's sleep. He knew it was Conrad because he got a glimpse of the fugitive going over his fence at 1:00 A.M., the time when Joe Gordon was visiting bars known to be Conrad's hangouts and patrolling the streets. When they received the first tip, the Gordons acted directly. They went together to Conrad's house, rang the bell, and demanded to see their man; Conrad's wife answered the summons. She insisted that he was not there and offered to let them search the house if they didn't believe her. They declined and returned to the car to plan a strategy.

"This could go on forever," Dave grumbled. "He's got

the money, what the hell does he care how long he has to run?"

"I think we have to scare him, let him know we mean business. It's pay up or else."

"How do we do that if we can't find him? Besides, I'm too old to run around with a club and a gun and I don't want to get my ass thrown in jail."

"There's a lot of guys who don't mind using a gun or a club or whatever it takes, and they know how to do it without going to jail. For a few bucks . . . at least by comparison to what the bastard owes us . . . we can send some other bastard around to knock on his door and talk to him. It will be somebody he doesn't know."

"If that don't convince him, then what?"

"I want my money. I want it bad. If we don't get it, I want to see the sonofabitch dead."

The brothers nodded to each other. They both wanted to see the sonofabitch dead if only to remove from the community an occasional reminder of their foolishness. There was also some possibility that Conrad would heed the warning and react favorably. A couple of phone calls to associates in the produce industry put Joe and Dave Gordon in direct contact with a professional terrorist, whose references included six previous professional murders. His name was Burt Hobart, although he was called a number of others, and he reported to the Gordons promptly. His assignment was to approach Conrad and convince him, either by scaring him or hurting him, to pay the Gordons, and if neither tactic worked, to cancel the debt by killing him. Burt Hobart accepted it as a routine assignment, gave the Gordons a telephone number, and said he would be there to answer twenty-four hours a day until Conrad was spotted again. Hobart would proceed as soon as notified to carry out the job with professional skill. He demanded and received $5,000 as a retainer, with a promise of $10,000 more upon delivery of either cash or corpse.

Seventy-two hours later in the soft gray of dawn the same neighbor who had spotted Conrad earlier heard the same outburst by the same dogs and peered out the window of the bathroom where he had been shaving to see Conrad going over the same fence. The light was sufficient to enable him to note that Conrad was carrying a small canvas bag of the sort used for athletic equipment or toilet articles on an overnight trip. The neighbor completed shaving and called Dave Gordon at home with the report. Gordon thanked him and immediately called Hobart who answered on the first ring, sounding alert and ready to move despite the hour. Hobart said that was all he needed and broke the connection.

Hobart, who had answered the phone and rolled to an upright position on the side of his bed in one quick movement, had managed to slip on his shoes while Gordon transmitted the information about Conrad. During the waiting period of such assignments, Hobart slept completely dressed with the exception of shoes. He slipped both arms through the yoke of a shoulder holster, fitted a loaded and cocked 9 mm Browning into the leather sling beneath his left arm, shrugged into a jacket, and moved out of his small comfortable apartment after only a few moments pause in the bathroom to urinate and splash cold water on his face. He wasn't sure how far he would need to take the Gordon appeal but his mind was clear and his resolve firm. It would go as far as necessary. Hobart had no way of knowing that Conrad was not only expecting him but preparing a greeting for him.

In the quiet old house where his wife slept deeply in their second-floor bedroom, Conrad moved from room to room with the canvas equipment bag. He was examining each possible entrance to the ground floor of the house. There were three ways to get in, front, back, and side, and several windows. He checked the vantage points that covered each and all of them. When he had determined what those points might be, he drew a fully loaded .45 caliber automatic from the equipment bag, jacked a cartridge into the firing chamber, and placed it at a point of quick access. The first floor of the house was a fortress awaiting the enemy attack.

It had been Murphy, of course, who had given Conrad the warning. Murphy, who made a point of crossing Conrad's path in the night shadows and found him sitting in the back booth of a small bar in Revere.

"There's an asshole by the name of Burt Hobart looking for you who is supposed to get some money from you or one thing or another. I know this kid has some capabilities from what I hear."

"Well, I guess I'd better say hello to him," Conrad said.

"Yeah, I guess you'd better. I'll see you around."

Burt Hobart parked his car in front of Conrad's house and left the keys in the ignition so he would not have to look for them on his way out. He walked casually but directly to the front door of the house, which had an arched oak door with a small window inset. Beside it was a doorbell. Hobart pushed it, shrugged his shoulder, and loosened the position of the underarm holster.

Conrad was standing in the kitchen finishing a cup of coffee when he heard the bell. He took a final swallow from the cup, returned the cup to its saucer on the kitchen counter, and dabbed at his lips with a dishtowel that was hanging in the elbow of the refrigerator door handle. He moved with reasonable haste toward the front room of the house, hoping that his wife had been at least partially aroused by the ringing of the bell but also hoping that she would remain upstairs to dress, her customary practice, before venturing to see who the caller might be. When he reached the front room, Conrad picked up the .45 caliber automatic from the coffee table about six feet from the entrance and proceeded to the door.

"Who's there?" he asked.

"Burt Hobart."

Conrad started firing and continued firing until the gun was empty, sending eight heavy slugs ripping through the wood of the door, momentarily deafening himself and arousing some of his neighbors. With a roar of surprise and fear, miraculously unscathed by any of the bullets, but sprayed with splinters and shards of glass, Hobart whirled and leaped approximately twelve feet from a standing start at the door to the walk in front of the house. By the time the last thundering blast had echoed through the peaceful morning he had started his car and was speeding away from the lair of a lunatic he vowed never to encounter again. While Conrad was calling a carpenter to repair the door, eight of his neighbors were calling the police —and his wife was pouring the first of the pain killers the day would require.

$ IX $

Bostonians, Proper and Otherwise

"The police," Murphy said, "are six ounces short of a pound of brains."

He was ready to move again. He had chosen the West-over Woolen Mill payroll, which ran in excess of $80,-000. The job had been sold to him three years earlier by the cousin of a former employee. Murphy filed it in his memory for just such a time as this when his whereabouts would be accounted for by the police who were following him. The key to it was having lunch at Vincent Foglieta's large, busy spaghetti house on Concord Avenue.

Foglieta was a short, narrow, migratory Neapolitan who liked to spend his days in the kitchen stirring sauces and making pasta while a swarm of cousins prepared the lunches and dinners that kept the place jammed from about eleven in the morning until midnight. His three sons tended bar, and his wife controlled every nickel that came in and out of the place from a perch at the cash register. The building in which the restaurant operated was actually three structures of red brick sitting side by side, with an additional parcel of land serving as a parking lot next to the restaurant. The building immediately adjoining the restaurant was used for storing supplies that the kitchen consumed at a rapid pace. The third building was used for the storage of equipment and cleaning materials, the items that were needed regularly but not constantly. And next to the third building was an alley that ran from Concord Avenue to the next parallel thoroughfare, a tree-lined residential street. There was a doorway, rarely used and obscured by boxes, that led from the third building into the alley. It was possible, in other words, to park a car in the lot on Concord Avenue, enter the restaurant, walk through the two buildings, leave through the alley door, and be on the back street in three minutes. Very few people knew this. Murphy was one of them. He chose a Thursday afternoon in April, 1965. The payroll would be delivered to the Westover Mill at two o'clock by armored car. If the police had paid attention, they would know that as well as Murphy did. They had driven past the establishment at least twice while following him. Jerry Sternweiss had also been there scouting, although they were not following him. Sam Gilardi had scouted it in his company truck and even Conrad had come there during his wanderings to avoid the Gordon brothers. He had even entered the building and applied for a job under the name Charles D. Gibson, which he had found under a picture in a book he had stolen.

Two weeks before the robbery, Murphy reached Fast Freddy by phone and arranged to meet him. He slipped Freddy an envelope containing $10,000, two sets of keys, and simple instructions.

The day before the robbery was to take place, a slight hitch developed. Sam Gilardi's foreman rewarded his excellent work record by changing his regular days off from Thursday and Sunday to Sunday and Monday and was somewhat surprised that Gilardi was not more effusive in his expression of gratitude at having the prize of consecutive weekend days. Gilardi consequently relayed word to Murphy through Conrad and, for once, Murphy did not take a variation in his plans as an omen of misfortune.

"It's a good thing," he said to Harry. "Connecting days off is a good thing. I never worry about the good things in life. They take care of themselves. I only worry about the bad things."

Shortly before noon on the day of the robbery, Harry and Murphy drove to the restaurant in the newest Cadillac—gold. They parked in one of the slots near Concord Avenue where the car could be observed from one and all of the eight police vehicles maintaining surveillance of Murphy. They seemed relaxed and casual as they passed through the green-painted outer door at Foglieta's. As they passed down the long bar toward the dining room, Murphy nodded to the bartender.

"Good to see you, Carmine. Set us up with a table in the rear. I'll just have a salad with some sliced oranges."

Harry's nose was tingling with the aroma of white clam sauce, but he indicated that he would have the same, knowing that he wouldn't be able to eat it anyway. They continued past the cashier's perch, smiling and nodding at Mama Foglieta, and into the men's room, where Fast Freddy was waiting in one of the two metal-paneled toilets next to the urinal. He handed Harry a brown paper bag containing six automatic pistols and the two sets of car keys. Each man put three of the pistols under his belt and one set of keys in his coat pocket, then moved out of the men's room to the table where salads and sliced oranges were already waiting. It was noon.

Harry stared at the salad wishing he could eat even that.

"Mix it up a little bit," Murphy said.

Harry moved a fork to tousle the lettuce around on the plate and Murphy did the same. They sat silently for ten minutes watching the door. When none of the police or anyone resembling the police had entered by 12:10, Murphy said, "Go ahead. I'll be right behind you."

Harry patted his already dry lips with a napkin, got up and ambled to the side of the restaurant door next to the kitchen entrance. The door led into a short hallway at the end of which was a second door into the second building. He picked his way through tins of tomatoes, boxes of supplies, and baskets of garlic cloves, which made him hungry and thirsty, and found the door to the third building. In a moment or two he was lifting the two-by-four braces from their slots against the door, pulling back the iron bolt and stepping outside. Harry turned left toward the back street and, once there, left again. His car, a new Pontiac, was parked in front of the third house on the left. As he looked down the street he could see Sternweiss and Conrad approaching. Without greetings, the three men entered the unlocked car with Harry at the wheel and drove away. A few cars back was a two-year-old Chevrolet with Joey Marcetti at the wheel and Frank D'Amato in the rear. Because of the surveillance being maintained on Murphy, it had been impossible to go through the customary drill Murphy conducted prior to a robbery, but he had managed, through one devious route or another, to approximate his system. Murphy emerged from the alley and walked to the Chevrolet. Again there were no greetings; instead, he began the Murphy ritual. Had they eaten? Had they gotten a good night's sleep? Did they know exactly what they were expected to do and, if so, would they please repeat it? He was simultaneously distributing the armaments. The same questions were being posed in the Pontiac as Harry directed it toward the Westover Mill. As Harry distributed the weapons, Conrad and Sternweiss were like errant school boys reciting a bowdlerized catechism; no, they hadn't eaten; yes, they had gotten a good night's sleep; yes, they knew what they were supposed to do.

The plan was simple. Conrad and Sternweiss would enter the Westover Mill building as soon as the armored car appeared in the vicinity. Harry would stay at the wheel. As soon as the guards entered with the payroll, Murphy and D'Amato would follow them, with Joey waiting at the second wheel. The guards would be confronted front and rear by four armed men half way down the hallway between the entrance and the accounting office where the payroll was normally divided into small brown envelopes for distribution throughout the plant. It was expected that the guards would not resist such complete coverage by so much fire power. Relieved of their weapons and the money sack and truck keys, they would be escorted to the truck, and locked into its rear compartment to await discovery while the robbers fled.

And that's exactly what happened.

"One minute in, one minute to settle business, and one minute out," Murphy had told them. A fussy cook could have timed a soft boiled egg by the operation.

Driver Richard Billings and guard Stanley Novack remained prisoners in the back of their armored car for forty-seven minutes. For the first thirty of that period they kicked at the sides and yelled for help until the commotion was noticed by an office supply salesman who was calling at the mill. The remaining seventeen were taken up in the rush from the central office of the armored car service with the duplicate set of keys to permit the men's release into the glare of flashbulbs and the cacophony of shouted questions. By that time both Harry and Murphy were emerging from Foglieta's Pasta Parlor with the casual saunter of men who have dined well, if not wisely, both rather ostentatiously chewing on toothpicks, which were the total of the disguises used in the holdup. Conrad was back in his own neighborhood walking toward his house carrying a supermarket shopping bag containing $87,643 —the Westover Mill payroll—keeping an eye out for the Gordon brothers or one of their allies and happy to see a police squad car cruise by—one of many now receiving the bulletin about the payroll robbery from the police dispatcher. Joey Marcetti and Frank D'Amato were in a small bar near Joey's garage, where Angelo, the community bookmaker, was taking their action on the races at a track in California; several customers would probably remember (if anyone ever asked) that Joey and Frank had spent the entire afternoon there drinking beer and wagering. Jerome Sternweiss was in an apartment on Boylston with a large portfolio of broadloom samples, charming a middle-aged housewife into five rooms of wall-to-wall at $7.50 a square yard, including padding, plus a small installation service fee. None of these men fit the descriptions that came from Billings and Novack as they remembered their sixty seconds of terror.

Murphy was as content as he ever permitted himself to be while they drove from the restaurant. The surveillance cars fell into their traditional patterns. He began to listen to their chatter on the radio receiver and permitted himself a chortle of triumph.

"There ain't a fuckin' way in the world they can

figure this out if everybody just does what he's supposed to do," he said.

Harry glanced at him, surprised at Murphy's contradiction in mentioning the good things instead of just
worrying about the bad.

"Yeah," Harry agreed. "If we don't fuckin' well
starve to death from missing meals."

Sam Gilardi's problem began with a routine
call to the Postal Inspection Service with a "sort of tip"
about the Plymouth mail robbery. The call was given
to Clappin. He almost brushed it off because the vague-
ness of the information challenged his compartmen-
talized, bureaucratic attitudes. But the caller identified
himself as a fellow bureaucrat and said he was following the rules by going to the agency in charge of the
investigation.

"There's this guy. I think he's got some of the loot of
a robbery, maybe the Plymouth mail robbery."

"Is this a known criminal? Who is it?"

"No, it's my brother-in-law, Sam. He's a laborer."

It's easy to see how the tip could have died there, but
Clappin had very little to do beyond sorting through
the dwindling number of surveillance reports about
Murphy and a growing number of newspaper accounts
about payroll and armored car holdups throughout the
area that seemed to follow the pattern of the Plymouth
mail job. There was one report that said Murphy had
come out of his house one night, walked up to a supposedly surreptitious surveillance car, and invited two
postal inspectors into the house for coffee because "you
guys look like you're freezing your asses off out here."
Another told of Harry strolling into a bowling alley to
bowl a few frames while Murphy got a haircut, asking

the FBI agent who followed him to keep score. In both instances, the officers declined.

A half-way vague tip was a pleasant change from that sort of thing and Clappin arranged a personal meeting with Alice's brother. But first he cleared it with his boss, which was not pleasant. Nothing about Humboldt had been pleasant for almost two years. Having come into the case with an untarnished reputation, and surrounded by the mystique of success, Humboldt had been expected to direct a quick solution to the case. He had even promised one publicly. He had grown increasingly bad-tempered as the days crawled by in futility and frustration. Clappin had forced himself to continue reporting personally to Humboldt simply to survive, although he felt that Humboldt had grown to detest him as a symbol of his first great failure. He decided to gamble that the information Alice's brother was offering contained some substance.

"We've got an unconfirmed scrap of information that indicates where the Plymouth mail money could be hidden. I'm checking it out. I thought you would like to know."

Humboldt wanted every detail. "I hope it's true. Keep me posted. Completely."

That was all he said. Clappin was relieved. He wasn't at the end of his rope. Yet.

The first meeting Clappin and Leibowitz had with Alice's brother took place in their official car. The informant was able to relax and ruminate about Gilardi's lifestyle and income, Alice's statements about the money Sam supposedly had, and how he thought these elements pointed toward the possibility that Sam was holding some loot, even if he had not participated in the robbery, and it could be the Plymouth loot. It was a patchwork quilt of suspicion. But it rang true. They noted that all of Sam's tools for his home repair work were of the highest quality, not the routine collection of hardware most amateur carpenters collect. Everything he used at his little jobs was the best, the most expensive, and not merely adequate and serviceable. It added up to the conclusion that Sam lived beyond his means—quietly and discreetly perhaps, but still beyond his means. Was he crazy, their informant asked, or was it worth checking?

"I think we've got something," Clappin said.

Reno and Castle still couldn't find Greek Billy or his wheezing tape recorder. But Murphy could. He dropped word that he was looking for the Greek quietly and casually.

"I ain't seen Greek Billy around," he would say to a waiter. "He used to come in here a lot."

The word got around. Greek Billy heard it. He made a point of solving the mystery of his absence. He came into Drew's Cafeteria one midday as Murphy was popping a wedge of ham steak sticky with raisin sauce between his wide, thin lips. Greek Billy was wearing a heavy beard, a strange black overcoat, and a black slouch hat that made him look like an East European refugee. He felt like one. He had been hiding in cellars with rats and spiders subsisting on fear—fear of himself, fear of prison, fear of Reno, fear of Murphy. He had lost about thirty pounds and staggered to the table and almost collapsed into Murphy's plate.

"Honest to God, I didn't tell them anything," he sobbed.

"Jesus, Billy, is that you? You look like a bum on a six-month binge. If you need a couple of bucks to get cleaned up and back on your feet I can help you out," Murphy said, reaching for a pocket.

Greek Billy grabbed Murphy's hand with both of his own.

"Honest to God, Reno and this FBI guy are going to send me back to prison if I don't rat on you, but I can't do it. They want you for the Plymouth job. They want me to set you up for it."

"Let go of my hand, will ya. I'm hungry and I want to eat and I don't know what the fuck you're talking about."

So Billy told him and Murphy listened—and ate—impassively. When Billy had finished his recital and stared at Murphy with a hollow-eyed plea for mercy, Murphy granted it.

"What you need is a lawyer, Billy," Murphy said. "They're trying to frame us both. Come on, I'll introduce you to one."

Gina Marcetti's days were crowded with excitement and fulfillment. Her exacerbated lusts appeared finally to have found a population to gratify them. Two mornings, there was the Drake's Cakes deliveryman, whose energy equaled the physical equipment he brought to his route. There would be calls at least twice a week from Rocky Gallagher to suggest an assignation, and he was followed, both in personal security and sexual activity, by his closest henchmen, the brothers Duke and Sean O'Brien. Gina's schedule was easily as complex as that of the Boston transit system. She was apparently the more successful, however, in moving large crowds. There was also the sudden and surprising munificence of her husband Joey, who had not only taken her to Las Vegas for a spree but had redecorated their house with approximately $26,000 worth of new furniture—all paid for in cash from the roll of hundred-dollar bills that

had replaced the gas station wad of singles he customarily carried. There was money in that roll for all
the new clothes and delicate lingerie she had time to
buy, which was seriously limited by the number of
times in any day she would undress, redress, and prepare her shapely body for the next visitor.

"I don't fuckin' believe this broad," Reno said to Castle as they watched the Marcetti home through binoculars from an apartment building across the street.
They knew from the tapes of Gina's phone conversations why the Drake's Cakes man spent thirty to forty-
five minutes delivering a loaf of bread, a bag of donuts,
and a pie to the house.

"Maybe he has a cup of coffee," Castle suggested.
The small jest annoyed Reno, a moralist. Further, he
could not reconcile the cast of characters in Gina's
private drama with the events that had taken place in
the Boston underworld. The struggle for control of
bars, whores, bookies, loan sharks, and extortion between the Irish and Italian factions had become a
bloody carnival. Forty known criminals were dead in
the streets or missing and rumored to have been assas-
sinated. Gallagher was the undisputed leader of one
faction, while Gina Marcetti owed at least her ethnic
loyalty to the other team.

As Reno watched the house, Castle sat on the floor
near the window, his back against the wall, smoking
and speculating on Gina's proclivities.

"I wonder how she does it," he said.

"What? What the hell are you talking about?"

"Most of those guys are only in there for fifteen,
twenty minutes. What does she do? Does she take them
to bed, bend over the kitchen sink, or what? She probably doesn't wear underwear. There just isn't time."

"What the fuck difference does it make?" Reno
snarled. It pleased Castle to annoy the city detective.

"It makes a lot of difference," Castle said. "She's got to be very good at it or they wouldn't keep coming back."

"Stop the bullshit," Reno demanded. "She's a cunt who'll fuck anything with a zipper. I want to talk to Marcetti about all the money he's flashing around."

"So let's talk to him," Castle said, agreeing against his better judgment. He couldn't expect Marcetti to divulge anything to them about the source of his money, and interviewing him would tell Marcetti that he was under surveillance and suspicion of involvement in the Plymouth mail robbery. But Castle also surmised that Reno, with his absolute sense of morality and righteousness, could no longer contain his violent reaction to Gina Marcetti's promiscuity. He had to take it out on somebody, if only a betrayed husband.

"There's that motherfucker Gallagher again," Reno said.

"Where are the O'Briens?"

"At either end of the block."

"Why don't we have them picked up for loitering? It would shake the shit out of Rocky to come out of there wiping his dick on his shirttail and find them both gone."

Reno turned from his surveillance to glare at him. "I'd rather have a bunch of guineas come along and blow their fuckin' heads off," he said.

Gangster lawyers, generally, are a rough, crude bunch who know courtroom strategy and jury psychology, as well as the process of bargaining with beleaguered prosecutors, far better than they know the law. Ethnicity means a great deal to them, for Irish gangsters tend to retain Irish lawyers, who try to put the cases before Irish judges, just as Italian gangsters

retain Italian lawyers to go before Italian judges, and
both retain Jewish lawyers, who are considered to be
smarter than any other variety, whatever the heritage
of the bar of justice.

Noel Eddington was unique in this milieu. Eddington was a WASP, a tall, angular, long-nosed, sunken-
eyed result of 350 years of Brahmin intermarriage. His
ancestors, as well as his wife's, had jostled politely to
be first off the first boat to touch New England. They
had signed declarations and constitutions, founded the
first mercantile establishments, organized the first
banks, created the first Society. That added something
almost indefinable to the riff-raff of the criminal element, who could only call it class.

It had been assumed by Eddington's family that he
would follow the well-charted course of his progeni-
tors into business and commercial law, possibly
finding a place on the Bench or, indeed, the strato-
sphere of power in some major sphere of government,
after having first added to the family fortune. He had
all the physical qualifications for such eventualities as
he began practicing with a rather distinguished Boston firm that handled the business and personal affairs
of one of his uncles: a cool aloofness, a serene dignity,
an autocratic sense of divine purpose. Unfortunately,
he also had bad habits. One was a taste for drink,
which he discovered as an undergraduate at Harvard,
and the others were pederasty and sodomy, which he
indulged in and had become fascinated by during his
years as an exchange student at Oxford. While the social register is stained with the renegades of fraud,
bribery, embezzlement, and corporate buccaneering
(which can be accepted as minor business peccadil-
los), Eddington's flaws were tantamount to being
crimes of passion and put him further beyond the pale
of acceptance by his peers with each incident, each

whisper of debauchery. And Noel Eddington gave them plenty to whisper about.

His indulgences also reduced his law practice to opportunists like Dan Murphy and a number of other criminal figures who wanted to go into court cloaked in Noel Eddington's outward aura of extreme respectability.

Greek Billy thought of Noel Eddington as a very classy guy who occasionally represented a bigtime hoodlum, and thus felt very reassured when Murphy told him casually that they would consult Eddington about Greek Billy's problems. None other than the great Noel Eddington. Billy felt reassured just being with Murphy, walking between the hulking Armenian and Harry into the Hale Building near the State Capitol, a quiet, marble-halled office structure whose own subdued character gave testimony to its occupancy by a long list of distinguished barristers whose offices were rich with gleaming oak, mahogany and teak panels, and occasional touches of frosted glass. Half-comforted, Greek Billy was twice as stunned as they approached the door to Noel Eddington's office when it flew open and a tall blond woman wearing only high-heeled black shoes, a white angora sweater, and a small cross on a delicate chain around her neck—but nothing else, not even underwear—ran screaming down the hallway. She glanced at Murphy, Harry, and Greek Billy with panic-filled eyes, screamed again, and ran off in the other direction toward the emergency stairwell.

"Jesus Christ," Greek Billy said. "What was that?"

"It looked like Rose Wilkopf, Gargolian's broad," Murphy said.

"Jesus Christ," Greek Billy repeated as Murphy led him into Eddington's office.

Greek Billy didn't know much about the life of Noel

Eddington, but he knew plenty about Joe Gargolian, a six-foot-five 280-pound professional killer who had graduated from training as a loanshark leg-breaker to murder-for-hire. Gargolian was considered a grade A monster by his employers as well as his victims. He enjoyed killing with his hands. He frequently dismembered his victims, who were said to number about twenty, not counting mere injuries, and rising steadily. Rose was his resident girlfriend, and Eddington had been his lawyer since Gargolian was picked up on suspicion of beheading an Irish hoodlum named Hanrahan with a tire iron.

The door to Eddington's private office was open, and Murphy led Harry and Greek Billy into the large, richly furnished room. Gargolian was standing at a large open window, with a pleasant view of the Capitol dome, holding Eddington by his ankles, the lawyer's narrow aquiline face pointed toward the pavement twelve floors below.

"I'll show you who the shtarker is around here, you motherfucker," Gargolian was shouting at Eddington, whose Phi Beta Kappa key and gold Patek Philippe watch were dangling from his vest pockets and hitting him on the chin in the high breeze that swept across the face of the building, while his pocket change, keys, and fountain pen were raining unnoticed on the street below. On the floor next to the desk were Rose's skirt, half-slip, and panties. Both Greek Billy and Harry were immobilized by the ghastly tableau, but Murphy, as usual, had the presence of mind to react positively to resolve the crisis as Gargolian glanced over his shoulder to note their arrival.

"Don't drop the sonofabitch," Murphy said. "We need him."

Gargolian was savage, but he wasn't dumb. Murphy was a power among the men who gave Gargolian employment and purpose in life. Even a Gargolian could not casually offend Murphy, as much as he might wish to release his grip on Eddington's ankles. Slowly he pulled the tall, lanky lawyer's frame back into the room, raised him above his head with a grip at the collar of Eddington's Brooks Brothers suit, and another at his waist-band, and hurled him eight feet across the office through the frosted glass windows into a service corridor off the waiting room.

"Okay," he said to Murphy as he straightened his own jacket and shirt. "But that's the last time I better catch him fuckin' my girlfriend up the ass. Which way did Rose go?"

"Down the fire stairs," Murphy said picking up her lingerie and skirt and handing them to Gargolian. "She's probably still there, because there ain't anywhere she can go in this neighborhood without these."

Gargolian nodded and left.

"See you, Joe," Murphy said. He locked the outer door of the office, told Greek Billy and Harry to look around for some booze and fresh clothes, but to be careful not to cut themselves on the glass, as he attempted the resuscitation of the crumpled heap of Noel Eddington. The lawyer seemed remarkably taciturn when he regained consciousness. He had only a small cut on the left side of his chin, which could pass for a shaving accident, and a collection of bruises. But nothing was broken, not even his dignity.

Harry found a replica of Eddington's torn and tattered suit in a wardrobe in a dressing room/toilet adjoining the office. Greek Billy found two bottles of Teacher's twelve-year-old scotch in a Victorian cabinet used as a telephone stand next to Eddington's desk. Murphy helped Eddington change clothes, and when the lawyer had trouble bending, Greek Billy had to tie his shoes. Harry found Eddington's ceremonial drinking tankard from Harvard on a shelf and filled it with scotch. Eddington raised it with two hands, drank it straight down, and nodded for a refill. When he had completed the second tankard, a process that took about half an hour, Eddington seemed to be completely restored and uttered his first words.

"Thank you," he said. "How can I help you?"

Whereupon Murphy told Eddington the story of how Greek Billy had been coerced by unscrupulous law enforcement officers, using blackmail as vicious as any practiced by a common criminal, to force him to become an informer in an attempt to frame Greek Billy's old pal Murphy for the Plymouth mail robbery. Greek Billy described the savage brutality Reno had employed in persuading him to accept the assignment while Castle had thrown the full weight of the FBI at him by threatening to appear personally before the parole board to revoke Billy's tenuous freedom. Not only that, but these cruel and ruthless men had also forced him to attach a tape recorder to his body in the hope that he would somehow ensnare Murphy in a web of self-incrimination.

The question that brought them to Eddington, Murphy said, was simply this: What could Greek Billy do to protect himself from these diabolical men without sacrificing truth, justice, and all things honorable to their evil machinations?

"The cocksuckers are trying to frame me," Murphy said.

"I see," Eddington said, turning to gaze out the window. He stared in silence for a full five minutes. Harry assumed he was thinking about his escape from the hands of Joe Gargolian. Greek Billy assumed he was drunk out of his mind. Finally he turned back to them.

"Take your shirt off," he said to Greek Billy. "If you would be so kind, there is a roll of adhesive tape in the medicine cabinet in my dressing room," he said to Harry. From a desk drawer, Eddington produced a small, expensive tape recorder which he used for memoranda and letters when his secretary was absent or he was traveling. He seemed to be approaching a smile as he looked to Murphy, the shirtless Greek Billy, and Harry, who had returned with a roll of tape.

"Since this is what the authorities have attempted to do in their zealousness to incarcerate you, it seems only fair that we do the same to them to prevent it."

Phil Kalis was the first to know that Murphy had resumed his banditry; he was finally getting his payoff for setting up the Plymouth mail robbery. As he had agreed with Murphy, his finder's fee for that one huge job would be a share—10 percent—of future forays against banks, payroll trucks, or supermarket money couriers. The money came to him in curious ways—one package of $8,000 in a shoe box delivered by parcel post; an envelope containing $3,700 tucked during the night above the sun visor in his car; $27,400 in a brown paper bag that looked like a workman's lunch handed to him by a stranger who took the seat next to Kalis's on the morning commuter train.

As any one of a hundred criminals might have told Kalis, Murphy kept his word. But the payoffs began to have an unexpected effect on Kalis. For the first time since he had gathered and bartered the information about the movement of weekend resort receipts on Cape Cod by mail truck, his position as an objective observer of the events that followed began to erode. Accepting the loot of the subsequent robberies made him feel like a participant in the crimes. He, too, became a thief in his own mind. He was not equipped for it. The awareness that he was profiting from robbery,

violence, and the threat of death at the hands of corrupt, unconscionable men, brought Kalis the additional burden of guilt, which grew in his gut like a
weed, nourished by the fertilization of each payoff.

He began looking backward over his shoulder to see
if anyone was following. He didn't like the feeling, or
the way that an almost imperceptible palsy appeared
from time to time in his fingertips and a small tic
would flutter at the edge of his cheek.

Phil Kalis got very, very frightened.

$ X $

Cracks in the Wall

Humboldt spent his days and nights in quiet desperation. He had little hope that Clappin would ever produce a lead that could break the case. His long and distinguished career as a postal investigator had died of attrition. One of these days he'd be asked to bury it. What was he doing here if he couldn't get this case solved, recover the loot, and put the bastards in jail? He needed no reminders, although they came to him almost daily in one form or another, that the cost of the investigation had exceeded $2 million while the five-year federal statute of limitations was within six months of expiring. The state law covering the robbery would carry the investigation five years beyond but he wanted a federal court. They were less subject to local influences.

Humboldt had long since considered butting his chief investigating officer out of the job. But who was there to take his place? It was an embarrassment. The postal inspectors were good but simply were not cops, at a time when he needed just that.

Humboldt occasionally considered retirement. He had twenty-seven years on the job, and qualified for excellent benefits. Plymouth was the only stain on his record. He detested the thought of leaving. It was beneath him. Consequently, he was vulnerable to the enchantment of even the slightest possible break.

"Chief," Clappin said, "I think we're onto a good lead." Clappin began to recite his suspicions, the fact that Sam Gilardi was living beyond his means, the coincidence of Gilardi's prosperity and the Plymouth robbery.

Humboldt's first inclination was to snarl "bullshit" and send Clappin back to his desk, but he scented something that needed to be brought into the open. It was the nuance of truth that every good cop learns to sense in his investigation, the fuel for the compulsion that carries the investigator deeper and deeper into the sea of misinformation, of unproductive suspicions, to that small lair where truth is hiding. Humboldt fired a series of rapid questions at Clappin, and the responses, to the credit of Clappin's sense of detail, were sound.

"Where was Gilardi during the Plymouth mail robbery?" "He had three days off." "Does he have any kind of criminal record?" "No." "Does he associate with known criminals?" "He has not been under surveillance but two of his neighbors report that occasionally Gilardi has had visits by 'strange men'." "How strange?" "Strangers to the neighborhood." "How does he pay for his tools and materials?" "Cash." "Big bills or small?" "All different." "How does the cost of these items figure against his income?" "He either scrimps and scrapes on food and clothes or he has an outside source of income." "Is he a known gambler, and a lucky one?" "No."

Clappin felt for a moment that he was the criminal

and this was his interrogation. Humboldt erased that thought with a few words of commendation.

"Good work," he said. "Get those guys who were operating the truck, Chaplin and Streeter, and find out where Sam Gilardi will be tomorrow morning. We're going to take them out and let them have a look at Gilardi and see if they can place him at the robbery. While we're at it, get hold of something with Gilardi's prints on it. We'll check the FBI files for a record under another name. Take as many men as you need and canvass that neighborhood. Get descriptions of those strangers who visited him and their cars. Find out where he buys his materials, get copies of their records. Ask the FBI to take a look at his bank accounts and slap a wire on his phone. And put his house and Gilardi himself under surveillance."

"I'll get right on it."

"We're going to pay a visit to Mr. Sam Gilardi."

"Are we going to ask him about the robbery?"

"No," Humboldt said. "We're going to ask him why he uses Tennessee White when he makes lamp stands instead of number 3 pine like the rest of us working people who have a shop in the basement and have to watch our pennies."

Sam Gilardi noticed two nondescript government-issued Chevrolets parked near his house as he was returning from work. Without so much as a glance at his own front door, he walked past the house and continued down the block to the delicatessen at the corner. He bought a six-pack of Budweiser from Cooley, the slender, bald proprietor, expressed a few pleasantries, and turned to leave. He stopped at the pay phone affixed to the wall beside the door and glanced into the street through Cooley's display-cluttered window. No one had followed him. He dropped a dime and dialed Conrad's number. It was a fortunate call. Conrad was talking to Murphy on another line. Sam's message was brief.

"The Postals are waiting for me at my house." He hung up and left the store with his beer.

Indeed, they were waiting for Sam Gilardi, and the lumpy presence of Humboldt, Clappin, and Leibowitz crowded the small living room almost to capacity. As soon as the first footfall touched the porch and Sam reached for the door handle, Alice flew toward him from the kitchen, a small bundle of fear.

"Sam, Sam," she cried. "The police are here. They want to talk to you. What did you do?"

"Just be quiet," Sam said. "I don't know what the hell you're talking about. I didn't do nothing." He turned to look at the three intruders. "Who are you? What do you want?"

"We're postal inspectors. I'm Supervisor Humboldt, and these men are Inspectors Clappin and Leibowitz." Humboldt paused for a reaction. There was none from Gilardi. Not so much as a blink until Alice screamed, "Who are they, Sam?" What do they want?"

"If you can't keep quiet until I find out, go sit in the kitchen." The brusque command startled Alice to silence. These were the first mean words Sam had spoken to her in fifteen years of marriage. Alice fell silent. Sam turned back to Humboldt.

"What do you want?"

"We're investigating the Plymouth mail robbery and we want to ask you a few questions. Why don't you sit down, Mr. Gilardi, this may take some time."

Sam turned to Alice. "Is supper ready?"

"Five minutes," she said.

"Who the hell are you to tell me to sit down in my own living room?" Sam asked. "It ain't going to take more than five minutes. I'm hungry." And to Alice, "Go get it ready and tell the kids."

Clappin had the distinct impression that the huge man they were attempting to interrogate would soon begin throwing them into the street bodily. Leibowitz tried to remember if he had worn his gun, without making a telltale gesture toward the unaccustomed bulge on his belt, while Humboldt tried to decide if Sam Gilardi was uncommonly dumb or unusually smart. Either way, Gilardi was not permitting them to slide easily into a seemingly friendly conversation that could turn into a difficult interrogation.

"What do you know about the Plymouth mail robbery?" Humboldt asked.

"Everything," Sam said.

Good God, Clappin thought. They had hit the jackpot.

"Tell us about it," Humboldt said.

"My ass," Gilardi replied. "They been printing bullshit about it in the papers every day for about the last four years. You can find out the same way I did. If you got no warrant, I'm gonna eat supper." He turned and walked from the room, leaving the three postal inspectors staring after him in disbelief.

"Should we take him down to the office and talk to him there?" Leibowitz asked. The familiar sounds of cutlery against china and of children squealing happily behind the kitchen door were a taunt to Humboldt. "Let's get the hell out of here," he said. "I need time to think."

It was no time to think for Murphy. He had to move. Cracks were showing in the foundation of his highly successful criminal system. When the call came to Conrad from Sam Gilardi, Conrad had been reporting to Murphy about the troubles Joey Marcetti was having with Reno and Castle. What the hell had gone wrong all of a sudden?

Reno and Castle were cleverer about approaching Joey Marcetti than Humboldt had been with Gilardi. They waited at the observation post until he returned home about 6:30 P.M. Through the afternoon, they had watched the departure of Gallagher and then the quick consecutive visits of Duke and Sean O'Brien.

"Sloppy seconds," Castle said.

Reno grunted. "You'd think she'd wear the fuckin' thing out."

The O'Briens were followed by a surprise visitor— Lorenzo "Little Larry" Vitale, a former jockey who owned a piece of the Forester Bar where Joey and Gina had stopped for drinks the night before. They mistook Vitale for one of Gina's children home early from school. "Nah," Reno said. "That's the little guy from behind the bar at Forester's. He's trying to cover his face like nobody should see him."

Castle wondered why. None of Gina's other visitors made any attempt to hide. Castle felt a touch of envy, possibly jealousy. She was a beautiful woman, but as accessible as a library book—anybody could take her. For a moment he toyed with the urge to be one of the users. Reno destroyed the fantasy:

"The little bastard better tie a two by four across his ass or he'll fall in," he said.

Castle did not talk to the detective for the next two hours. He suspected that Reno knew what he had been thinking and had made the crack deliberately to refocus his thoughts on the surveillance.

As was his custom, Joey Marcetti had gone directly

from the front door to the shower, stopping only to exchange a brief kiss of greeting with Gina. He stood under the hot water for almost half an hour, trying to scrub off the stink of gasoline and the grease that penetrated the pores of his hands. Gina and the children were waiting for him when he emerged. So were Reno and Castle. Marcetti recognized Reno immediately and greeted him with expansive familiarity.

"Hey, Lieutenant. How're you doing? Who's your friend? Get the guys a beer, Gina, or maybe they want something stronger."

Through all this good-natured jabber, Gina was smiling at them and handing them two cans of beer and apologizing for the condition of the house, which was immaculate. Castle wondered when she had the time or the energy to clean it and he felt that the smile that came with the beer was more provocative than mere courtesy would warrant. He wondered if Gina was trying to put the make on him right there as her husband buttoned up his clean shirt and expressed casual interest in why they had come to see him. Maybe he was imagining things, Castle thought, but it would explain how she acquired so many part-time companions. She was even more attractive up close than he had thought. He forced himself to stop looking at her and join Reno who was taking inventory of the room.

"You got a lot of new furniture, Joey," Reno said. "Where did it come from?"

"Hey—what is this?" Joey asked with what seemed to be geniality. "Where does furniture come from? We got it at the store. What was the name of that joint, sweetheart?" Marcetti threw himself into a large plump club chair and bounced on the springs. "Great stuff, ain't it? Gina picked it out." Gina had taken a seat on the arm of the chair and slipped one hand to the nape of her husband's neck where she toyed with his thick hair. Castle still thought her glances at him were suggestive and sexual. Maybe she couldn't look any other way. Her skirt had ridden over her knee and toward her thighs because of the position she had taken on the chair—or perhaps she had done it deliberately. Castle felt himself gazing under the hem of her skirt, and with a twist of guilt, turned to look at Marcetti, who seemed blithely unconcerned, if he had in fact noticed. Jesus, maybe he was one of those guys who liked . . .

"Listen to me, you asshole," Reno said. "Where did you get all this furniture?" Marcetti seemed stung, almost hurt, and his voice was rich with indignation. "Oh, you think I stole it. That's what this is all about. Well, I bought this goddamned stuff. I gave it to Gina for our anniversary. Honey, go get the receipt. It's over there in the desk someplace."

Gina slid off the chair arm, more leg, more skirt, more thigh. Castle was convinced that she was pointing it at him. She was a bitch and a half. He wanted to lunge across the room after her and drag her into the nearest bedroom. She came prancing back from the desk with a large yellow delivery receipt form listing the furniture and its cost. She ignored Reno, handed it to Castle, bending over unnecessarily to do so. It was an invitation to peer down her blouse and he accepted it. She had great tits. He hated her for what she was doing to him, berated himself for being so vulnerable. Could Marcetti be so blind or dumb that he didn't know?

Castle glanced at the receipt without reading it. The numbers were a blur. He was trying to remember the telephone numbers of three or four girls in Cambridge who would provide instant, if superficial, relief for this arousal. He handed the receipt to Reno.

"See, it says paid right there on the receipt," Marcetti said.

"I can read what it says," Reno said. "It says that three weeks ago a guy who takes home maybe $400 a week tops out of a fuckin' gas station had $26,000 cash in his pocket, and maybe he had a lot more because he was free to spend the whole bundle on a bunch of goddamned furniture. Where did you get the money, Joey, all of a sudden like that?"

"Oh, *that,*" Joey said. "Sure, I hit a streak. I had a month there like you wouldn't believe. I couldn't lose a bet. It didn't matter what. It was like all I had to do was look at a horse and it'd win, or I liked a team and I'd take the odds and suddenly the bookie is crying all over me telling me he doesn't even want to take my action. Ain't that right, honey?"

"Yeah," Gina said looking directly at Castle. "It was a miracle. It started right after you went to church with your mother."

Reno leaped to his feet. "You goddamned grease-ball," he shouted. "You haven't been to church since you were in prison. I'm gonna bust your fuckin' head open if you don't tell me where you got that money."

"On my mother," Joey said raising his hand to his heart. Reno reached down and grabbed the front of Marcetti's shirt and bunched the fabric in a tight fist, half lifting him out of the chair.

"You'd send a saint to hell to save your ass. You wanna give me the names of the bookies? You wanna give me the bets? You're in with Dan Murphy and you got that money from the Plymouth mail job."

"Honest to God," Joey whined. "I don't know what you're talking about."

Castle glanced at Gina. She smiled slightly and winked at him. Reno dropped Joey back into the soft folds of the chair cushions and straightened up.

"I'll find out if you're lying," he said. "You'll never know what hit you when I do. Let's get out of here before I throw up on this scum bag."

He led Castle out the door and the FBI man resisted the impulse to look back and wave to the lovely Gina. He didn't need to. He expected the vision of her to fill his mind for days. In the car as they drove away, Castle remarked, "He gambles, we know he gambles. Do you know who his bookie is?"

"I know he gambles," Reno said. "Your people in Vegas told us he loses. He robbed that money off somebody."

"You think we can connect him to Murphy because they were in jail together ten years ago?"

"That ain't the connection I'm looking for," Reno said. "It's Gina. She's twice as smart as that dumb prick and she knows twice as many wise-guys. She's the woman who was part of the Plymouth gang." Reno looked to see if the suggestion had shocked the FBI man. He was surprised to see Castle was smiling.

"You think that's funny?"

"No," Castle said. "I was thinking about something else."

He was thinking quite happily that if Gina were a suspect, he might have to sacrifice himself for the investigation and let himself be seduced in the line of duty.

Murphy's gloom was a bottomless pit. Joey Marcetti had been waving money around like a drunken millionaire. The dumb sonofabitch had done everything but have a sign painted. The only saving grace was that Marcetti was a professional. Reno could ask him questions forever and never get a straight answer about anything up to and including the time of day. But the questions wouldn't stop and Marcetti would be under continuing close surveillance, which complicated things at a time when Murphy did not need complications.

Sam Gilardi was something else. Murphy could not understand how the suspicion had come to Gilardi. He was the least flamboyant of them all. He had no criminal record. He never did anything except go to work everyday, tinker in his basement, and occasionally rob a bank or a payroll car. How could the Postals, the dumbest of the people chasing them, have tumbled to the idea that Gilardi might be a part of it? Even Gilardi's wife was utterly devoted and seemingly incapable of providing a clue to Sam's involvement. Murphy was positive that she had no idea whatsoever of her husband's criminal activities. Maybe he could find the answer interrogating Gilardi himself, but there was no time for it and they obviously could not be seen together.

"Drop me off at Filene's," he told Harry. "Take this thing and park it someplace obvious where they can watch it. Tomorrow about noon you be standing on the corner of Mass. Ave. where they're digging a hole for the Prudential Building. A car will go by and blow the horn twice. You get in quick. Don't let anybody follow you there."

On that, Murphy was out of the car and part of the swarm of pedestrians who always crowded the sidewalks around Boston's leading mercantile establishment. He moved so swiftly that he was gone into the labyrinth of the store before Harry could pull away from the curb. If any of the police following them had noticed, they would never be able to get out of their cars in time to catch up with Murphy. He was gone.

For all Harry could tell, the cluster of cars that customarily followed the gold Cadillac remained unchanged. He didn't pay any attention to them most of the time since Murphy, who saw everything, kept track of them. Murphy even noticed when they brought in a new vehicle for the surveillance, because they invariably used their old plates on the new car. A man whose head was a camera was very difficult to fool.

Harry felt a great sense of loss as he looked for an obvious place to park the Cadillac—lonely and slightly discomfited, until he realized what had happened. Murphy had given Harry his first twenty-four-hour break with nothing to do except keep an appointment the following day. The realization stunned him. He could look back on all that time and see that when they weren't simply riding and looking, adding to the encyclopedia of Murphy's information, they were scheming, then stealing, then running, then cruising again. Harry had been home only a few consecutive hours in all that time to change clothes, and make sure his mother was all right. Harry glanced out the car window and noticed that he was opposite a police precinct house. Murphy wanted an obvious parking place, didn't he? Harry drove quickly into the parking lot across the street, turned the Cadillac over to the parking lot attendant, promised to return for it eventually, and strolled away. He felt almost giddy with a sense of freedom, however momentary it might be. He knew the surveillance teams would assume that the placement of the car was part of a scheme of some sort. They would have the lot staked out as long as the car remained. Then he decided to give himself a feast. He thought carefully and chose one of Boston's finest restaurants, an age-encrusted establishment of dark paneling and brilliant damask linens set with gleaming silver and crystal. A cab took him to its doors in an alley just off the Boston Common and a $50 bill got him an immediate table for four—all for himself. He started with Clams Casino—a dozen—and six sauteed soft-shell crabs with a light garlic sauce. The first bottle of Pouilly Fuissé— the wine steward's choice—was gone, and he switched to a Montrachet with Lobster Savannah, a two-and-a-half-pound beast. Then he cried encore for both lobster and wine. Four hours later, he was stuffed.

Harry took a cab home, left a trail of clothing from the front door to his bedroom, and collapsed. He slept for fourteen hours and awoke just before dawn and then only from the insistent pains of bladder pressure which forced him out of bed. He felt incredibly good and decided to dress carefully for the day ahead, which could turn into a week or a month of the old schedule with Murphy. He exchanged a few words with his mother in the kitchen where he went for coffee, but his wife was nowhere around. The mother only shrugged when he asked where she was. He couldn't remember if she had been a presence in the house during the night.

After he completed most of his wardrobe he went to the closet and reached for the new shoes that served as his private safety deposit box. The four $10,000 packets of bills were gone. So was his wife, he knew.

Murphy had disappeared into Filene's basement. Humboldt was certain that it had something to do with his unsuccessful interrogation of Sam Gilardi, just as Reno was certain that it related to his conversation with Joey Marcetti.

"How could anybody that big and that ugly just vanish?" Humboldt demanded of Clappin as soon as he heard about the interruption of surveillance. Clappin could only lay it to Murphy's acknowledged cunning, and his taste for dull, drab clothes. Moreover, most of the men on the street had failed to notice Murphy step away from the gold Cadillac, which was the focus of their attention.

The bizarre story of how Harry had parked the car opposite a police station, then gone on a gluttonous orgy by himself made no sense. What was that all about? Was there a falling out among Murphy's gang? Were they making mysterious moves in response to the police intrusion into their territory?

"I think we've got something in Gilardi," Humboldt said. "I just don't know what the hell it is. And I'd hate to have to explain why I think so."

"You want to bring him in?" Clappin asked.

"That won't do any good. The key to this may be his wife. She was very nervous, wasn't she? Let's go back over there this evening and spend about an hour with her just before Gilardi usually gets home. We can probably get her spinning like a top, and then let's see what Mr. Sam Gilardi wants to talk about."

"Good idea, chief," Clappin said. "What do you make about that business with Harry and the car?"

"It's bullshit," Humboldt said.

The dull decor and the static routine of the FBI seemed more claustrophobic than ever to Castle. He wanted to rip the dull gray uniform of the investigator from his tingling flesh, let the sun sear him and the wind sweep away the cobwebs of bureaucracy and law enforcement, as he ran naked down a white sandy beach beside a coral sea—hand in hand with Gina Marcetti, of course. Somehow, he had to make contact with her again . . . alone. She was only a telephone call away, but if he picked up the black instrument on his desk and dialed her number it would be the end of his career. The director would have him on a plane bound for assignment to the office in Nome, Alaska, within twenty-four hours after the transcription of the call came off the tape that was being made of Gina Marcetti's telephone conversations. Or he might even be fired. Then it would be goodbye to the charming little apartment in Cambridge, farewell to the sweet little potheads who never shaved their armpits, addios to la dolce vita. He would make a rotten truck driver. His stomach churned with jealousy at the thought of the Drake's Cakes deliveryman. He was swept to hatred for every man who had known the body of beautiful Gina. And there were so many.

Just as suddenly, he detested her. She was evil. She was base. She was vulgar. She was a nymphomaniac. She was . . . a goddess. And he wanted to crawl on his hands and knees to her side, or at least to the side of her bed. How could she share such beauty and spirit with a swine like Joey Marcetti? The moment he had a vision of Marcetti's oil-stained hands touching her sweet flesh, the blood pounded in his temples and Castle wanted to pull the stubby .357 magnum from the holster beneath his jacket and empty it into her lovers. Christ, he told himself with bitter savagery, that would decimate the adult male population of Boston.

What was happening to him, Castle wondered? He was a user of people and situations and he felt helpless with both this woman and her circumstances. To the best of his knowledge, he had never been in love with anything but his ambition, and he wondered if love was what was happening to him. Castle was revolted by the conjecture. How the hell could you fall in love with a bum like Gina Marcetti? Reno was right about her: She was an open manhole that anybody might fall into. Yet the thought of her, the scent of her, the promise in her eyes, obliterated his reason. "Insanity," he said loudly.

With a wrench and a small groan—he glanced around quickly to make sure he had not been heard—

he forced himself to return to the language of the report he was reading, then tapped his teeth with the end of his ballpoint. Maybe if he just dropped her a note, they could meet somewhere, like Venice or Oahu.

Reno was glad to be rid of Castle and back in the office alone. The guy wasn't worth shit in the interrogation. He sat there like a stuffed owl trying to sneak a peek up the broad's skirt. Didn't he know she was scum like the rest of them? A guy like that could blow the whole investigation, chasing hot-pants nookie when he was supposed to be concentrating on connecting the Marcettis to Murphy and Murphy to the Plymouth mail robbery. It surprised him that the FBI had a guy like that on the job. Next thing you knew they would have faggots with pink pistols.

It was perfectly clear to him that Gina Marcetti had been part of the robbery. You had to look at her like a guy, Reno thought, and forget that she was a broad. Look at the nerve she demonstrated fucking around the way she did. Look at the brains she had for juggling a schedule of dates, places, and people. She had everything and the greaseball she was married to had nothing. He probably couldn't change a spark plug without a chart. But Gina, she was the one. She was the blond on the overpass. And he'd get to her one way or another.

Reno was pursuing the thought when he charged into his office and ignored the gesture of the cop sitting at the anteroom desk. The man probably wanted to tell Reno that Greek Billy was in there waiting, a shrunken, unshaven version of the Greek Billy who had disappeared with his tape recorder. Reno stopped abruptly and glared at Billy. The Greek cringed. Reno resisted an impulse to snatch the chair out from under him and smash it over Greek Billy's head.

"Where the fuck have you been?"

"Around," Greek Billy said.

"You little sonofabitch. You're going back to prison and I'm going to kick your ass through the gates."

"I was afraid. I was afraid you were going to kill me and Murphy was going to kill me."

"When I get through with you, you'll wish somebody had."

Billy sank deeper into the chair, trying to crawl into himself.

"I did what you told me. I tried to get him to give me fifty thousand dollars from the Plymouth job. He just laughed at me."

"Where's the tape?"

Greek Billy dug into the folds of his ill-fitting suit. Reno's tape recorder was hidden in the folds of the fabric and Billy pulled it out and held it forward with a trembling hand. Reno snatched it.

"If there's anything on here that's important and you've been holding it back . . ."

"Play it, play it," Billy pleaded. "There's nothing. I swear. He laughed at me. He said if I knew where fifty thousand dollars was, he'd help me go steal it. Honest to God that's all he said."

"I'll play it. You better be right."

Reno sat down in his chair behind the desk and studied Billy. The man was a mess. He needed a bath as well as a shave. He needed a spine.

Reno said, "Have you seen Murphy since then?"

Billy shook his head. "I'm afraid."

"What are you afraid of? You used to rob banks with the sonofabitch, remember? He's a friend of yours. He's a rat just like you are. You get along like brothers. All you got to be afraid of is me."

"I don't want to do this. Just leave me alone."

"I'll leave you alone, you little sonofabitch. I'll leave you alone in a grave under six inches of garbage. That's where I'll leave you alone." Reno took a set of keys out of the back pocket where he kept them wrapped in a handkerchief so they wouldn't jingle when he was attempting to take a culprit by surprise. He opened a desk drawer and found a stack of $20 bills.

"Here's your money." He threw the wad at Billy. "You ain't earned it, but now you will. You are going to be with Murphy every chance you get." He removed the cartridge in the old tape recorder, replaced it with a fresh one and handed the machine over. "I want every word that Murphy utters. And let me tell you something. If you ever disappear like that again I'm going to put out a shoot-to-kill pickup order on you as a suspect in one of our unsolved cop killings. The first guy who finds you will blow your ass off. You get a bath and a shave. You stink."

After Reno sent Billy trembling from his foreboding presence, he shuffled a stack of telephone messages on his desk and threw most of them in the wastebasket. The first to go were the ones from departmental superiors. They had no contribution to make to his investigations and merely used his time seeking information for their own purposes, usually political. Next he threw away call slips from Homicide, which was deeply involved in the gangland murders that were occurring at the rate of one a week. Reno knew most of these characters, victims and killers alike, but he really didn't care if they killed each other. They were the scum of the earth. He hoped they would go on with it until there was only one survivor left standing with a smoking gun. That was the one Reno would like to have for himself and the only one worth bothering with. There was one call that attracted him—from Sgt. Arthur Klemberg of the Danhurst precinct. An old friend, a tough Kraut filled with the same hatreds that churned in Reno. Klemberg had gone on the job about the same time Reno had but his career was interrupted when he walked into a tavern holdup and was shot twice before he was able to get out a gun and kill the two bandits. Klemberg recovered and went to a desk job in a precinct near his home. That's where Reno found him when he returned the call.

"What do ya say, Dutch?"

"Whose head did you break today, Reno?" They both laughed, hard laughter of a shared intimacy known to men on the line.

"I've got to come and straighten you out one of these days," Reno said. "What do you need?"

"Did you ever hear of a guy named Conrad—about five-eight, built like a bowling pin, very nervous?"

Reno thought. Klemberg gave him the silence. "I don't hear any bells. What does he do?" Reno finally answered.

"The last thing he did was shoot the shit out of his front door with a .45 and wake up half the fucking neighborhood around here."

"Drunk?"

"I don't think so. He says somebody was trying to break in. Maybe it was his imagination, because we never found any sign of the other guy."

"What's that to me? Am I supposed to give the guy target lessons?"

"Fuck you, you couldn't hit the ashtray with a cigar butt. Well, we've got this guy Conrad here, talking to him, and after he makes a phone call, somebody I understand you're interested in was up to see if he needs any help squaring the situation."

"What somebody?"

"Dan Murphy. I don't know if it means anything but I thought you'd like to know for what it's worth, since a dumb cop like you couldn't find shit in a pasture with a hundred fat cows."

"Give me the address you got on this guy, Dutch. And thanks."

When he had the meager information Klemberg gave him, Reno sat for a moment with a pencil and made a list. Murphy, Harry, Marcetti, D'Amato, Conrad. He put a question mark after Conrad's name, then went back and wrote Gina in front of Marcetti. Five of them. Maybe.

Klemberg would have been a hell of a cop if he hadn't taken those slugs. The Dutchman knew that crime was like a broken window. You collected all the bits and pieces and laid them out on the table. When most of them were there, you could tell what had shattered the surface. He picked up the phone and called Castle.

"I've got another tip for the wire guys," he said, giving him Conrad's address and identifying him as a friend and possible confederate of Murphy's. Castle was dubious about the value of such a connection and this annoyed Reno. "Just have your weasel put the fuckin' bug in there, will ya? And if you're thinking of boffing that guinea broad, take your hand away from your zipper before you fuck up a grand theft indictment." He dropped the phone in the cradle.

As soon as the kids were off to school, Alice Gilardi made sure there was a scarf in her purse and hurried off to St. Malachai's. She found one of the assistant pastors on hand and confessed a few imaginary transgressions to purify herself, lighted a votive candle to the Virgin and knelt in prayer. If God was anywhere in the vicinity of Boston that morning, He got an earful about the problems that had been visited upon

the Gilardi family—by Humboldt, Clappin, and Leibowitz. The main problem was her fear for Sam, whom
she assumed the Lord knew was one of the finest, hard-
est working, and most loving husbands around.

Alice extolled her husband's virtues for almost an
hour, giving details and, in some cases, specific dates
and times of his special kindnesses toward his family.
Further, she protested his innocence of any and all
crimes that might have been attributed to him. Oh, he
didn't go to church a lot, Alice conceded, but she said
that she was working on that problem and would one
day whip him into shape. As big as he was, Sam did
pretty much what she wanted him to do and it was just
possible that this brush with the authorities might
convince him of the necessity of having some backup
protection against the twists of fate by joining her before the altar on a regular basis.

That said, she hurried home to return to her knees to
scrub the kitchen floor. The kids were so messy. She
ran a spotless house. Humboldt, Clappin, and Leibowitz noted that. They were waiting for her.

"Hello, Alice," Humboldt said. "How are the kids?"

The big, moon-faced man was holding a dagger to
her heart. For the next few hours, he displayed no reluctance about plunging it home. Where did Sam get
his extra money? My, that's nice—what did it cost?
Where does he go on his days off? Who are his friends?
Does he know a man named Dan Murphy and how
long have they been friends? And Harry—how long has
he known this fellow Harry? Look at these pictures,
Alice. Have these men ever been here to see Sam? Not
a very nice looking bunch with the numbers across
their chests, but everybody has a friend or two who
may have gone bad. Now let's go back to the money.
How much does Sam give you every week to run the
house . . . ?

The Alice Gilardis of the world are hardly prepared for the onslaught of a police interrogation. They know little about the rights of silence or counsel. Miranda could be a name on a cigar box.

By the time the children returned from school, Alice Gilardi was on the edge of hysteria. She called her mother and asked her to take them for the evening, for as long as need be. By the time Sam returned, she was a glob of guilt-wracked gelatin, quivering in her clothes, intermittently sobbing, pacing, wringing her hands.

Both Clappin and Leibowitz loosened the revolvers in their holsters when they heard the heavy-footed approach of Sam. Who could tell what reaction the sight of his wife's discomfort would provoke in this somnolent giant?

Alice ran across the room and threw her arms around Gilardi as he came through the door.

"Sam, Sam—what have you done? What do these people want with us?"

Gilardi stroked her with a large hand. With customary gentleness, Sam told his weeping wife, "It's all right. It's all right. You go into the kitchen now and let me deal with this. It's all right."

With a few moments of borrowed strength, Alice regained some of her composure and turned toward the kitchen. Humboldt was glad to see her go. In some reservoir of decency, he felt repugnance for using this technique to get to Gilardi. But time was running out. Humboldt conceded that he would have run his own mother through a gauntlet of questioning if he thought a solution lay at the other end. He had to know. They had to break it.

"You cocksuckers want anything here, you ask me," Gilardi said flatly. "You ever bother Alice again, I'm going to come up behind you some night and kill you with my bare hands. Maybe I'll let your family watch. Understand?"

They understood. Gilardi put his lunch bucket down on a small end table, folded his arms across his chest, and waited. Clappin and Leibowitz looked to Humboldt, who also felt some admiration for this taciturn man who seemed so capable and contained.

"I'm going to ask you some questions, Sam," Humboldt said. "For your own sake, for the sake of your family, I hope you give me honest answers. One way or another we're going to find out, and it will go easier on all of you if you help us now. I want you to know that we have information connecting you to a lot of money about the time the Plymouth mail robbery was pulled. Do you know who did it?"

A long pause. A thought of Alice. A thought of the future and the past. "I know a lot of people."

A wild flash of intuition and hope swept Humboldt. He suddenly felt the direction he must take, turning away from the culprits and toward the object of their crime.

"I won't ask you who they are. We're already aware that you know Dan Murphy and Harry. But I don't care about them right now. Let's talk about money. There's no way of hiding the fact that you spend more than you've got or earn. It comes from somewhere. But I'm not even going to ask you where."

"I gamble," Gilardi said. "I win a little now and then."

"Sure," Humboldt agreed mildly. "We all gamble. But there's something else. I want to put a situation to you and see what you think. Say, some guys go out and pull a big robbery with a great deal of cash involved, like a million and a half. And these guys have some records or criminal associations that people know about. It figures that these guys are going to be questioned and watched very closely. Right?"

Gilardi nodded.

"Now what is the first thing they have to do? They have to get rid of the money and put it in a safe place. Well, now, we know that these particular types of individuals are not going to go down to the Shawmut Bank and open an account, don't we? And they are not going to carry it around in a shopping bag where it will be found. What are they going to do? They are probably going to give the money to a friend they can trust, a friend who does not have a record or shady past. Somebody they can use as a bank until they are ready to take the money and split it up. For this, they pay a fee—just like they would have to pay rent on a safety deposit box. How does that sound to you, Sam?"

Clappin and Leibowitz considered the line brilliant. Humboldt was giving Gilardi an opportunity to escape the onus of accusation as one of the participants in the robbery with the suggestion that he might be "banker" of the funds for a small service charge. Whatever Gilardi thought, once they had the money they would have the thieves.

"Well, Sam?"

"It could happen," Gilardi said.

"A friend could be holding the money for them?"

"It could happen."

"Did it happen?"

"I said it could, I didn't say it did."

Humboldt worried about setting the hook on this first nibble on the bait of his suggested immunity. He wanted the money back—if, indeed, it was in this house—but there was an overriding consideration that had probably not occurred to Sam Gilardi. If Gilardi gave up the money with the suggestion that he had been hiding it for a friend, it would be an easy step to the identity of that friend. Then Humboldt would not only have the money, but also a *witness* who could take it back to the robbery. That was more important than any of it. A witness!

"I know what you're saying," Humboldt sighed.

"I didn't say anything," Gilardi replied.

"I know, I know. We're going to go now, Sam. I'm sorry if we upset Alice. We won't bother her anymore. You'll be around, won't you?"

"I'll be around," Gilardi said.

Both Clappin and Leibowitz were astonished that they were leaving and Clappin said so in the car after they had pulled away from the small ranch style house.

"You were so close, chief," Clappin said. "We could have broken him. I had the feeling we were standing right on top of the money."

"We were," Humboldt said. "But only a goddamned fool would try to force that man to rat on his pals. You couldn't break him if you hit him with a sledgehammer. But . . ." and Humboldt's face lighted with a smile ". . . if we give him a way to protect that family he loves so much and save his own ass in the bargain, then we've got him and a witness against all those other bastards. You also may have noticed we've been doing all this without a warrant of any kind."

Humboldt even chuckled at the thought. With only a few months left until the federal statute of limitations would run out on the Plymouth mail robbery, the Postals finally had a break in their biggest and most humiliating case.

"Besides," he said, "that money ain't going anywhere."

The don of dons, the boss of bosses, and whatever else he may have been called, with due respect, as he governed the six states of New England from his power base in Providence, was sorely troubled by his failing health (diabetes and a heart murmur), the situation in Boston (only the funeral directors were getting rich), and some of the grumbling in the ranks (two of his rising young hoodlums had declared that their chief was a faggot because he dressed so fastidiously in tailored chambra suits and silk hose and shirts). It was bad, all bad. Least tolerable of all was being called names. It meant a lack of discipline. He could always get a good doctor, and the gang war in Boston would eventually be over. But who needs a boss of bosses who could not control his fiefdom? Through couriers, he turned to Murphy. The problem was placed before the hulking bandit in the lobby of the hotel where Murphy kept a weekly Thursday assignation with a beautiful red-haired prostitute. Murphy's response was instantaneous. He said the offending minions must be plucked out and destroyed before the insults provoked a rebellion.

There was no objection, but it contained a problem, because of the closely knit family relationships between the dissident hoodlums and the local assassins. The don did not wish to use local talent. He required an outsider who would be just as effective. Murphy understood. First, Murphy sent himself on a reconnaissance mission to Providence to study the habits of the pair of condemned men and the territory they prowled. As always, the essential element of the crime in Murphy's view was not merely committing it, but getting away with it.

As a man under surveillance and an eclectic expert in its techniques, Murphy handily slipped out of Boston, went to Providence, and tracked the potential victims. It took him three days, a period of bewilderment to Boston authorities because they couldn't find him.

As suddenly as he vanished, he reappeared to take up the game of fox and hounds. Also to send Actor Sternweiss to Providence to eliminate the don's problems and accrue to Murphy considerable obligation.

Except for an occasional robbery, Sternweiss had been relatively inactive in his professional capacity as a killer and looked forward to the fact that the don would pay the generous wage of $25,000 a head for the successful plucking of the thorns in his side.

Sternweiss told his wife that he would be out of town for a day or so on a wholesale carpet acquisition trip. He packed an overnight case, kissed his children good-bye, and headed for Interstate 95 in his gleaming white Thunderbird armed with nothing more than his psychosis. As had been prearranged, Sternweiss stopped at a Howard Johnson's waystation on the outskirts of Providence to have a cup of coffee, leaving his car unlocked. Upon his return to the vehicle, he noted that two fully-loaded weapons—a 12-gauge shotgun containing OO buckshot, which made each shot comparable to firing a dozen .22 caliber slugs simultaneously, and a 9 mm Browning automatic containing fifteen hollow-point cartridges—were on the floor behind his seat, wrapped innocently in an old blanket. All three, shotgun, pistol, and blanket, were stolen property and could be traced back only to their point of origin so long as Sternweiss did not touch them with his bare hands. In the glove compartment of his Thunderbird was a pair of skintight leather gloves from Milan to prevent such an amateurish happenstance. Sternweiss had also been given verbal descriptions of the two rebels, their habits and homes, hangouts and friends. All of this he had committed to memory. The choice of time, place, and technique were his. If he determined that neither weapon was suitable for the occasion, a call to a number he had also memorized would bring whatever he required instantly. He settled on the shotgun.

It was the practice of his two intended victims to travel together to a small specialty store in a suburban business section of Providence to collect extortion payments once a week. Although both men had reason to expect some form of disciplinary action, they were remarkably self-confident about their safety. They were pocketing the money and helping themselves to the shop's delicacies when a dark nondescript car pulled up to the curb to deliver a tall handsome man carrying a rolled up blanket. By the time they asked themselves why he was wearing gloves, it was too late. Both men were virtually decapitated in a few thundering seconds and Sternweiss was back in the car, down the block and around the corner before the first resident of the area reached for a telephone to report a shooting.

He was back at his motel within twenty minutes. He had kicked the shotgun under the stolen black car and tossed the Browning down a sewer en route. Sternweiss slept soundly for five hours. The news media took care of reporting the success of his mission. He needed the rest, for in the morning he would visit carpeting wholesalers and acquire the inventory he had mentioned to his wife—as well as a reason for being in Providence if the question should arise. Then he must return to Boston, for Murphy had indicated that these were perilous times and his presence and his proficiency might be required.

$ XI $

There Goes the Neighborhood

On the day of Actor Sternweiss's successful foray into Providence, Chief Inspector Humboldt was savoring his own success. He was so confident that Sam Gilardi would provide the first break in the investigation of the Plymouth mail robbery that he needed to share his enthusiasm. He called a meeting of the other law enforcement officers at the Boston postal annex—Reno of the Boston Police, Castle of the FBI, and Manning of the state police. Clappin and Leibowitz were there as well. Chewing on a cigar, Humboldt told them what he had done, how the situation had evolved, and how he planned to carry it further by easing Gilardi into a situation where he would be pitted against his cohorts as a witness. Almost in unison —with the exception of Clappin and Leibowitz—they shouted protests.

"Grab the goddamned money if it's there. That makes Gilardi an accomplice whether he's a fuckin' witness or not," Reno said.

"Do you think Murphy is dumb enough to let this

happen? Without knowing about it and doing something about it?" Manning shouted. "Who the hell do you think we're dealing with, Peter Rabbit?"

"As soon as a court opens anywhere in this city, we're getting a warrant and going into that house," Castle declared. "Now, goddammit, you start dictating an affidavit about all this so we can give it to the court!"

Crestfallen and overhwelmed, Humboldt started dictating. By morning, the affidavit was ready to take to U.S. Commissioner Peter J. Nelligan, who was persuaded to issue the warrant for a foot-by-foot search of Sam's house for the Plymouth loot.

Shortly after Sam Gilardi left for work, Alice packed her two children off to parochial school classes, each carrying a small brown paper bag containing peanut butter and jelly sandwiches, an apple, and an assortment of cookies. She had shopping to do as well and planned to visit Sears shopping center to investigate the possibility of acquiring a new washer and dryer. The old ones were worn out with the heavy loads of Sam's grimy work clothes and the kids' stuff, combined with her own fastidious nature.

Her departure in a black 1961 Chevrolet station wagon was noted by two postal inspectors and two FBI agents who were maintaining a surveillance on the house. The men posted outside Gilardi's house were instructed to maintain their observation of the house and the movements of its occupants until they were relieved, or until search parties arrived with warrants that would permit them to invade Sam Gilardi's domain. All four noted that Alice walked out of her house at 8:23 A.M., backed the family's 1961 Chevrolet station wagon into the street, and drove off. Although Sam had been followed to work, she was not. Both the inspectors and the agents checked with the central communications unit set up at the FBI office for instructions. They were instructed to remain in position. Alice Gilardi was considered to have absolutely no value as a connection to the Plymouth mail robbery gang except as a weapon to be used in dealing with her husband.

At 8:50 that morning, Harry walked out of Drew's Cafeteria, picking the remains of a pecan and raisin sweet roll out of his teeth, at the moment that a 1961 black Chevrolet station wagon with grime on the windows and mud splashes on the license plates pulled to a stop in front of the cafeteria. The horn sounded twice. Without interrupting his stride, Harry walked around the car, opened the driver's door, and got in beside Murphy who had slid into the passenger's seat.

"Is this Sam's car?" Harry asked.

"It will do," Murphy said. "Let's take it over and park it in his driveway."

At 9:00 A.M., a prosecutor from the U.S. Attorney's office led the postal authorities into a session with the U.S. Commissioner. By 9:30, the warrant had been issued and the officers were ready to leave. They were already twenty minutes too late.

At 9:10, the four officers maintaining the surveillance on Sam Gilardi's home had noted the return of the 1961 black Chevrolet station wagon. One of them commented that it looked like Alice had been driving through mud puddles. Because Gilardi's driveway swung around the back of the house to the garage, which was connected to the house, and Alice had left the garage door open as a matter of convenience, they did not see Murphy and Harry emerge from the car and move quickly into the house. The two men went swiftly into Alice's immaculate kitchen, down the stairs to the basement, and into the equally neat work room.

"Do it neat," Murphy said as Harry picked up a chisel as a prying tool and began to work on the wall board. "Don't leave any marks."

"No problem," Harry said. "He's just got this fuckin' thing up with thumbtacks."

They had the wall board off by 9:13. There were still eight mail sacks containing approximately $900,000 behind it. Each of them carried two sacks, and they made two quick trips to the station wagon, threw the sacks into the crawl space in the back of the vehicle, and covered them with a blanket. By 9:30, as Castle and Humboldt emerged from the court building and half-walked, half-ran to the waiting cars containing a crowd of postal inspectors and sledge hammers, pinch-bars, crowbars, hammers, and even acetylene torches for cutting metal, Murphy and Harry were pretty well out of the neighborhood. Again, the movement of the vehicle was noted by the surveillance teams. The caravan of postal officers was just coming into the neighborhood when Alice Gilardi was walking across the Sears parking lot and getting into her 1961 black Chevrolet and Harry was turning to Murphy to ask:

"Where did you find this thing?"

"What difference does it make, I found it."

"Okay, where are we going with it, or are we just going to drive around with all that money back there?"

"Dominic's Nursery in Salisbury."

"This is a hell of a time to buy a tree for your lawn."

"We're going to bury the fuckin' stuff in a green-house under the pile of dirt he's got there for putting in flower pots."

Harry felt pleased that he was associated with such genius. He glanced at Murphy and smiled. "Did you tell Sam to get rid of anything else he might be holding from the other scores?"

"I don't tell anybody fuckin' anything," Murphy said. "I just do it."

Although Humboldt had gone through the formality

of knocking at Alice Gilardi's door fully aware that she was not there, he desired not to enter the premises and begin the search until she returned. If by the most remote possibility she knew anything about a secret cache of money, she would probably reveal it as she witnessed the destruction of her home in the process of a total search. They waited slightly less than fifteen minutes before Alice returned. Her face furrowed in concern and her heart pounded with fear as she noted the presence of so many obviously official vehicles when she turned into the driveway. The four original surveillance officers noted without comment that she had probably gotten the station wagon washed and concluded that was the reason for her second trip. She parked the car in the driveway and stepped out to be greeted by Humboldt.

"Mrs. Gilardi," he said. "I have here a warrant authorizing the search of your premises issued to the United States Postal Service by United States Commissioner Peter J. Nelligan. We want you to open the door and permit us to enter the house now or we will be forced to make entry any way we can."

"What do you want?" Alice Gilardi cried in a wrench of torment. "Why are you doing this to us? What do you want from us?"

"We want the money that was taken on August 14, 1962, by six armed men who robbed the United States mail of approximately $1.5 million dollars at Plymouth, Mass. We have good reason to believe that this money is hidden in or around these premises with the knowledge of your husband, Sam, and we intend to search for it unless you are now prepared to divulge its whereabouts."

"I don't know what you're talking about. This is crazy. You have no right to do this."

Humboldt extended the folded white legal-sized

sheet of paper labeled "warrant" and said firmly, "We have every right under the law, Mrs. Gilardi, and we intend to make the search. Now let's get on with it."

Alice faltered in her step. She felt dazed, confused. She felt that she would somehow be betraying Sam if she admitted these men.

"All right," Humboldt said, "break down the door."

"No," Alice cried. "I'll open it." She searched for keys in her purse with trembling fingers, forgetting in her panic that the back door was unlocked and usually remained so in this quiet residential community, where a hundred neighbors now peered through blinds and curtains at the awesome congregation of police armed with the tools of destruction. She led Humboldt and the others to the front door, tried unsuccessfully to fit the key to the lock, and then with a soft sob, handed the keys to Humboldt, who quickly unlocked the door, returned the keys, and gestured to his men to enter.

It took Murphy only twenty minutes to bury the $900,000 under the mixture of top soil and peat moss at Dominic's greenhouse and to pay Dominic $10,000 cash for this temporary banking service. But it took Humboldt and his men fifteen hours to destroy Sam Gilardi's house. They broke through every wall in every room and ripped open all of the wall tiles. They tore apart the furnace and the water heater as well as the dishwasher and the washer and dryer. They cut open and drained the water storage tank. They ripped open every floor and tore open every ceiling. They pulled down every shred of insulation from the rafters in the crawl space of the attic. They smashed into the cinder block of the foundation and they opened every drawer and cupboard and spread out the contents of each, and finally, they ripped up the back patio, probed every inch of the yard with steel rods, pumped out the septic tank, took away the earth above it, and smashed in its concrete in order to look even there.

In the end, working into the night under portable floodlights, they had obliterated what was once a small and charming house and had left nothing untouched except the false plumbing extensions where Sam Gilardi had hidden several hundred thousand dollars accumulated in other robberies. The total of their discovery was this: one .45 caliber automatic, loaded but unregistered; $300 in $10 bills that had been hidden under a hat in Sam's bedroom closet; one .45 caliber weapon clip, empty.

Gilardi had returned home early in the evening as the search was about half completed. He seemed impassive and unmoved although Alice knew what tortures he must have been suffering at the sight of so much of his effort and skill being cannibalized. He insisted that she take their crying children away from the awful scene to the sanctity of her mother's house. He would join her there later. Silently, he watched until the search concluded, when Humboldt approached him.

"Where did you get this .45, this $300 we found in the closet, and this clip that looks like it came from a machine gun?" Humboldt asked.

"Go fuck yourself," Sam said and walked away. Humboldt did not try to stop him. There was time enough for that after they checked the serial numbers on the money and tried to trace the origin of the pistol and the cartridge clip.

When Murphy and Harry abandoned the twin 1961 Chevrolet station wagon, having first removed the bogus triptych license plates, they went for a short stroll down the quiet streets of Dedham until the gleaming white Thunderbird with Actor Sternweiss at the wheel pulled up at the curb and they climbed in. Murphy was deeply troubled by the pressure being brought on Sam Gilardi. There wasn't anything he could do about it because he couldn't figure out how the Postals and the Feebees had stumbled onto Sam. The lines of communication were so clogged with listening devices and surveillance teams that there was no way he could investigate. Through Fast Freddy and a couple of other intermediaries, he managed to send a message of some reassurance to Gilardi which was expressed in the pragmatism of the criminal who believes that loyalty is necessary but survival is paramount above all things.

"You do what you have to do and I'll do what I have to do." That was Murphy's communication.

Now he had other problems. Sternweiss, an unknown quantity to the police because he had no criminal record and seemed to come out of nowhere *after* the Plymouth robbery, was able to move more freely than any of the others in the environment of the underworld. The Actor had some disturbing intelligence to report to Murphy: Rocky Gallagher and the O'Brien brothers had been seen around Joey Marcetti's gas station and it had become general knowledge that all three of them had joined the legions that were tapping Marcetti's wife, Gina. That they wanted Gina was understandable. But what were they doing with Joey?

Murphy glared out the window of the Thunderbird and indicated his concern only by increasing the rate of consumption of digestive mints: one, crunch, crunch; two, crunch, crunch, crunch; three, four, five, crunch, crunch, crunch, crunch.

"Gina talked too much," he said. "Rocky didn't climb

down out of a tree yesterday. He knows. They're shaking Joey down."

"Maybe you could talk to Gallagher," Harry suggested. "He's got nothing against you. Maybe you can
take the pressure off."

"Keep gangsters the fuck away from me," Murphy
said. "The only place you find gangsters is in prison or
the graveyard and I don't want to go with them. Gallagher's an animal. He's gone crazy with all the blood.
The only thing to do with something like that is to put
him away immediately. It's a danger to everything.
Even our families are in danger."

"Joe Gargolian maybe," Harry said. "He'd love to do
that and it would look very good."

"If Gargolian could take Gallagher or the O'Briens
he would have done it already. Somebody like that
won't get anywhere near them," Murphy said. He
glanced at Actor Sternweiss. "It would have to be somebody they don't know. Somebody a lot smarter than a
salami like Gargolian. With Rocky Gallagher you only
go to bat once. You can't miss."

Actor Sternweiss was listening very carefully, however casual he may have seemed as he drove Murphy
and Harry into the heart of the city.

Rocky Gallagher's final assignation with Gina
Marcetti took place on the Tuesday evening following
the conversation between Murphy, Harry, and Sternweiss. Joey was playing cards with Frank D'Amato in
a high stakes game in the basement of a shoe repair
shop in the near North End.

When Gallagher emerged from Marcetti's house, the
O'Briens were waiting in Gallagher's car, both of them
in the front seat. Gallagher took the rear compartment
so he could stretch his legs out across the seat.

"That's some broad," Gallagher sighed in what was certainly a redundancy to the O'Briens. "She's going to fuck me to death if this keeps up."

The O'Briens laughed, and Duke, who was at the wheel, added, "It ain't a bad way to go."

They took their customary route down three blocks to Hillbrook Street then left at the stop sign. Duke O'Brien had barely begun to accelerate out of the turn when the heavy 30-06 caliber copper-jacketed rifle bullets began ripping into the limousine roof and windows from a sniper's vantage point on the flat rooftop of one of the two-story red brick row duplexes along Hillbrook. Rocky Gallagher took seven of the fifteen bullets that hit the car; three in the legs, two in the right shoulder, one on the left forearm, and the seventh in his right hand—his shooting hand—blowing away two of his fingers and a portion of a third. The O'Briens were killed instantly. They took rifle slugs in the head.

Without stopping to watch the car careen off the street and onto the lawn of a house on the opposite side, Actor Sternweiss held the rifle by its barrel and swung it like a baseball bat, heaving it as far as he could over the neighborhood rooftops and into an alley about sixty yards away. He then proceeded over the rooftops to the end of the street, down a fire escape, and into a second alley where he could walk to his car.

Although it was one of his few "failures"—Rocky Gallagher managed to survive the wounds—it was the end of Murphy's problem with the extortion of Joey Marcetti's share of the loot and Murphy was satisfied with the results. The only loud voice of regret came from Reno.

"Too bad the guineas didn't kill the motherfucker," he said. "Things might have quieted down around here."

For all his outward taciturnity, Sam Gilardi was seriously shaken by the destruction of his home. It was not just a house; it was a home, and Alice and the children had filled it with love for him while Murphy had packed it with money. The threat of being arrested and convicted as a bank robber was not so frightening to him as was the possible destruction of the love. He was a bank robber, certainly. He also was a devoted husband and father, a fine family man who had constructed his middle-class paradise on the quicksand of crime.

Further, Gilardi did not share the excitement of being pursued and getting away that most of his cohorts enjoyed. He did not think quickly enough or with the same degree of ruthless cunning—and he knew it. He needed a Murphy to train him, inspire him, and direct him. But the line of communication between them was clogged with listening devices, detectives sitting in cars and stationed at every point along his daily path, men who looked as if they might be cops who even rode the bus to work with him.

After Sam had ensconced Alice and the kids at his mother-in-law's house, he set about the massive job of rebuilding his home—by hand, and by depleting his small bank account. He began going to the site of the devastation every morning at the first powder blue indication of dawn to personally resurrect a house from the shambles. He also had to protect all the money he had hidden in the plumbing before some scrap dealers swept down and appropriated all of the pipes for a junkyard. At least the police were good for one thing: They were guarding the ruins in their around-the-clock surveillance. They were there when he arrived in the morning and still there when he returned in the evenings, and he knew they were there through the night. But it was wearing him down, that constant presence and some of the tactics they were using.

Almost every day, the police would come to his place of work with the postal carriers who had been driving the truck that had been robbed, and they would shout the same questions: "Are you sure this isn't the man who was with the robbers? Look again and see if you can remember. Does he move the way one of the robbers did? Is there anything about him that resembles one of those men? What about his hair? Did any of them have that color hair?"

They did it at different times and different places but it was always the same. There was not much comfort for him at home, either. Alice wept almost continuously, a great river of bereavement for a lost existence that had approached perfection. She was likely to burst into tears at any moment—at dinner, giving the kids a bath, in bed, handing him a cup of coffee in the morning. She cried like a widow and there was nothing he could do to console her except give her back her home. He strove to do just that—and wondered just how many desperate hours he had left to achieve it. They knew the truth. Where was Murphy to help him through this dark night?

The men of Reno's intelligence squad, who accepted a great deal of aberrant, ruthless behavior on the part of their commander, seriously thought one morning that they were going to witness history's first self-induced human explosion. Greek Billy had slipped into Superior Court that day and filed for an injunction which would forbid Reno or anyone else in the department from using Greek Billy as an agent to help trap the Plymouth mail robbers under threat of fouling up Billy's parole. Greek Billy said that he had tape recordings to substantiate his complaint, made surreptitiously while Reno was snarling at the helpless ex-con.

What made Reno so angry was that they had him cold. The court might not permit Eddington to introduce the tapes but he was in a great deal of trouble if it did, and he made an attempt to fight the injunction. It was Reno's first real humiliation at the hands of his adversaries.

"They're six ounces short of a pound," Murphy said of the great force of investigators pursuing him, "and they get worse when they get sore. They don't think. They run around yelling at each other and blaming everybody else for their own stupidity."

The use of Greek Billy as an informer stopped. When he reported for his semi-annual parole hearing, there were no problems. When it came time for Greek Billy to report again, he failed to appear.

And he hasn't been heard from or seen since.

Murphy was burdened with a growing concern about the loot he had planted under the humus pile in Dominic's greenhouse. The cash was safe enough from the elements in the heavily oiled canvas mail sacks, but he was wary of avarice. Dominic was honest—$10,000 honest—and trustworthy to a point. With a $200,000 reward outstanding, he might reach that point quickly or report that his nursery had been burglarized of its humus pile some dark night.

Murphy decided it was time to make another split— roughly $250,000 six ways—and begin putting the rest to work.

Ducking the surveillance again, Murphy, Harry, and Sternweiss moved through the night to the nursery.

Murphy had already sent two messages about the money and its further concealment, one to Noel Eddington, the other to Marcetti and D'Amato. The two thugs were playing cards in the basement of a clam bar about three hundred yards from the historic Boston waterfront. D'Amato's car was parked in plain sight in front of the tavern. Eddington was in his office drinking Scotch from a delicate Dresden teacup and discussing a divorce action that had come to him unexpectedly in the person of a twenty-eight-year-old dental hygienist married to a philandering dentist. While Eddington normally did not deal in divorce litigation and the young woman was utterly plain, the lawyer noted that she had a remarkable posterior and he was developing a strategy for combining pleasure with business. He never had to look at their faces until later anyhow.

As D'Amato left five hundred on an open-ended four card straight, and Marcetti kicked in five hundred more with a full house of sevens over fours, and Eddington led the dental hygienist into a discussion of her marital sex life, Murphy and his companions were digging the eight bags from beneath the humus and carrying them to the Thunderbird. Murphy knew exactly what each contained. He directed that three of them, containing a total of $300,000 in small denominations, be separated from the rest. Marcetti and D'Amato were to run as much of this as possible through their cash businesses, and gradually exchange the rest for larger denominations in bars, restaurants and other business establishments around town. Working under a flashlight held by Dominic, they completed the evacuation in ten minutes and were back on the road heading into the city. While Harry drove, Murphy and Sternweiss removed bills totaling $100,000 from the other five bags. Their first stop was the middle of a dark street two blocks from the clam bar where D'Amato and Marcetti were bemoaning the loss of the pot to a third player whose full house of jacks over deuces had swept the table. A good pot, too, containing about $13,000.

Murphy located the 1960 Plymouth, a standard backup car with a finely tuned engine that one of Marcetti's employees had parked two days earlier with a "delivery" sign on the turned-down sun visor. The trunk of the vehicle was unlocked. Sternweiss and Harry threw the three bags containing $300,000 into the trunk, slammed it, and got back into the car to head for Eddington's office about ten blocks away.

Eddington had finished with his new client when Murphy called him from the lobby pay phone to ask him to get clearance from the custodian who maintained a night vigil on comings and goings of the building's occupants. The dental hygienist was rearranging her clothes thinking that Scotch had never done this to her before. On the other hand, she had never had more than three or four drinks in her life, and this was a very emotional situation that, Eddington assured her, would soon improve, just as he promised her the pain would go away and turn to pleasure. Murphy handed the phone to the custodian and Eddington instructed the man to bring the elevator to his floor for the departure of a client. As the man did, Harry and Sternweiss returned to the Thunderbird while Murphy turned his back to the building entrance and pretended to make another phone call to avoid being seen by the dental hygienist. After she had left, Murphy suggested to the custodian it would be worth a considerable reward if he could find three cheeseburgers and three cups of coffee, one of them for Mr. Eddington, who was going to work late. The custodian said that he couldn't do that since the nearest source was an all-night coffee shop on the edge of Scollay Square eight blocks away. The rustle of two $20 bills and a glimpse of their denomination in the dim light of the lobby changed his mind; that and Murphy's assurance that the building would remain safe. The man departed quickly, and as soon as he turned the corner, Sternweiss and Harry dragged the remaining bags of money into the building, threw them on the elevator, and ascended to Eddington's floor with Sternweiss at the controls. The young killer smiled and confessed that he had once spent a summer vacation from school operating the elevator in a large department store, where he also had the opportunity to be seduced by an assistant buyer in dry goods when he stopped the elevator between floors and pretended that the controls were jammed.

Eddington was prepared for their arrival with four new but inexpensive plastic and canvas suitcases in the dressing room adjoining the office. The money from the five remaining mail sacks—minus the $250,-000 Murphy had held out for distribution to the gang —was quickly repacked into three of them and the empty sacks themselves went into the fourth. The three suitcases containing the money would be picked up by individual couriers over the next several days. A total of $350,000 was headed for integration into the heavy flow of cash at a casino in Las Vegas. It was a simple banking arrangement and the money would be held until Murphy was prepared to make a withdrawal. The fourth suitcase containing empty sacks would be picked up by Fast Freddy who would see that it was soaked in charcoal starter and torched in the coal-burning boiler of a small factory.

The porter was waiting with the burgers and coffee when Murphy, Harry, and Sternweiss returned to the ground floor. Murphy told the man to enjoy the lunch as well as the change he had pocketed, and to forget the source of both. The look in Sternweiss's eyes as he smiled and waved farewell convinced the custodian to do just that.

D'Amato and Marcetti were leaving the poker game at about the same time, several hundred dollars poorer, by separate exits. D'Amato took the front door. Inherently flamboyant, D'Amato made his departure as obvious as ever, standing on the sidewalk in front of the tavern with two of the other players, stretching and yawning, bemoaning his losses, glancing at his watch to indicate that he was waiting for someone. It was a wasted demonstration. There weren't any police around and no one noticed. Marcetti, meanwhile, had left through the rear door and was at the wheel of the Plymouth driving off into the night toward his own neighborhood—but not to the home where Gina and the children slept. His destination was the same apartment building across the street where Reno and Castle had set up their surveillance post. Marcetti had rented a smaller vacant set of rooms two floors below the surveillance team. He had made the choice as a matter of convenience when Murphy had called for an apartment or room where the change could be counted and rolled and the small bills cut into packets of $100 each for exchange throughout the city. The surveillance apartment was empty as Marcetti dragged the three money sacks into the rear door of the building, locked them in a closet in one of the vacant rooms, and then drove the Plymouth to his auto repair shop to pick up his personal car for the return home.

"Let the motherfuckers tear down somebody's house and try to find the money now," Murphy said, as he got out of the Cadillac a few blocks from his own house and went in to feed Friskies to his pet cats, one spoonful at a time, as he teased them with babytalk.

The gun was a standard blue-black Colt .45 automatic, with checkered walnut grips. It was the standard sidearm issued by the American military during World War II, Korea, and Vietnam, and there are millions of them in private hands around the world. It's a big gun, with a big hole at the end of the barrel where the fat, stubby bullets come out. It is also a favorite gun—at least it used to be—with bandits, because its appearance is awesome and frightening. This was the gun they had found at Sam Gilardi's house. It fit the description given by the guards of the guns carried on the Plymouth job. It had Gilardi's prints on it too, but it was not one of the guns used in the robbery. Those were 9 mm Lamas, heavy Spanish automatics with the same general configuration as the Colt .45, but not the same guns at all.

That gun now became something of a mystery within a mystery. The authorities discovered, or at least they said they had discovered, flecks of yellow paint under the walnut grips on Sam's gun that were identical to paint on the stolen sawhorses used to divert traffic during the robbery.

It was nothing if not miraculous that the right paint could turn up on the wrong gun belonging to the right man—and just in the nick of time.

Now they had something.

$ XII $

The Clock Runs Down

While Murphy managed to control outward signs of tension and maintained a phlegmatic if gruff composure, he watched the calendar as closely as Humboldt, Manning, Reno, and Castle. He could anticipate a rising pressure for indictment and arrest. Yet it was difficult for him to remain in close communication with his crew. He had hoped that the discipline he had instilled, the threats he had invoked, and the punishments that all accepted as the potential reward for deviation or betrayal, would cement their resistance to attacks by the police. That was the real honor among thieves—the danger of suffering a great deal more at the hands of friends than from the law enforcement agencies.

Murphy's inner tensions were apparent to Phil Kalis, who managed a local meeting with Murphy at Drew's Cafeteria. Neither felt that Kalis was being compromised at this stage. Murphy was obviously a focal point of the Plymouth mail robbery investigation; Kalis was a journalist covering the story.

In those days just before the expiration of the federal statute of limitations, Kalis felt a concern if not apprehension about the conversations he was having with Murphy. He was still attempting to keep Murphy informed about the movements of the postal inspectors and the other agencies reporting to Humboldt, Clappin and Leibowitz, but there was very little information for him to give. Humboldt seemed to have closeted himself with his own gloom. Not even Clappin or Leibowitz could provide scraps of information about what their chief was doing and, more importantly, thinking and planning. As Humboldt received confidential reports in the privacy of his office, and made calls about them on his private line, he locked his notes in his safe without divulging their contents. That frustrated Kalis. Murphy would add to these small anxieties during their meetings by becoming philosophical about his existence. Accustomed to the idiosyncratic nonsense about birdshit and funeral caravans as good or bad omens, Kalis now heard Murphy talking about his real fears. Murphy said one day that he could not stand the idea of being incarcerated again. Whatever kind of life he had, Murphy went on, with the police in pursuit and his friends and family in jeopardy, it was still far better than the blankness of an eight-by-twelve cell, the container of nothingness.

Murphy told Kalis that he was not concerned about the police, the Feebees, or the Postals being able to prove anything against him or the other members of the gang. He did not underestimate the police, but he believed the Plymouth mail robbery and subsequent jobs had been flawless. His real concern, he said, was their dishonesty and deviousness, which could lead to an attempt to frame him with phony evidence and/or false witnesses against him. That was his big worry— to be arrested on false charges, to be taken away from his family and friends to a cell where he couldn't breathe, to be sent to prison for something he hadn't done because they couldn't get him any other way.

The effect of these unexpected insights behind Murphy's normally glacial reserve was at the least unsettling to Kalis. This man across the table was the master of them all, the finest mind that Kalis had ever encountered. Was he cracking under the strain of two decades of dodging the law and five years of intense scrutiny? Kalis felt his gut tighten. What would happen if Murphy cracked? Would they all go down the drain with him?

"It's not going to happen if you keep your head, Dan," Kalis said.

Murphy stared at him. Kalis would normally have turned aside from the piercing gaze, but he realized Murphy was not seeing him but was looking inward.

"What's really bothering you, Dan?" Kalis asked. When the reply came, it was an unfamiliar voice, softer and almost gentle in contrast to the hard rasping snarl that was Murphy's style.

"What really scares me, Phil," he said, "is that one of these days I'm gonna die and nobody is going to care. I'm not going to leave a mark of any kind on this world. They will just say he's dead and not give a damn. All my life I really wanted to be the best and the biggest of something. I tried to be that at gambling once, years and years ago, and wasted away eleven million dollars in cash on everything—dice, horses, cards. When I was in the joint, I realized that I was an asshole and so were all the other gamblers. Gambling gets you nothing but grief. So I gave it up. I never bet a penny on anything again. I tried with women for a while. I tried to have all the women in the world and all that got me was a pain in the ass. And then this. I tried to take some people with capabilities and make them into something that I knew they could be even though they were nothing when I started with them. I have been the best there is at this but nobody knows and nobody cares. Now I think I'm gonna die one of these days, and it will be the same thing because nobody will know and nobody will care."

Kalis thought about it for a moment. All he could say was, "Don't worry about it, Dan. I'll see you soon."

Murphy nodded. Kalis left.

Despite what small reassurance he offered to Murphy, Kalis felt the first real paranoia that had touched him since he had laid out the job for Murphy more than five years ago. It was the first crack in the shield of utter confidence that surrounded his relationship with Murphy. Naturally, it came after his first glimpse of something less than superhuman in Murphy's character. Kalis had profited mightily over the last five years with his 10 percent share of Murphy's jobs. He had well over $250,000 cash in safety deposit boxes that no one knew about, not even his wife, and all of his mundane middle-class financial problems like mortgage, car, furniture, and recarpeting payments had been washed away. There was even a paid-off summer retreat in Vermont. It was easy street, the good life. It was also suddenly dangerous.

Irrationally and impulsively, Kalis found himself walking away from his customary route back to the postal annex and the small office where he wrote while he was in the city. He found himself moving toward Ashbourne Street, which was little more than an alley between two major avenues and contained the entrance to a large old tool-and-die plant as well as a small coffee shop and an even smaller sporting goods store, "Blake's—Guns, Fishing Tackle."

Exchanging as few words as possible with Blake himself, Kalis bought a gun, a .25 caliber Barretta automatic, small enough to conceal in the palm of his hand or even a vest pocket. It was, Blake assured him, just as deadly as anything else used for self-protection. Blake showed Kalis how to load it, arm it by sliding the chamber housing backward over the barrel, and how to make sure the safety was in position to prevent accidental firing. Kalis asked Blake for permission to use the men's room, carried the unfamiliar weapon there, and tried to decide where to conceal it. He felt that it bulged monstrously in any pocket. He even tried one of his socks, but the elastic was weak and Kalis jumped as the weapon slipped out and clattered to the floor. He caught a glimpse of himself in the toilet mirror and realized he had a perfect hiding place—the sweat band of the inside of his hat. He tucked the gun in the band and placed the hat back on his head. It was somewhat uncomfortable but felt reassuring, much more reassuring than Murphy had been.

M urphy was a much more practiced paranoid than Kalis. Continuing to chew Rolaids at a rate that probably influenced the retail company's distribution program, Murphy also sought release from his tension sexually. Like everything else he did, his approach was slightly aberrant. He maintained a once-a-week ritual—every Thursday night—of spending two hours with an attractive hooker in a hotel room. He did not have intercourse with the young woman, the sister of a North End hoodlum. For two hours, without removing his shabby clothes (except possibly his hat), Murphy performed cunnilingus, to the hooker's pleasure and occasional puzzlement. He would pay the prostitute twenty-five dollars.

Murphy was essentially monogamous about this activity. His closest associates could recall only two, possibly three, women with whom he had had a similar arrangement over a period of about twenty years. Murphy did not seem to mind as they grew old in service, and it was invariably the hooker who terminated the relationship, by drifting off into marriage, an easier line of work, or by simply disappearing.

In addition to loyalty, Murphy showed understanding in this situation. When he was otherwise occupied on Thursday evening, he made certain that the woman was paid for the time she had set aside for the appointment. This helped create the sort of loyalty Murphy needed in desperate times.

The police were aware of the habit since it was about the only consistency in Murphy's entire social and business scheme. Not the intimate details, just the pattern.

The hotel was Murphy's destination the afternoon he spoke to Kalis. He walked there since it was only a few blocks from the cafeteria, paused briefly at the registration desk to learn that he was in room 611 without the bother of registering. In the custom they had established, the woman was nude and in bed. Murphy, who neither stood nor knelt on formality, tossed his hat on a dresser and approached the woman to take his pleasure.

"Wait a minute, Dan," she said. "I have to talk to you."

"What the hell is there to talk about?"

She hesitated. Murphy had a fearsome reputation, even among hookers. She considered it a prize to be his girl because of the power he could wield in other areas of the underworld. As long as you were Murphy's girl, no one came around and demanded the weekly fealty for the mob. But she had to tell him.

"The police have been to see me. They picked me up at my apartment. You're gonna get picked up."

"Who was it, and I'll straighten it out."

"It wasn't a roust. It was about you. It was some guys with the post office. They said you were a bank robber and an armored car bandit and maybe a murderer who ought to be in jail. They said I had to help them or they would have me picked up every time anybody saw me."

"That's bullshit. A good lawyer will fix the fuckers in five minutes. What are you supposed to do?"

"They said they would fix the door so they could get in quick even if you locked it and threw the bolt. Then when we was doin' our thing, y'know, I start screaming 'rape' and they bust in here and arrest you."

"Then they take me off to jail and try to get me to confess to a lot of other things I didn't do so they can make it look good. What a bunch of assholes. What happens to you after I go to jail? They give you a life-time job at one of the windows selling stamps?"

"They said there's a lot of reward money."

"You've got about as much chance as a fuckin' go-pher of collecting it."

"I know. I told them that. They said they would give me twenty-five thousand dollars cash, a new Chevy convertible that they confiscated in a raid or some-thing, and something they called immunation, or like that."

"Immunity. That means you don't get arrested."

"Yeah, immunity. They said I could murder some-body in Boston and get away with it 'cause they'd make everybody agree to keep hands off."

Murphy yanked back the covers from her body. "That's enough talk. Let's have some fun." He climbed onto the bed.

"But what should I do?" she asked parting her knees.

"Tell 'em you'll take their offer," Murphy said as he proceeded to take hers.

Standing at the window of the small apartment across the street from Gina Marcetti's home, Castle continued to play games of fantasy and fulfillment, with the realization that he was probably neglecting his job and would ultimately have to answer to higher authorities if he could not bring himself under control. But he also believed that the only cure for this sickness was gratification. He had to have her. Somehow, somewhere, he had to have her. He was toying with the idea of following her on one of her shopping expeditions, meeting her "accidentally" at a counter in one of the stores and then suggesting that they lunch together as part of an "interrogation." It was legitimate that he had to ask questions; no one could fault him for that. A few questions, a few glasses of wine, and their mutual lusts would find a confluence of gratification. Maybe, as the old joke went, they would never be permitted back in the restaurant, but . . .

He heard the key turn in the lock and turned to face Reno, whom he had not seen for seventy-two hours. Reno offered no greeting but strode to the window and looked out.

"Anything?"

"Nothing. She seems to have quieted down since Rocky Gallagher and the O'Briens were hit."

Reno grunted. "She's probably giving thanks that she wasn't sitting on Gallagher's dingdong when the lead started to fly. That would have been a fuckin' riot."

Castle wondered if he could take Reno. Maybe, maybe not. Castle had the standard Judo and hand-to-hand combat training of the FBI Academy, much more thorough conditioning than anything available to the average policeman. But he recognized Reno's muscu-

lar frame as containing possibly the most ruthless
street fighter he had ever encountered. It was almost
worth trying. Perhaps Reno felt the energy of the
anger that suffused the FBI agent. He turned from the
window and looked at Castle steadily but without ma-
levolence.

"Don't even think about it," Reno said. "We got
things to do. Humboldt has the number on Sam
Gilardi, and we're going after him. You should be in on
it."

Reno was spreading the risk by involving all the police agencies in the confrontation with Sam Gilardi
over the discovery of paint under the grips of the .45.
It would diffuse the suspicion that any one of them had
set up Sam Gilardi with questionable evidence. Further, it would bring the pressure of their combined
weight down on Gilardi and reinforce the sense of
jeopardy that Gilardi must feel.

Without knowing it, Reno and Castle were at that
moment very close to the Plymouth mail robbery loot.
Two floors down and two apartments to the west, Joey
Marcetti and Frank D'Amato were sitting on the floor
of their vacant suite of rooms, the venetian blinds
closed and overhead lights glowing on a pile of money.
They were arguing about ways to steal it. It was
D'Amato's idea; Marcetti was the reluctant participant.

"We'd never get away with it," Marcetti said. "Forget
it."

"I tell you there's nothing to it. You don't even have
to do anything. I'll take care of it. I'll bunch up a lot of
newspapers in the closet and stick a candle in there
with a little bit of kerosene. When it goes, we'll both be
the fuck on the other side of town. What does Murphy
do, call the arson squad?"

"Maybe he calls Jerry Sternweiss and has *him* investigate the fire. Are you ready for that?"

"Ah, fuck the Actor. He doesn't scare me."

"Then you're crazy, because anybody who isn't scared of Sternweiss is crazy. And I don't want to talk to anybody as nuts as that. Just count the money." They counted, slipping rubber bands around the bills in $100 packets.

"This is a pain in the ass," D'Amato said. "How much money have you got all together, what can you lay your hands on?"

Marcetti thought. "Ten, maybe fifteen large," he said.

"You're on your ass, right?" D'Amato pressed.

"Well, I bought a lot of things, and I settled with the bookie."

"Then what the fuck, let's do it," D'Amato said, gesturing to the money.

"It's a crazy idea," Marcetti said. "Murphy would never believe three hundred thousand got burned in a fire. Especially *his* three hundred thousand."

D'Amato began to work himself into a rage of self-justification. It was his style. It was the way he got into arguments and fights and occasionally got his ass whipped when he underestimated the opposition.

"It ain't his three hundred thousand," he shouted. "It's just as much ours as his. So where's the split? He takes it from Sam's house and he moves it to the greenhouse. He takes it out of there and he gives most of it to the lawyer to put in the bank. So where's ours? Where's our cut? Where's our share?"

"We always get our end," Marcetti said. "If he didn't think it was too dangerous, he'd spread it around."

"What's wrong with having the money that's coming to us?" D'Amato demanded. "We worked for it, it's ours. I want mine. You should have yours. You keep losin' the way you've been, you'll have to put Gina on the street to cover your action."

Marcetti was amused. "Gina on the street? You're lucky she's not here or she'd bust your fuckin' head for you."

"I'm tellin' you, we gotta do something."

As he continued to count and stack the bills, Marcetti was torn by temptation, loyalty to Murphy, and the awareness that money washed through his hands without adhering, the same way water spilled off the grease that soaked into his skin during his hours at the garage. He wished that the idea had not even occurred to D'Amato. Gina was expensive. His luck was cold on the crap table, in the sports he bet, in the cards he challenged. He could really use an extra $150,000 if they could get away with it.

"Tell me this," he said. "We take the money, we torch this joint, and we tell Murphy that it went up in smoke. Then what do we do? Where do we hide it?"

A slow smile spread over D'Amato's handsome face. He was aglow with avarice. "I already got it set up," he said. "A guy I know in Maine—we used to do cars together—for 10 percent he'll take this shit and give us C-notes."

"That's thirty large he gets."

"Nothing's cheap. You still come out with better than a hundred twenty-five thou."

"Who knows, besides this guy with the money?"

"He don't even know. Just you, me."

"And Murphy? That sonofabitch ain't human. What if he finds out?"

"Fuck Murphy. He don't know everything. He don't know enough to give us the dough that's comin' to us. What do you say?"

Marcetti looked down at the stacks of money on the floor. "Yeah," he said.

D'Amato picked up double handfuls of the money

and threw them into the air, cackling happily at his good fortune. Marcetti smiled at his antics, but there was some trepidation behind his smile. Murphy was not the easiest man in the world to cross, nor the safest. And he had never done them any harm from the time he had guided them through the right patterns of behavior in prison to freedom and the big time of larceny.

For a man who was rarely imprudent, Humboldt was quick to approve the plan for the trapping of Dan Murphy in a hotel bed with a hooker screaming "Rape!"

The young woman was amenable to all the suggestions. She promised a dramatic rendition of the protest and an encore performance in court, if an arraignment of Murphy should be necessary to prolong his incarceration. There were some details to iron out first, however. One of them was the deposit of $25,000 cash to her account. The second was clear title to a brand new Chevrolet convertible, preferably yellow, but she would settle for bright blue. Third, she insisted on a letter of some sort that would be tantamount to immunity from arrest, a license to sin generously without fear of retribution or even interruption. All of it was arranged quickly.

Clappin, meanwhile, was given the job of seeing that software dowels were substituted for steel bolts in the door of the room customarily assigned to Murphy for his Thursday assignation. Unfortunately, he had to enlist the help of hotel personnel.

Two weeks after the physical and financial arrangements had been completed, the young woman was waiting for Murphy at the appointed hour, postal investigators were lurking in fire exits as well as a room across the hall, and Murphy was strolling from his car to the hotel entrance. The hotel owner was, at the same time, more than customarily visible as he moved across the hotel lobby.

When the tall bulky robber pushed through the door and strolled across the lobby toward the desk, the hotel manager intersected his path and said, "Dan, if you go upstairs, you're going away."

The manager continued on to his office, and Murphy made a sharp right turn and departed through the side door of the hotel. Two or three hours later, the young lady rose from her siesta and walked out of the room. She was aware that Murphy would not appear, but rather than waste the time entirely, had taken a nap.

Clappin stopped her in the hallway.

"Where the hell are you going?" he demanded.

"I gotta go check my service," she said. "I probably got work to do."

"But where is Murphy?" he wailed.

"How the hell do I know? He was supposed to come up here and rape me and he never showed up. What do you want me to do, go find him so he can do it on the street?"

They were unwilling to let her go. And they suspected quite accurately that she had informed Murphy of the plan. The young lady was transported to the postal annex and interrogated.

When push came to shove between the postal inspectors and the hooker, the bottom line was that they wanted their money and their Chevrolet convertible back. Also the letter. The girl told them to go screw themselves, which was at the least a redundancy since they had already accomplished that. What she was willing to give them was a large farewell, for she had already packed, transferred her bank account to another city, and was leaving in the morning with the top down and the wind streaming in her long red hair.

All of the threats and incantations the officers were able to muster were to no avail. The young lady made the final point that she was acting on the advice of her attorney, who also happened to be Dan Murphy's attorney, who had explained to her that what the postal inspectors were attempting to do was entrap an innocent man in a devious plot, to frame him for a crime that he had not committed and they could not otherwise solve. As a matter of fact, that very same lawyer was on the telephone at the moment, inquiring of the young lady's welfare and whereabouts. They informed him that the lady in question was just leaving.

At Reno's suggestion, Sam Gilardi was picked up by Clappin and Leibowitz as he was finishing his work and brought to the Postal Inspection Service offices for questioning.

"Think of the problem this sonofabitch has got confessing anything in front of that broad he's married to," Reno said. "For Christ's sake, she *believes* in him."

They had no warrant, but Gilardi did not argue. "We just want to talk to you, Sam," Clappin said. Sam was shaken enough by the events of recent weeks to accede. Alice would think he was working the evening hours on the restoration of their house, or negotiating a loan for the $18,000 in materials he needed, and would not be alarmed until after dark.

Humboldt conducted the questioning while Reno, Castle, Clappin, Leibowitz, and Manning stared at Gilardi with varying degrees of suspicion and hostility. Arrayed across Humboldt's desk were the items of "evidence" the investigators had gathered: the .45 caliber automatic taken from Gilardi's home; beside it the lab report dealing with the discovery of paint flecks under the grips of the gun and the matching of those flecks with the scrapings from the roadblock signs; the $300 that had been found hidden in Gilardi's closet; a copy of Gilardi's income tax return paper-clipped to an appraisal of the value of his house and the improvements that he had made on it before its destruction during the search. Gilardi was not impressed by any of it nor frightened by its presence until Humboldt started to talk.

"We've got you, Sam," he said. "We've got your prints on this .45. We've got paint under the grips that matches the paint on the roadblock sawhorses used in the Plymouth mail robbery. Either you or somebody else used that gun butt as a hammer, maybe to nail one of those things together. That would be the kind of job they'd give you. You're a handy guy with things like that, all this carpentry and stuff you do. That puts you at the robbery, or the preparation for it. Over here we got your income tax statement, and we got a good appraisal on all the stuff you put in your house. It doesn't match. You spend a lot more than you earn."

"I win at gambling," Gilardi said.

"Don't give me that shit, you miserable fuck," Reno snarled. "You never made a bet in your life. And I know where everybody in this city pisses away his money."

"Just three hundred dollars," Humboldt went on. "You didn't find it under a rock, and you didn't win it gambling. Once again, it's more than you earn. Buying all that stuff, all those tools, all that quality material. We know you know Dan Murphy and his pal Harry. They've been to your house. You think those neighbors of yours don't watch what's going on when creeps like that come into the street? They lock up the kids and the dogs and hide the silverware if they've got any. Do you know what all this means, Sam?"

Gilardi looked around the room. There wasn't an iota

of mercy in anything or anyone he saw. He shook his head in the negative and rubbed his chin and its shadow of bristle with one huge, calloused hand. "No," he said, a half-muffled grunt behind banana fingers.

"We got an indictment," Humboldt went on. "We got enough to put you into the robbery and nail you for it. That's not guesswork, Sam. That's hard evidence. A jury's gonna look at it and say this big dumb sonofabitch had to be one of the guys who took the mail truck at Plymouth. They're gonna convict you in about fifteen minutes, and the judge is gonna send you away for something like ten to twenty years."

"Maybe longer," Castle said. "They'll figure that because you won't talk and help us recover the loot, that you have to hang for all the others involved. The judge won't care that we'll get them eventually. All they know is that we've got you. And we've got you, Gilardi —you can see it right there for yourself."

"Were you involved in the Plymouth mail robbery, Sam?" Manning asked.

"I don't know," Gilardi said.

"Book the sonofabitch," Reno shouted. "Throw his ass in a cell." Reno pointed a stubby finger at Gilardi's eyes. "You helped steal a million-and-a-half fuckin' dollars. You're a goddamn robber. You think you can hide behind a regular job and your old lady's skirts? Well, fuck you. You're going away for a long time, and I hope you rot in the cell while those so-called pals of yours are out spending the money, riding around in Cadillacs, chasing broads, and guzzling booze."

Humboldt raised a hand to interrupt. "Take it easy, Reno," he said. "Maybe he wants to help us. Maybe he wants to cooperate and see if the court will give him a break because of his attitude."

Reno smashed a hand down on the desk. "Book him. Lock him up and throw the fuckin' key away. Throw the fuckin' key in a sewer."

Gilardi had never been arrested before. He was not familiar with the psychological tennis game in which the suspect is the ball being volleyed between the "bad cop," who threatens the worst of all possible consequences, and the "good cop," who holds out the hand of mercy and understanding.

"Gilardi, were you part of the Plymouth mail robbery?" Humboldt asked quietly.

"Maybe," Gilardi said.

"Was the money in your house?"

"Yeah."

"Where did it go?"

"I don't know."

"Who put it there?"

"I . . . I'm not sure about that."

"Was it Murphy?" Castle asked.

"Maybe. Yeah."

"Who else?" Reno asked.

"Well . . . I don't know."

"Did you actually take part in the robbery?" Manning asked.

"I . . . not exactly."

"What the fuck is this exactly stuff?" Reno demanded. "What did you do?"

"I just had the money for a while."

"But you knew where it came from. You knew what was going on," Castle said.

"Yeah."

Humboldt looked at Clappin. "Wheel a typewriter in here. Mr. Gilardi is going to give us a statement telling us how Murphy and Harry arranged to hide the loot from the Plymouth mail robbery in his house, and maybe some other things."

Clappin hurried out of the office. Humboldt turned to Gilardi again. "Sam," he said almost gently, "we can't promise you anything, but the more you tell us, the better it's gonna look for you. There are judges who will look at this as a public service, and I'm sure the D.A. can be convinced to recommend that you be shown full consideration for your cooperation. Do you understand?"

"Yeah," Gilardi said.

When Clappin returned, the six officers guided Sam Gilardi through an affidavit, which he signed and they all witnessed. In the document Gilardi declared that Murphy had arranged to hide the loot from the Plymouth mail robbery behind a loose wallboard in his basement workshop. He denied personal participation in the holdup or any knowledge of its planning and execution.

When it was done they let Sam Gilardi go home. They warned him that he would be kept under surveillance and that any attempts he made to contact Murphy would be considered a violation of the new ties of faith and trust that bound them together for the solution of the crime and the conviction of its perpetrators.

Gilardi refused transportation from any of the police agencies. He went home by bus and arrived at his mother-in-law's at about 11 P.M. Alice was worried, more frantic than usual. Gilardi calmed and reassured her, reminded her that he could take care of himself, and said that their troubles with the police were ended. He would not explain.

He made Alice go to bed alone and sat at the kitchen table with a can of beer, thinking. He had to communicate with Murphy. But how? To try to go see him or call him on the telephone was out of the question. All the old subterfuges were pointless in the face of his commitment to the investigative forces. There would be cops all over the place, watching every move he made.

But Murphy had to know. Gilardi finally decided on

the course that no one, particularly the postal inspectors, would expect him to take. He would write Murphy a letter, have Alice's mother mail it on her way to church one morning. Using a pencil stub he found in a kitchen drawer and the lined tablet Alice kept for grocery lists and reminders to herself about domestic matters, Gilardi scribbled out a few sentences about the .45 Colt and the paint chips and how he had been forced to respond to this frame-up. There was no date, no salutation, no closing signature. Murphy would know all that. Gilardi folded the note in an envelope and addressed it to Murphy in care of the hotel bar that was the one place he knew Murphy would be with regularity, and certainly a place where no one could expect him to be receiving mail. Gilardi went to bed at 1 A.M., curled a huge arm around Alice, and slept.

W hat does the hunter feel when he finds the fresh track of a great beast that still lurks hidden in the dark forest? Anticipation, excitement, lust for the kill? Fear, too. Fear that he has misread the spoor, that the beast's cunning is greater than his own, some doubt that he is worthy of this denouement. Exhilaration. Adrenalin pours, blood pounds, muscles tighten, all the senses sharpen. Humboldt felt it, they all felt it in one way or another. Vindicated. They had the sonsofbitches. Now it was only a matter of closing in and pulling the trigger.

Humboldt himself went to the U.S. Attorney's office in Post Office Square to bring the affidavit from Gilardi as well as a collection of selected reports about the activities of Murphy, Gilardi, and Gina Marcetti. The case against the woman was extremely weak, but her flamboyant amorality coupled with Reno's insistence that the woman had been involved in the robbery, en-

tangled all of them in a bizarre effort to substantiate
their suspicions. There was a great deal of mileage to
be had in an indictment and trial of this notorious
"blond in the case."

Daniel Hartigan, assistant state's attorney for the
Boston area, took personal charge of the case. He said
he would take it to a Grand Jury for indictments as
soon as everything was pulled together. There might
be some holes in the structure of their prosecution, but
they had to move soon before the federal statute of
limitations ran out.

Murphy's response to Sam Gilardi was simple
and direct, and a reminder of his earlier message. He
wrote: "You do what you have to do, and I'll do what I
have to do."

As Murphy fed his pedigree Siamese cats
whenever he returned home, so also did Harry feed his
pet German Shepherd and take the large dog, Wolf by
name and disposition, for a walk through the dark
streets near his home. It was agreed by the investigators that such a moment would be ideal to approach
Harry, for a couple of reasons. There would be some
surprise, and second, no warrant would be necessary
for a curbside meeting. As soon as it was reported that
Harry had parked Murphy's car near his home and
entered the house, Clappin and Leibowitz moved into
the neighborhood, parked their own vehicle, and
strolled toward Harry's residence. The wheelman
emerged twenty minutes later with Wolf on a leash.
The animal decorated two trees and a shrub, then
began barking fiercely at the figures of the two postal
inspectors standing in the shadow of a tree between

the sidewalk and the street. The barking turned into a warning snarl as they stepped forward.

"What the hell is this?" Harry said.

"We want a few words with you. Hold that dog."

"I can't hold him. He's too big. You come a step closer and I'm letting go of the leash."

"If that goddamn dog comes at me I'm gonna shoot him through the head," Leibowitz said.

"He'll tear your throat out before you have a chance," Harry warned.

The lights went on in Harry's house. His mother appeared at an upstairs window. Her voice carried through the neighborhood over the dog's continuing slavering snarls. "What's going on?" she shouted. "What's happening?"

"Call the police," Harry shouted. "They've got a gun. I'm being robbed."

"Wait a minute," Clappin said. "We're postal inspectors. We want to talk to you."

"Hurry up," Harry shouted to his mother. "They've got a gun. They're ready to kill me."

His mother screamed. Harry gave the dog another four or five inches of leash, and it snarled even more fiercely at the two officers.

"Hold that fuckin' animal," Clappin shouted.

"Help! Help!" Harry cried. "Call the police." Harry's mother continued to scream.

"Let's get out of here," Leibowitz urged.

"We just want to talk to you," Clappin said. "Get that goddamn animal back. I'm warning you." The warning was punctuated by the sirens of two city police cars coming into the street from opposite directions with roof lights flashing and sirens wailing in answer to several reports of mayhem in the neighborhood. Clappin and Leibowitz couldn't leave if they tried. Their best estimate of the immediate situation was that if they weren't attacked by the dog they would be shot down as fleeing bandits. The quiet street was in an uproar. Heads were appearing at lighted windows on both sides of the street. Men and women were shouting.

"There they are!"

"I see them."

"Here come the police."

"Get your shotgun, George."

In a moment, Clappin and Leibowitz were surrounded by four burly, blue-jacketed officers, their guns drawn. In the pandemonium, Clappin and Leibowitz had a difficult time explaining. Their official identifications saved them. But Harry had disappeared into the house with his animal, and there was no other conversation between them. Harry's parting words had been a threat to appear at police headquarters the following day to seek a warrant for their arrest. The neighborhood, like an occasionally erupting volcano, settled back to sleep with grumbles and snorts.

There was a momentary interruption in that calm three hours later when Harry, who had been asleep, was awakened by the sound of an automobile horn beeping insistently in the street. He rose from bed and looked out the window. It was Reno alone in a police car with his snubnosed .38 in his hand and his rage completely out of control. He pointed the gun in the general direction of Harry's window, and pulled the trigger twice before Harry could duck.

"I'll get you yet, you motherfucker," Reno shouted, and drove off.

The state police said they had come up with three witnesses for the U.S. Attorney. One was an airline pilot who said he saw Gina Marcetti standing along Route 3 with a man in a uniform on the evening of the robbery. The pilot said he wasn't very good at faces, but he never forgot a body—and Gina's was more than memorable. Another was a dentist who said he'd know Sam Gilardi anywhere, especially after seeing him on the overpass near the scene of the robbery the very day it happened.

And the third was a housewife who was absolutely positive she saw Dan Murphy in a state trooper's uniform at the roadblock on Route 3. They were all positive—positive—and the net began to grow tighter.

Because Sam Gilardi's affidavit gave the investigators a sense of security, a certain inattentiveness developed in the routine of surveillance, and members of the gang were moving around freely—with the exception of Sam, Murphy, and Gina Marcetti. Gina's husband and D'Amato were able to slip away from the surveillance teams assigned to their respective garages, get to the apartment opposite Marcetti's house, and leave with the money. They were spotted again when they showed up at D'Amato's garage. They drove the car they were using into the garage and it was assumed that the purpose was mechanical and not conspiratorial. But once inside, they stashed the money in the concrete enclosure D'Amato had built into the addition on his garage.

Behind them at their rented flat, they had left a stack of newspapers sitting next to a saucer containing about an inch of gasoline and half a votive candle.

They now took special pains to put as much distance as possible between themselves and the anticipated fire. They took the day off and went bowling, driving slowly for the convenience of the police on their tail. Their departure was noted through the FBI communications center and the information forwarded to the other agencies. Humboldt received it with some interest. He had a serious morale problem on his hands after the fiasco of the confrontation with Harry's dog. Humboldt summoned Clappin into his private office.

"I want you to go over to Gina Marcetti's house with Leibowitz. See what she has to say," Humboldt said. "We've left her pretty much alone and I'm not as convinced as Reno that she's really the one we want. But maybe he's right. As long as her husband's out and her kids are in school, spend some time with her. Try a friendly approach. She's a girl who screws around a lot and seems to respond to male attention. Flatter her. Maybe she'll drop something. You know what to look for."

It was a brighter, more hopeful Clappin who collected his partner and hurried out of the postal annex. His step was jaunty and his look was narrow-eyed and determined as he supposed a detective should look. This renewed sense of purpose and spirit was noted by Reno and Castle from their observation point across the street.

"That asshole looks like he's going to a Saturday night dance," Reno said as he watched Clappin lead Leibowitz up the walk to Marcetti's house. "He's almost as cute as you are."

Castle went over the edge.

"You're a fuckin' flannelmouth," he said. "One more crack and you'd better be prepared to back it up or eat it."

Reno noted that the FBI agent had unbuttoned his jacket and that his hand had remained in the general area of his belt buckle. The man looked ready to draw on him—and it occurred to Reno that Castle would probably beat him if it came to that. Reno preferred to use his hands as weapons. Castle's eyes told him this was not a moment to make a mistake. The man might be a pussy, but he had his limit and they had reached it.

"Take it easy," Reno said. "We're here to do a job." "That's all we're here for, so let's stick to it from now on. Okay?"

It was a difficult word for Reno and an unfamiliar one. "Okay," he said. They both turned to look out the blinds of the window and both could feel the tension rising from their bodies like clouds of steam.

Clappin and Leibowitz were apparently in the house. The porch was empty and so was the car.

"I hope he doesn't blow it," Reno said. "I'd like to hit her right between the tits with a warrant before she has a chance to talk to anybody."

In a way, Gina Marcetti had welcomed the arrival of Clappin and Leibowitz. She was bored and lonely. The Drake's man only came around once a week now. Both the O'Briens were dead, and God only knew where all those bullets had hit Rocky Gallagher. He might be singing soprano for all she knew, and since he got it only a couple blocks away, he probably wouldn't be coming back. Who wanted to drop in and boff somebody's wife while the cops were taking down the license number and running a check on the registration? And any guy in the bar who offered to buy her a drink might turn out to be some bum cop who only wanted to get his hot hands on her safety deposit key.

As Clappin settled into a large club chair that was Marcetti's favorite, and Leibowitz found a place on the couch, Gina seemed unusually pleased by their presence but said she didn't know why they were bothering with her. As long as they had, would they care for a cup of coffee? Leibowitz declined, Clappin took his black. After all, he had instructions to be friendly. Clappin noted that while Gina was well-dressed, her skirt was shorter than those being worn around the city and her blouse was one size too small and suffering severe button strain.

"Have you read much about the Plymouth mail robbery, Mrs. Marcetti?" Clappin asked.

"Oh, sure, everything. Especially since those two bastards—well, the one from the FBI wasn't so bad, the other one was a real creep, that Reno—they came here and started to put the pressure on my husband about it." She laughed and covered her mouth delicately as her body shook with paroxysms of amusement. "And him, he couldn't rob a kid with a lemonade stand for ten cents."

"But you've heard some things about the robbery, I imagine. You travel in a pretty fast circle. I imagine they talk about the robbery."

"Oh, sure."

"What do they say?"

"Say?" She giggled again. "They say they wish they knew where the fuck—excuse me—the money was so they could get their hands on it."

"Besides that, what else do they say?"

"Are you guys carrying tape recorders?"

Both men protested their innocence of such stealth. Clappin held open his jacket and Leibowitz mimicked the gesture. Gina got up and walked to the couch.

"Let me make sure," she said, leaning over, running her hands up and down Leibowitz's chest, ribs, and then back. "You're clean, as the cops say." Clappin rose from the deep club chair as she approached him. She went through the ritual of the frisk, concluding it by pinching the nipple of his right breast.

"Gotcha," she said as Clappin jumped and blushed.

Leibowitz thought the discussion was getting out of hand.

"Look, Mrs. Marcetti," he said, "this isn't a joke. Your

husband could be in very serious trouble, and you, too . . ." Clappin's sudden glare turned Leibowitz away from divulging the purpose of their visit, and Leibowitz picked up a new track quickly: ". . . with those kids to feed while he's in the joint, if it comes to that."

"Well, if I have anything to say, I'm not going to say it in front of a witness because it's only gossip and I don't want it to come back on me, if you know what I mean."

"What does that mean?" Clappin said.

"Well, I know a little bit about the law. I mean if I tell you something and you go out and find out if the gossip's true or not, that's okay. But if I tell you something in front of a witness and you decide I'm telling you because I was involved or maybe my husband was involved, then it can come back on me."

"Do you have something in mind you would like to tell me?" Clappin asked. "I mean alone."

"Uh huh—yeah."

Clappin looked at Leibowitz and shrugged. "Why don't you wait in the car," he said.

"It's okay with me," Leibowitz said. "I think this is all bullshit anyhow." Clappin returned to the chair and sat down as Leibowitz went out the door.

"All right," he said. "What do you want to tell me?" Gina crossed the room as sinuously as a leopard, slipped into his lap and put an arm around his neck. She stuck her tongue in his right ear and whispered, "I would like to sit on your face."

Reno and Castle watched with some surprise as Leibowitz returned to the car, got in, slumped down on the seat, and pulled his hat over his eyes.

"What the hell is he doing in there alone?" Castle muttered.

"Three guesses," Reno said.

Castle turned away from the window and walked

toward the exit of the apartment. "I'll see you later," he said. The thought that another investigator in the case might be enjoying the prize that tempted him so sorely was intolerable. He felt physically and emotionally bludgeoned as he opened the door and walked into a cloud of heavy gray smoke.

"Hey," he shouted to Reno with a cough. "The fuckin' building's on fire!"

The last days of July, 1967, were dark for Daniel Murphy. While the sun shone on the rest of Boston, he learned at 9:00 one morning that Joey and Gina Marcetti had tried to drive to Canada the previous night. They were stopped at the border and turned back when Marcetti refused to open the trunk of the car for inspection by Canadian immigration officers. Marcetti did a lot of public shouting about being a citizen of a free country who was entitled to take a vacation without opening his car trunk for anybody. Privately, word was around that he had panicked in fear of Murphy's anger over the loss of $300,000 in the fire that had gutted half the apartment building opposite Marcetti's house.

By 10:00, Murphy had learned from a detective with whom he occasionally traded information vital to both of them that a Federal Grand Jury was returning indictments against him, Sam Gilardi, and Gina Marcetti for the Plymouth mail robbery. By 11:00, he went to Noel Eddington's office with the thought that Eddington could arrange his surrender and release on bail without having to spend more than a few claustrophobic moments in a cell, only to find Eddington sprawled out face down on his carpet with an empty Scotch bottle in his hand.

$ XIII $

Trial and Error

The Federal Grand Jury, sitting for the Northeastern District of the United States, handed down three secret indictments charging Daniel Murphy, Sam Gilardi, Gina Marcetti, and "other persons unknown" under Title 18 of the United States Code, section 2114—specifically, with robbing two United States Postal employees of $1,551,277 and putting the lives of those two postal employees in jeopardy. Conviction carried a minimum sentence of twenty-five years.

Sam Gilardi expected it because he had been told it would happen by Humboldt and was assured that the U.S. Attorney's office would recommend consideration of his cooperation as a witness against Murphy when a conviction was obtained and it came time for sentencing.

Gina was surprised, considering all the nice things she had done to and with that cute little postal inspector, as well as the fact that she had not been anywhere near Plymouth on the day of the robbery (she tried for a while to remember who she was with that evening but gave it up as a hopeless mnemonics exercise).

Murphy responded to Eddington's incapacity by making an extremely important decision. He turned his defense over to a new lawyer—a young, vigorous Boston Irishman who had become one of the country's most famous criminal lawyers, F. Lee Bailey. After five years of skirmishing, the battle lines were drawn exactly two weeks before the expiration of the federal statute of limitations on the Plymouth mail robbery.

Sam was arrested at his home by U.S. marshals; Gina and Murphy surrendered through their attorneys.

"Boy, did you turn out to be a rat's ass," Gina said to Clappin when their paths crossed at the bail hearing before United States Commissioner Francis H. Farrell on Monday, July 31, 1967. They were ordered to appear before Judge Charles E. Wyzanski, Jr., for formal arraignment August 15. All three were released immediately—Gina on $5,000 bail, Murphy and Gilardi on bonds of $25,000 each. Both Murphy and Gilardi were represented by Bailey; Gina by Joseph Balliro, a Bailey associate.

Between the hearing before Commissioner Farrell and the arraignment before Judge Wyzanski, the press turned Murphy into something of a folk hero. He gave interviews to anyone who asked about the charges and suggested that it might be a good idea to go to trial, to be done with it once and for all after years of harrassment by the police, constant invasion of his privacy, and a bitter ordeal for his innocent family. There was no way that the government could convict him of the Plymouth mail robbery, he went on, because he was innocent. And that was that. Even his old pal Phil Kalis interviewed him two or three times and reported the same message to the public. A poor man, Murphy said of himself, he would now be hammered into the abyss of poverty through extraordinary legal expenses under the weight of the government's effort to persecute, the word he consistently substituted for prosecute. Gilardi said nothing and remained the "mystery man" of the case until the prosecutor's office suffered a small leak that said Gilardi had been seen by witnesses on the Cape Cod highway diverting traffic at the roadblock while occasionally talking with a tall beautiful blond, one Gina Marcetti. Gina remained mostly silent except to point out that she hadn't dyed her black hair blond until approximately two and one-half years *after* the Plymouth mail robbery and her hairdresser could testify to that. And no, she wasn't having more fun because she always had a lot of fun except when the cops bothered her.

They went before Judge Wyzanski August 15. Each pleaded not guilty. Judge Wyzanski set trial for November 6.

Bailey moved immediately to test the strength of the prosecution. He filed a plea for a change of venue on the grounds that "massive prejudicial publicity" would make it impossible for any of the three to receive a fair trial. He also demanded access to the minutes of the Grand Jury. Gina's lawyer, Balliro, simultaneously filed a plea for separation of her case from that of Murphy and Gilardi. The uproar over the indictments, which Bailey said should have come within six months after the heist and not four years, eleven and a half months later, brought an immediate order for a crackdown on the press coverage from Judge Wyzanski. He banned interviews which might affect the outcome of the case, pictures of the defendants, and any other activities that might come under the scope of what he described as "prejudicial to the due administration of justice."

That didn't leave much, but by then most of the damage had been done. Operating under his own doctrine of "fairness," the judge was ready by September 1 to permit Bailey to examine the minutes of the Grand Jury session, a transcript that is normally held in total secrecy. It became public knowledge for the first time that the government had made extensive use of electronic listening devices and wire taps. Bailey filed a motion for dismissal of the charges.

Meanwhile, Attorney Balliro filed a motion demanding that the prosecution provide a "bill of particulars" describing what they would attempt to prove in their case against Gina.

Wyzanski was prepared to rule on all of the motions by the middle of September. The judge denied the motion for dismissal of the charges. He denied the motion to separate (or sever) Gina's trial from that of the two men. He granted the motion requiring the U.S. Attorney's office to provide a bill of particulars on the role that Gina Marcetti was alleged to have played in the robbery. And he stunned the prosecution and the rest of the city by granting the motion for a change of venue, choosing to move the trial to the jurisdiction of the northwest district of the federal judicial system, specifically, to the court in San Francisco.

Judge Wyzanski expressed the hope that he would be the trial judge in San Francisco because he was now completely familiar with the case, the defendants, the lawyers on both sides, and the legal questions involved —a collection of insight and information that would require many days, if not weeks, for another jurist to obtain.

"You worried about this thing?" Harry asked Murphy as they sat near the window of a small restau-

rant in West Roxbury drinking coffee and watching
the flow of traffic in and out of a bank branch across
the street.

"Fuck 'em," Murphy said. "The one prosecutor's a
drunk and the other's a bum and they got nothing.
They couldn't convict John Dillinger of purse snatch-
ing."

"You always say to worry about the bad things. What
if they get lucky?"

Murphy ignored the question. "You notice how the
guard at that park over there always slips out to the bar
down the street at 10:15 every motning?"

The estimates of the cost of the Plymouth mail
job investigation ranged from double the loot to $20
million—and involved 104 years of man-hours. It all
depended on the paper of your choice.

The prospect of bringing Murphy and the others to justice in San Francisco caused a widening
schism between the U.S. Attorney's office and the
court. The prosecutors were appalled at the idea of
having to transport witnesses, most of whom lived in
the immediate vicinity of the robbery scene, and defendants and the judge, more than three thousand
miles, with the attendant difficulties of housing, feed-
ing, and protecting them. The government looked forward to a horrendous new expense after five years of
endless costs that had put only three of the suspects
before the bar.

Judge Wyzanski was also having his problems with
his own superiors. They let it be known that they were
reluctant to assign him to hear the case in the north-

western district, despite Wyzanski's logical contention that he was the only justice in the federal system completely familiar with the circumstances of the robbery and the cast of characters. They assigned a panel of three fellow justices to review the matter and the panel concluded that there were other justices just as competent and qualified in the west and that the government could be spared Wyzanski's hotel and travel bills. On September 18, Wyzanski called both sides to his courtroom to announce that he had decided to transfer the trial to New York City instead of San Francisco, obviously to enhance his own chances of serving as the presiding judge. The action came as a surprise but Murphy had a bigger one. He collapsed while walking into court for this hearing, clutching his broad chest and turning pale with pain. He was taken to New England Baptist Hospital where the seizure was diagnosed as a heart attack, a coronary embolism. The doctors were able to handle it, and so was Murphy, but for the moment, at least, he was out of action.

The Gordon brothers, who had been driven to the point of murder as well as bankruptcy, called Conrad to seek a truce. They had an even bigger problem than the thousands of dollars he had skimmed.

The man they had sent to kill Conrad and who had fled a sleetstorm of .45 caliber slugs, had returned to haunt the Gordons. The would-be assassin was virtually living in their offices, demanding more and more money, helping himself to anything that struck his fancy, from a variety of foodstuffs to a new calculator and including the pretty young bookkeeper. They couldn't refuse him; he was a killer and let the brothers know that they were bound to him by their excursion into vengeance. Further, if he couldn't kill Con-

rad, he could always kill them—and they were terrified.

When the brothers swore that they no longer desired
restitution from Conrad and insisted that they were no
longer angry with him, Conrad agreed to a meeting
and heard their lamentations. Conrad liked the situation. He had the answer, but it was not going to be
cheap and the brothers realized that they were going
to the financial wall again.

"I've got just the man for you," Conrad said, smiling.

The federal court's assignment panel was unwilling to accept Judge Wyzanski's transfer of himself
to the trial in New York City. The panel could not disal-
low the change of venue, but made it clear that Wyzanski was not going to be the presiding judge. The U.S.
Attorney's office, which had opposed the change of
venue in the first place and considered Wyzanski un-
reasonable toward their best efforts at prosecution, accepted the circumstances. F. Lee Bailey did not. After
examining the bill of particulars against Gina Marcetti in which the prosecution said it could provide
witnesses to place her at the scene of the robbery and
in conversations with Sam Gilardi, he felt that the
prosecutors were overreaching in desperation and that
Wyzanski's knowledge of all of the circumstances and
all of the individuals involved was crucial to his defense. He went back into court on September 29, with
Murphy sufficiently recovered to attend, and withdrew
his plea for a change of venue, asking instead that the
trial be held in Boston where there would be no question about Judge Wyzanski presiding. Bailey denied
suggestions that he was attempting to dictate selection
of the judge who would try the case and complained
that, in fact, the defense was making a major sacrifice

on the question of venue in order to get a fair trial under the proper circumstances.

Wyzanski agreed. He set the trial to commence on November 6 before the bench he occupied.

It was a lonely time for Harry. After so many months of constant movement, he was suddenly immobilized. There was nowhere to go and very little to do while Murphy limited his movements and rested his heart. Conversely, it was not a time to carouse or be careless. At any moment he might be picked up as one of the "other persons unknown" in the indictments.

His friends were sympathetic and tried to ease his boredom. Harry was sleeping fitfully on a cool night in late September when he was aroused by the beeping of a horn in the street.

It was about 3:00 A.M., and remembering Reno's visit and promise, Harry approached the window cautiously to peer into the street. It was the Actor in his Thunderbird.

"What the hell do you want?" Harry shouted.

"I got a present for you, Harry," Sternweiss said. He opened the passenger door of his car and with great effort, pulled out a 400-pound hooker who worked the worst dives of Scollay Square. "Have fun!" He propelled her toward Harry's door and headed for his car.

"Go fuck yourself!" Harry shouted. "And I'm not Jewish!"

There seemed to be a minor depression in the carpeting industry and Actor Sternweiss was spending more than the customary amount of time at home. Much of that time was devoted, in the privacy of his basement gameroom, to his practicing to perfection the business of death. When he emerged, it was to pursue his second major interest, organized sports. Baseball had given way to football on television and he was wagering heavily—as much as $7,000 to $10,000 per game depending on the point spread.

Because he liked to watch the events with complete concentration, Sternweiss frequently rented a hotel room, so that he could order a drink if he felt like having one, but primarily because of the isolation. If Sternweiss could be assured of silence during the actual play, he might invite a few of his associates to watch with him. They could talk business during a commercial or half-time breaks. He learned during one such break that Rocky Gallagher had emerged from the hospital minus two fingers of his right hand and carrying two bullets that the surgeons has found inoperable. Because of the condition of his hand, Gallagher found it difficult to quickly draw the revolver he normally carried in a shoulder holster, and he was now appearing on the streets carrying the gun in a brown paper bag that looked like a lunch.

Sternweiss was amused. He said it was a good system except in the rain, and it rained a lot in Boston. During another station break, he learned about the Gordon brothers and their problem with the ineffectual killer they had hired and could not now abide. Conrad solicited his help with the situation.

When the game continued, Sternweiss's amusement faded as he watched an incomplete pass, two fumbles, and one dramatic recovery, which cost him $7,000 in a wager. Enraged, he picked up the nineteen-inch RCA color television set which was bolted to a tripod metal stand and hurled it through the window of the eighth floor room, then stalked out. The others left hurriedly by whatever exits they could find, hoping not to stumble onto accidental victims of Sternweiss's rage.

After examining the evidence of widespread wiretapping by various police agencies, Bailey filed two motions with Wyzanski on the basis of "espionage" by the government in preparing the case. He asked for dismissal of the charges and, failing that, for suppression of the evidence obtained through wiretapping. Wyzanski reserved decision on both motions. The adversaries were locked into positions of combat.

In the last several days before the start of the trial, a lot of odds and ends got needed attention.

Rocky Gallagher left his house at 6:00 one morning, carrying the brown paper bag. He waited at the curb to be picked up by two young hoodlums he was attempting to train as replacements for the late O'Brien brothers. They were not punctual. As he stood in the morning coolness, a workman in overalls wearing a yellow metal hard hat and carrying a lunch pail approached him from some distance down the street, not an uncommon sight in Gallagher's neighborhood. Rocky ignored the man and concentrated on his impatient search for his transportation. When the workman was precisely behind Gallagher, the man raised the lunch box at arm's length, pointed it at Gallagher's head and fired two shots from a .38 caliber pistol concealed in an opening that had been cut into the container. Gallagher pitched forward and died in the gutter where he had lived as the workman strolled away.

A minor hoodlum who had proclaimed himself a paid killer (but had never successfully substantiated the claim) found himself in a ten-minute conversation with Actor Sternweiss. The man departed Boston within an hour of the conversation to take up residence in Los Angeles, and one of the problems of the Gordon brothers abruptly ceased. Conrad divided his $50,000 fee for the service with his friend and associate.

Six days before the trial commenced, Sam Gilardi got a phone call he said was "just Harry with some bullshit," and told Alice that he couldn't stand the strain of the constant harrassment by police and the news media while waiting for the trial. He told her that he had to get away for a few days. It was an unhappy parting, but Alice recognized its necessity. She assured her husband that she would be all right in his absence, that the children would be protected and comforted.

Gilardi made arrangements to leave in the middle of the night by taking his station wagon to a nearby garage for servicing. He slipped out of the house at 2:00 A.M. with spare keys in his pocket, walked to the service station, and drove off in a new car.

It became apparent in the days just before the trial that the proof of the charges was hanging by two delicate threads. One was proof that Gina Marcetti had helped reconnoiter the movements of the mail truck and had been one of the several heavily armed individuals who committed the robbery. The other was Sam Gilardi's affidavit that put the loot in his house. The prosecution hoped to entangle Murphy in these threads and bind him neatly for delivery to a federal penitentiary.

It was not a formidably strong situation for the prosecution, and Murphy's confidence was not shaken although his paranoia about being framed received considerable fuel. He knew as well as anyone that Gina had not been anywhere near the robbery, nor had she taken part in any of the planning. He also knew that the connection that had been made between the gun found in Gilardi's house and the detour sawhorses was fabricated. Sam worried him, but Murphy had considerable confidence that Bailey could protect Sam from additional manipulation by the Postals. His major concern was his experience with the coronary embolism. It was a well-kept secret from all but his immediate family that this had been his second such episode. Murphy believed the then extinct medical theory that most victims only get three—the third being customarily fatal.

So he tried to stay calm and confident.

It was a confidence shared by Gina Marcetti despite some nervousness on the part of her husband. She knew she hadn't been there. Her preparation for the trial, in addition to consultation with the attorneys, included a shopping spree with funds provided from the sudden surge of affluence that her husband seemed to be enjoying. Gina began a round of her favorite boutiques, acquired seven or eight outfits ranging from a light blue tailored wool suit with a fox fur collar to a smart, patterned silk dress appropriate to cocktails or tea in the elegant mezzanine lounge of the staid old Ritz-Carlton Hotel on the Boston Common. She wanted to enjoy her acquittal in style.

Sam Gilardi spent his self-imposed exile pacing a small motel room in West Attleboro, smoking an endless chain of cigarets. He had put his friends and himself in an extremely vulnerable situation. He had promised Alice that he would be home without fail on the day before the trial. Sam was desperate for Murphy's counsel. Murphy had guided him through a long, schizophrenic career as honest, hard-working family man and part-time bank and payroll bandit to the point where he was extremely wealthy, without a prior police record, and well loved and respected in his home and neighborhood.

If he had some idea of turning the affidavit against the prosecution in court, he needed Murphy to tell him how to make it work. But the connection between them had been broken. The manager of the motel would report eventually that apparently Gilardi left his self-imposed isolation only twice, returning shortly with brown paper bags containing food and cigarets. There was nothing sinister looking about him, and he was assumed to be a distraught husband who had taken refuge from domestic disagreement. On the night of November 5, that hypothesis was put to a challenge. The motel manager noticed that a previously unobserved dark sedan of late vintage appeared in the lot and pulled up in front of Gilardi's room. It contained two men, neither of whom was clearly visible to the motel manager or anyone else in the vicinity. But the men were obviously acquaintances of the distraught guest, who had registered as "B. Anderson, Bangor, Maine" and paid for his room in advance, with cash. They were admitted without delay, remained for approximately five minutes, and emerged with the guest, who departed with them in the car.

Mr. Anderson of Bangor Maine was never seen again and, of course, neither was Sam Gilardi.

At 2:00 on the morning of November 6, Alice Gilardi, who had sat up through the night staring into the darkness from the large, overstuffed couch that she had shared with her husband, got up and left the house. She drove to Murphy's house, approximately eight miles away, in the beat-up second car the Gilardis seldom used. She parked in front of the house, went to the door, and rang the bell. Murphy, who slept lightly when he slept at all, answered the door in an old flannel robe.

Alice did not give him an opportunity to speak. Pointing a finger at his face, with tears brimming in her eyes, she shouted:

"You murdered my husband!"

She held his gaze in hers for a long moment, then lowered the accusatory finger, turned, and walked back to her car. Murphy watched her drive away, then closed the door. He stood transfixed in the small foyer of the house, then went to the phone and dialed Harry's number.

"Yeah," Murphy said to Harry's sleepy mumble. "Alice was just here. She pointed a finger at me and said I murdered her husband. I think she's probably on her way to your place."

Acknowledging Murphy's record for accurate projections, Harry pulled on a robe and went downstairs to wait at the front door. He heard the noisy old car pull into the quiet neighborhood, then the rapid footsteps on his walk. He opened the door before she rang. Again, the hand rose and the finger pointed. The words were the same:

"You murdered my husband!"

Again there was a long moment. Again, she finally lowered her arm, turned away, and went back to her car.

Harry stood watching her in the morning cold, shivered, and went back to bed. It was a short respite.

Alice Gilardi drove home in a haze of tears, choking with grief, and called the police to report a murder, her husband's. She named Murphy and Harry as the killers. Since there was no corpse or smoking gun, the police were dubious—until she explained who her husband was. Within an hour, Murphy and Harry had been roused from bed again, this time by police, and taken in for questioning. Both said simply that they didn't know what the hell Alice was talking about and demanded to call Bailey. The lawyer responded immediately. They were all his clients, including the purported victim. When the police said they wanted to look into the matter, the lawyer said they were only looking at hysteria. He demanded that they either book Murphy and Harry for murder so he could bail them out, or free them. Either way, he had to get to a trial in a few hours.

The police released them without charges.

As long as they were so thoroughly awake, Murphy and Harry gave up any hope of sleep.

The trial commenced at 9:00 A.M., the first Monday in November, 1967. Gilardi's absence was noted immediately. Neither defense nor prosecution could offer an explanation for his absence, although Bailey suggested outside the court at a later date that Gilardi might have been kidnapped by gangsters who hoped he would lead them to the still unrecovered loot of the Plymouth mail robbery. Less flamboyant but given more credence was the suggestion that Gilardi had become a fugitive to avoid going to prison or to escape the vengeance that might follow his testimony in amplification and substantiation of the affidavit he had given the postal inspectors. Finally, there was Alice's theory.

Judge Wyzanski issued a bench warrant for Gilardi's arrest, granted a motion for severance of his case from the remaining two, and ordered the trial of Murphy and Gina to proceed.

Behind the sensational contributions to the media made by Gilardi's disappearance and Gina's stunning beauty in a wardrobe of unparalleled elegance for an alleged bank robber, the trial was uniformly routine. The jury of eleven men and one woman, with two male alternates, was selected by the prosecution and defense with no great difficulty in less than an hour. The prosecution introduced a group of extremely shaky witnesses who performed so badly that Judge Wyzanski ordered the Grand Jury to investigate two of them for possible perjury. The pilot who had been willing to place Gina Marcetti at the scene found himself unable to remember the dimensions of Gina's bustline—even after she put on a tight sweater for the witness's benefit. The entire court seemed to agree, with a good deal of laughter, that her bosom would make a lasting impression on any reliable witness.

The pilot testified that he later recognized Gina beside a swimming pool at a West Yarmouth motel where he had been asked to meet a postal inspector. But questioned by Balliro, he admitted that he did not see the long scar on her abdomen, even though Gina was wearing a two-piece bathing suit.

Fifteen minutes of surveillance film of Murphy, Gilardi, and Gina was shown to the courtroom, and spectators laughed when Gilardi was shown taking snapshots of the inspectors who were photographing him.

Twelve days of this and the case went to the jury for only sixty-one minutes. Gina and Murphy were declared innocent.

Murphy said he was going home to shovel snow from his front walk. Gina pointed out that she had obviously neglected both her husband and her children during this unnecessary extravaganza and winked suggestively at one of the jurors on her way out of court.

The last word in the federal case against Daniel Murphy was had by Judge Charles E. Wyzanski, Jr. At the opening of the trial Judge Wyzanski had criticized the media for overplaying the case and ordered the jury "locked up." Now, as the press broke for the door to report the verdict, the judge demanded that they return to their seats. In a prepared statement, he applauded the jury's verdict and declared his opinion that "this result could not have been as easily achieved . . . had you been subject to the errors deliberately or ignorantly circulated by . . . the press . . ."

Speaking on the responsibility of both the media and the courts, Wyzanski went on, "For a long time it has been known, not only to this Court, but to the proprietors of the Boston newspapers, that the news which they circulate with respect to this Court is incompetently gathered, inaccurately written, and melodramatically published. Unreal reports of nonexistent controversies have been spread in the public prints merely to make money for the press and to titillate the constant desire for sensation. . . . For some time the reporters who cover this Court have felt offended that they were not allowed to rummage in the Court files. . . . As a kind of petty revenge, some of the press chose to present in their least lovable aspects the images of some of the judges most responsible for strict regulations." Suggesting that some judges might be afraid to speak out against the press, Wyzanski concluded, "One needs the spiritual integrity, the intelligence, art, and independent character of a Dante properly to assign judges as well as others to their appropriate places in the three eternal realms. The Boston press awaits a successor to the famous Florentine."

And the word began to circulate that Sam Gilardi had "gone to Argentina," a mob colloquialism for permanent departure. A few days after the trial, on application by Bailey, Sam was declared dead by the court so Alice could collect his $25,000 insurance policy. She could always give it back if he turned up.

$ XIV $

A License to Steal

It is insufficient to say that Reno was furious. He entertained fantasies of personally destroying the members of the Plymouth mail robbery gang. Maybe that was the only way to get them. He had the list and he knew where they lived. He knew also that they had relaxed now that the first challenge to their corruption had been passed so handily. Not a feather had been ruffled on any of them. Only that poor dumb slob Gilardi was gone. His remains were moldering in the freshly poured cement of a construction project or disintegrating in the acid bath of recycled wastepaper. If the elimination of Gilardi had not been ordered by Murphy, so Reno thought, it had certainly been condoned when some of his associates suggested that Gilardi's affidavit and his projected testimony would fall too closely to the truth. They were all murderers as far as Reno was concerned and it was his absolute conviction that murderers should be removed from society—permanently.

He was also convinced that they were maintaining

an uninterrupted program of payroll and bank banditry throughout the area despite any attempts to
maintain a protective surveillance over them. Murphy
was just too goddamned smart for most of the police
who were trying to put him in jail.

The acquittal in federal court was, for a man like
Murphy, a license to steal, pure and simple. There was
another five years to go on the Massachusetts state statute. But what the hell difference did it make, Reno
wondered, if you couldn't come up with reliable witnesses or keep the ones you had alive long enough to
testify? Reno thought about the jobs that had been
going down. He was positive that Murphy had been the
mover behind several major robberies involving some,
if not all, of his gang. The Brinks truck that was robbed
of $131,000 cash on July 22, 1966, when four men wear-
ing halloween masks and carrying machine guns way-
laid the guards outside the Mitre Corporation in Bed-
ford. And four days later at the Jamaica Plain Veterans
Administration Hospital where three men wearing ski
masks shot and wounded two guards to escape with a
$68,000 payroll in a stolen panel truck (followed by
three other men in a white sedan who were apparently
serving as armed escorts to the robbers).

Then the Quincy armored car job. On April 1, 1967,
only a few months before Murphy would be brought to
trial for the Plymouth job, two guards left an armored
truck to pick up receipts at Sandy's discount store in a
Quincy shopping center. This time the bandits took the
truck that had been left parked in front of the store.
Two officers in an unmarked police car saw the robbers transferring the loot to two cars in a nearby parking lot and gave chase. Within the next half hour,
thirty police cars were in pursuit of the getaway vehicles. They were unable to stop them. One of the escort

cars was found abandoned a mile or so away with $94,-
000 of the $400,000 loot, but none of the rest of the
money was found and none of the robbers captured.

Reno was convinced that was a Murphy job, too, in
planning if not in execution.

A little less than two months later, bandits were
waiting in a Brockton bank as a Brink's truck arrived
with cash. The guards were jumped and slugged as
they walked into the bank and were relieved of the
cash. The take was $630,000.

Reno was certain that was Murphy too. Now he
knew there would be more, much more. The man had
to be stopped.

"There ain't a way in the world they can get
us," Murphy said after the trial. He felt hugely relieved
after the catharsis of having faced the indictment and
beaten it. So did all the others. While they still faced
possible prosecution under the state statute, they all
felt a lessening of the surveillance and the pressures
from the Feebees and the Postals at least. The revela-
tions of the widespread use of wiretapping in gaining
such evidence as was offered at Murphy's trial had
helped them. The authorities began pulling their
wires to protect themselves from charges of unconsti-
tutional incursions into the privacy of the suspects and
the fringe characters in the case.

It was such a relief that Murphy felt more and more
secure in meeting with Conrad, Jerry Sternweiss,
Harry, and even Phil Kalis. He was not so certain about
Frank D'Amato and Joey Marcetti, who remained valuable members of his attack team. The fact was he
simply did not believe the story about losing $300,000
of the Plymouth loot in a fire. He knew they had the

money or had gambled it away and he was wary of putting himself in a position of vulnerability with them. If there was no honor among thieves, there must be caution.

"Maybe you ought to retire now," Phil Kalis suggested to Murphy one afternoon in March of 1968 as they sat in Drew's Cafeteria and watched cars and buses splash the muddy residue of winter onto the sidewalk. It was this suggestion that elicited Murphy's boast of invulnerability.

"Retire, my ass," he said.

"But you got enough money. What the hell more do you want?"

Murphy thought about that for a moment, then said, "I want all I can get."

Murphy was the new hero of the underworld. He reveled in it. He was the man who had pulled the big job—everybody knew it. Many claimed notoriety by association in claims of having taken part. And he had gotten away with it in a stunning victory over the agencies that wanted to send him to prison.

He continued to move through the underworld with the same frenetic, peripatetic style, picking up information, seeing everything, planning new activities. Even thieves love a winner, and his close associates believed implicitly that he spoke the truth when he said there was no way to interrupt the operation he had created. Consequently, clusters of bandits gravitated toward Murphy, offering to cut him in on jobs if he would take over the strategic planning—tendering banks, payrolls, and armored cars for his consideration and asking only a percentage of the take in return; trying to be recruited into his small company of robbers for the obvious benefits of the "sure thing." Because his own manpower was suspect, Murphy used a few of the volunteers in small ways but he never permitted any of them to get close enough to gain an insight into his activities to an extent that would have made him vulnerable. Murphy was well aware how angry the investigative agencies were as a result of his victory in court. His fear of being "framed" filled his nights and days and contributed to his pattern of insomnia.

But it didn't interfere with his work. Quietly, as he did most things, Murphy had sent to Montreal for another unusually talented technician who went by the name of Shorty LeClerc. His specialty was the making of keys. Because the lines were strong between the criminal elements in major North American cities on both sides of the border, LeClerc did an active business with U.S. criminals seeking easy access through otherwise impregnable steel doors. Like any other minor genius, LeClerc's success depended on the secrets of his skill. He never divulged his methods but it was known that he could provide a device to unlock any set of tumblers created by man—if he could be given two or three minutes in close proximity to the locking device. Thus it is impossible to explain how he did it and is still doing it. While other lock experts required long periods of time to take wax or soft metal impressions of locks before being able to fashion keys, LeClerc was able to do it instantly.

A small, dark man with a mousy, nervous manner, LeClerc went through the world mostly unnoticed, slipping over the fence of a parking lot where armored vehicles were kept, or being boosted into a high window that gave access to a private garage for such vehicles.

If the quality of his work was high, his rates were higher. Murphy paid him $50,000 cash for a forty-eight-hour visit to Boston. During that period, LeClerc brushed against approximately twenty armored cars from various delivery services—over the fence and through the window in some cases, but also while the trucks were parked and the guards were away from the vehicles taking meal breaks in heavily trafficked commercial areas. Murphy soon had twenty keys, Le-Clerc was back in Montreal, and hardly a payroll in Boston was safe. The only problem was picking the best of them—a job, say, like the one that became known as the Canal Street job, pulled off three days before Christmas 1968, when the slush piled high in Boston streets and the day was cold.

There was always a lot of cash floating around during the Christmas period and it was safe to assume that most armored cars in commercial areas would be loaded with it. The driver guards parked their vehicles on Canal Street in the North End section of Boston and stepped out of the truck for a coffee break at a small lunch counter. Left behind in the truck with the promise that he would be provided with a container and a doughnut, was a messenger whose usual job was to carry the money in and out of establishments. He later told police that he was highly surprised when two men wearing black ski masks and carrying machine guns entered the armored car by unlocking the door and climbing in. While one of the bandits manacled the messenger, the other drove the truck to a parking lot three blocks away where $1,068,949 was transferred to a station wagon driven by a third man.

It was immediately assumed that only Murphy could have come up with the means of unlocking the door and walking in on all that loot. The assumption was correct. It was also one of the first jobs of its kind pulled within the city limits—Reno's bailiwick. The fact that Murphy was home in bed, quaking with high fever and the chills of influenza, in no way lessened his responsibility for the robbery—either in fact or in the enraged awareness of Lieutenant Reno.

Castle expected to be out of a job momentarily. His performance on the Plymouth mail robbery and so many other robberies that were taking place in the New England area of his responsibility was unacceptable to the Bureau and its aging, crochety director.

Castle had filed report after report, gone out into the street checking leads that were so infinitesimal that most law enforcement officers would have considered them mere dust specks on the surface of the case rather than potential cracks that would lead, if explored, to the heart of the mystery and its solution. Castle felt that he now knew every example of human vermin in the Boston underworld and he tested each of them. None of the information Castle had been able to gather was of any value in leading to Murphy, and a number of his informants had turned up strangled, shot, stabbed, or drowned as part of the continuing conflict for control of the criminal fiefdom in the area.

Castle knew that it was Murphy who was behind much of it. They all knew it, from Reno to that nitwit Clappin at the post office, that miserable excuse for a detective who had partaken of the fleshly delights that were rightfully Castle's. Oh, he knew about that.

Castle had begun to think about the possibility of resigning before he was transferred in disgrace and moving on to one of the reasonably remunerative security jobs that were usually available to former agents (unless they were driven from the agency under a cloud). He forced himself to pick up the telephone and call Reno to see what was happening on the Canal Street job.

Conrad was bored. He was also encouraged to show a sense of capriciousness, a complete contradiction of his normal attitude, by Murphy's renewed vigor and confidence. As usual, he had been testing the weapons used in the new series of robberies that the gang had launched. When he wasn't reading, he kept his hands busy making silencers for various weapons by packing short lengths of steel tubing with unsoaped Brillo pads. Fitted to the muzzle of the weapons, these highly illegal homemade devices efficiently muffled the blast of any handgun. They were ineffective after the third shot, though, because the gases from the exploding shell packed the Brillo pads so tightly that the noise started coming out with the bullets.

Six days after the Canal Street job, Conrad was en route to a meeting with Sternweiss and the wan but recovered Murphy in the storeroom of a small Armenian bakery that Murphy owned in his mother's name. Conrad was still suffering from his New Year's Eve hangover, which may have been a source of his uncharacteristic whimsicality. As he drove toward the bakery, Conrad noted that he would arrive fifteen minutes early for the meeting and he was not pleased with the prospect of waiting for his friends in a hot stuffy storeroom. He stopped at a corner phone booth. Through the information operator, Conrad got the number of the Washington headquarters of the FBI and dialed it. He deposited a long stream of quarters that had been part of the change in one of the robberies, and when an operator answered, he asked to speak to FBI Director J. Edgar Hoover.

"I want to confess to the Plymouth mail robbery," he told the operator, "but only to J. Edgar Hoover." The call was quickly given to an agent assigned to deal with cranks, nuts, and phone freaks. The agent believed he had a better grade lunatic on the line with Conrad, but was patient, and expressed a willingness to assist the caller in his confession.

But Conrad was adamant. He wanted to confess only to J. Edgar Hoover and would not settle for a lesser authority. The agent tried to persuade Conrad to relieve himself of his guilt at this preliminary stage, but without success. He transferred the call to his supervisor with a short explanation. The supervisor was equally gracious and patient. Conrad was equally adamant.

"No," he said. "I'm gonna confess to J. Edgar Hoover. It's a big crime and I don't want to talk to no low-level cops about it. If you think this is a joke, you'll be sorry if you brush me off." The supervisor was 98 percent certain Conrad was a crank. But even 2 percent doubt in a case as significant and frustrating as the Plymouth mail robbery could not be ignored. After several additional attempts to get the information from Conrad, who was pumping quarters like a slot machine addict, he finally transferred the call to an assistant director with an additional quick explanation of what was happening.

Once again, Conrad repeated his demand for the ear of the Director. Once again the FBI and the confessor repeated the *danse macabre.* Conrad was about to hang up. The operator had twice interrupted the call to demand additional payments. Conrad was also about to run out of time. Murphy did not like to be kept waiting; it heightened his paranoia, which at that point was already as unscalable as Mt. Everest.

"Hang on a moment," the assistant director said.

"Okay," Conrad agreed, "but don't try to trace the call. It's just a fuckin' phone booth in the middle of the snow and I'll give you the number here if you want it."

The assistant director put Conrad on hold. He thought deep and hard for a moment. It was a difficult decision. But the alternatives were far more dangerous than meeting Conrad's strange request. He put through a call to the director, and explained quickly and succinctly the nature of the call.

The next words Conrad heard were these: "This is J. Edgar Hoover. What can I do for you?"

Conrad took a deep breath and spoke. "I want to confess to the Plymouth mail robbery," he said. "But first, you miserable little sonofabitch, I want to tell you that if you put $2 million up there in your office in the Federal building, we'd steal that too." The line went dead. Conrad laughed all the way to the bakery.

"You should see the tits on this broad," Harry told Jerry Sternweiss. "They're about the size of watermelons, and they stick straight out. You could put dinner plates on them, pull up a chair and have a meal."

Harry was describing Murphy's new romance. It began at an automobile agency where Murphy was trading in his car. The woman on the switchboard was Francine DeVoe, and the dealer who sold Murphy the new Cadillac had thrown in Francine as a bonus.

"I don't know what the hell he wants with her," Harry said. "She's the biggest pain in the ass I ever met."

Melons, as Francine became known to Murphy's crew, was a lady who liked attention, a great deal of it, without consideration of the source. She would flirt outrageously in restaurants or bars and then bring the interest of the male stranger to Murphy's attention.

"That creep is bothering me," she would say to Murphy after provoking attention while Murphy was away from their table making a phone call or in the men's room. And she made it clear that she expected Murphy to do something about this supposedly unwanted notice. He would. Or Harry or some of the others would.

That was the point of the conversation Harry was having with Sternweiss. He was explaining that he had come late to their meeting because he had to drop Murphy off at Melons's apartment (a new one, a surprise gift from Murphy) and he had had to disabuse a paint salesman of his interest in Melons by waylaying the man in a parking lot.

"What are we supposed to do," Sternweiss asked, "go around leaning on people because this broad has a problem?"

"I guess that's the idea," Harry said.

"Horseshit," Sternweiss dismissed the idea. But it came to pass in the next several days that this was not a casual involvement for Murphy. He was deeply enamored of Melons and demonstrated his interest by moving her from the new apartment, when she complained about the quality of the neighborhood, to a small house in Jamaica Plain, and then to a large apartment in the city when she complained about the house being "in the sticks."

It was the first instance in the knowledge of any of his associates that Murphy had become a slave to his emotional involvement. Heretofore, to their way of thinking, he had correctly categorized sexual activity along with such problems as having the oil changed in his car. He gave his wife $75 a week and his hooker of the moment $25 or $50, and that was the way it should be. But that was not the way it was with Melons.

Murphy began bringing Francine along to meetings with Harry, Sternweiss, Conrad, Marcetti, and D'Amato. Her demeanor was overbearing and impatient; she treated Murphy's associates like employees who were present to protect the inviolability of her status as Murphy's paramour.

Sternweiss was the first to rebel. He concluded one meeting with Murphy where Melons was present and being generally obnoxious by rising from the table abruptly, turning to Murphy and saying, "Tell that broad the next word she says to me is her last."

He left the restaurant. Because of Sternweiss's temperament, which Murphy had nurtured and fully appreciated for its deadly potential, the occasion was the last in which Sternweiss and Melons were ever in the same room together.

Marcetti and D'Amato were the next to excuse themselves from any sort of meeting where she might be present although they were less pungent in their expression of animosity. They simply weren't available. Conrad also began to avoid her. And that left Harry, who found himself leaving the table with greater frequency for periods of longer duration at the bar while Murphy and Melons were dining.

Their disengagement from the core of Murphy's operations was made a great deal easier by the fact that Murphy seemed to have stopped working.

"He acts like a fuckin' goofy teenager who just got into the pants of his first broad," Harry complained to Sternweiss.

"Talk to me about something else, Harry," Sternweiss would say.

But Sternweiss, like the others, was seriously worried. The romance had brought a halt to their activities and kept a pall over their moods. Murphy, meanwhile, bought Melons a new Pontiac, which she didn't like, and later traded up to a Chrysler, which she considered barely acceptable.

They began to think of a variety of solutions. Sternweiss, naturally, proposed taking Melons for a twelve-mile ride out to sea on a fishing boat to determine if she could float back to shore. Marcetti and D'Amato suggested introducing Murphy to another woman, or two or three other women, to distract him. Harry proposed buying her a ticket to Los Angeles and making sure she was on the plane with an injunction, delivered by them en masse, against returning to the Boston area. But it was Conrad who came up with a scheme to distract Murphy.

He tried it out on Harry, who thought it might work, then Sternweiss, who agreed wholeheartedly. They met Murphy for a cup of coffee in a seemingly casual encounter and put the plan before him. Murphy listened, then thought, then smiled. He liked it.

"I knew you had to be good for something besides giving me grief," Murphy said.

They were going to collect the Plymouth job reward —if they could.

The police did not believe what they were hearing when word filtered through to them that Murphy was ready to talk about the possibility of telling authorities how they could recover the loot from the Plymouth mail robbery, if he could be given immunity from prosecution as well as reward money. Reactions were mixed.

"Don't trust that motherfucker two inches," Reno said.

"We ought to talk with him if he wants to talk," Castle said.

"When and where?" Humboldt asked.

"It's worth looking into," Manning concurred.

Word went back through the same devious route that the police agencies were willing to raise the white flag of truce with Murphy for as long as it took to discuss and negotiate a possible deal.

Four days later, Manning received a call from Murphy.

"Yeah," the bandit said. "I'll be at the corner of Comm. Ave. and Beacon Street at eleven tomorrow morning if you want to talk."

The car that picked up Murphy contained Manning, Castle, and a representative of the state attorney's office. Humboldt felt that the Postal Inspection Service could not take part without compromising itself and should remain in the background as an observer.

Reno said they were all nuts and walked away.

The three officers were struck by the relaxed, expansive attitude that Murphy brought to the meeting as he climbed into the car, shook their hands, and greeted each of them by name. They were more accustomed to the twitching, blinking informant who was worried about being able to walk away from any confrontation with the police. Not Murphy. He had the situation and himself in complete control.

"Well, Dan, I understand you want to tell us where the money is from the Plymouth robbery," Manning began.

"First, I want to know where the reward money is, and how much I'm going to get," Murphy said.

Thus began the negotiations.

The officers had too much respect for Murphy's intelligence and too much eagerness for the recovery of the Plymouth loot to attempt any subtle or devious suggestion that Murphy confess to his role in masterminding the robbery. Instead, they concentrated on the realities of a business transaction, the exchange of the reward money or at least a portion of it, for information that would lead to the Plymouth money, or what was left of it. The officers made the point that the return of the money would take a good deal of the pressure off the suspects in the case although it would not free them from eventual (and inevitable) further prosecution. It had gone too far to just forget about it, of course, and even Murphy understood that. The officers reminded Murphy that there was no statute of limitations on income tax evasion and that if the men who took the money could not be convicted for stealing, they could always go to prison for not paying taxes on their ill-gotten gains. Prison is prison, they noted, and pointed out that the return of the Plymouth money would probably eliminate the tax problem.

Murphy noted these considerations matter-of-factly and made the point that money was just as important to individuals as it was to governments. His family, for example. He had to provide for them, and it was a time of rising costs. Jesus, had they looked at their heating bills for the last winter?

There was a double meaning and a barely obscured significance in each comment or thrust on both sides. At this late date, the law enforcement officers were no longer interested in accusing Murphy of having taken the money. They knew he had taken it, and they suspected that he still had it in his possession. Murphy, for his part, also felt beyond bothering with denials. He had done that in court. Anything but a relatively straightforward negotiation for the exchange was a ridiculous redundancy.

"All right," the officer said. "Just what is it you want?"

"All right," Murphy said. "Two hundred thousand dollars."

There were groans of protest. The reward, totaling $200,000, was for the return of the money and information leading to the apprehension and conviction of the bandits. But Murphy was asking for all of it, in return for approximately one-third of its designated purpose. It didn't add up, and they could not justify paying it. Murphy replied that he could not take the risks entailed for anything less. There were dangers, serious dangers, for anyone involved in assisting law enforcement agencies in such circumstances. They knew that. So did he. It might be necessary for him to leave the Boston area for an extended period. Perhaps he would have to take his family with him. That was expensive.

That was his problem, the officers said. Theirs was justifying the payment of the reward money for limited services. They couldn't stretch it.

What did they have in mind, Murphy asked. They proposed $50,000 in return for a partial return of the money; $75,000 for as much as a million, and $100,000 for the full $1,551,277. Murphy said that was unacceptable. He asked for time to think and suggested that they give the matter thought themselves. They agreed to meet two days hence in the same place and drove Murphy to the same corner where they had met him.

A mass hysteria took hold of the officers involved in the negotiations with Murphy. After so many years of frustration, they had their first scent of a moment of triumph. They would all look like heroes if they could return to its rightful depository a large portion, if not all, of the Plymouth loot. Their eagerness colored their judgment and fogged their suspicions of Murphy. They felt that they had maintained a strong unified front in their negotiations with the bandit. They believed that he was as sincere as he could get, that he must feel the Plymouth loot was too hot either to use or distribute and that his only hope of profit was turning it back for a portion of the reward.

Only Reno stood aloof from this narrow perspective. He insulted them collectively and individually. He told them that Murphy had outsmarted every one of them at every step of the investigation. He made the point that Murphy had probably been the mastermind of two-thirds of the bank and payroll robberies in the Boston area over the last seven years and could not be suffering from a shortage of funds. They were dreaming, he insisted, and he prophesied that this would turn into a nightmare.

Reno was very succinct. "You're out of your fuckin' minds," he said.

They proceeded anyway.

There was a good deal of merriment among Murphy's associates about the forthcoming finalization of the arrangements to trade loot for reward. Murphy recounted in meticulous detail what each participant in the negotiations had said and how he had responded. As usual, he missed nothing, including the taint of alcohol on the prosecutor's breath, the perspiration on Castle's palm when they greeted each other, and the difficulty of the state police official in supressing his embarrassment at being put in this position.

He was equally careful in his preparations for the adventure ahead. He acquired, for a few hundred dollars, a used Chevrolet four-door sedan, noteworthy only for the roominess of its trunk compartment. He drove the car over to Marcetti's garage with an eighteen-year-old hot-rod enthusiast. Their assignment was to turn the engine of the vehicle into a speed monster, tuned to the limits. With that in progress, another craftsman was given the job of hinging the back seat that rests against the metal wall separating it from the trunk compartment. The supports and bracings were cut away. The result was instant access from the trunk to the rear compartment. The seat would fall down with a slight push and the release of a small catch that held it in place. Murphy also ordered a pair of wide gauge wheels for the rear of the vehicle for added traction. When the work was completed the car looked like any beat-up old crank on the road, but it was a fireball. In the hands of a driver like Harry, the car was probably untouchable by anything east of Indianapolis. Then Murphy went back to meet again with the investigators.

The cast was the same; the scene they played slightly different. This time, the normally obdurate Murphy permitted himself to be beaten into a grudging retreat from his demand for $200,000. He tried for $150,000, finally settled for $100,000.

The arrangements for closing the transaction were relatively simple. They would meet on neutral ground, a street in Brookline. Two of the officers—Castle and Manning were agreed upon—were to come to the meeting with a satchel containing $100,000 cash in unmarked bills of any denomination they chose. Murphy would come with Harry in Harry's car. The officers would come to the car, hand over the money, and Murphy would tell them where the Plymouth mail robbery loot could be found. He said it was almost a million, but not quite.

The meeting was set for 4:00 P.M. the next day. They dropped Murphy back at the corner.

Harry made a number of test runs in his new car. There were a few astonished witnesses to its speed and maneuverability, among them Actor Sternweiss, who went along for the ride and the amusement. Stern-weiss laughed all the way. The car jumped away from the newer, racier, and seemingly more powerful vehicles as if they had been nailed to the pavement. At the last minute, before picking up Murphy, Harry remembered to disconnect the brake lights and turn indicators. They wouldn't know which way he was going or when he was slowing down, and the only thing that would stop him was a concrete wall.

Castle and Manning arrived early. They had picked up the money at the Postal Inspection Service and again heard Humboldt's anxious request that they call immediately after the exchange. His entire department was alerted to be ready for a move on the Plymouth mail money. They had an armored car available for picking it up, and the plan was to use at least four additional vehicles as escorts. The money would be brought back to the office for counting and then placed in a vault under guard pending its disposition.

Castle and Manning remained silent, sitting at the intersection where Murphy was to meet them. There was little traffic. Each felt an occasional twinge of doubt, the unspoken echoes of Reno's warnings. But they were very close now and the moment seemed rich with potential for success. Each of them thought of the wasted effort, the weary attempts to actually solve the crime. Each pondered the bitter irony of having to pay a reward to the man they knew to be the thief.

Exactly on schedule, Harry's car came slowly into view. It was a filthy old wreck, just as Murphy had described it. It pulled up about forty yards away. Harry was visible at the wheel but Murphy was not. They assumed he was slumped out of sight, as he was known to ride from time to time, occasionally napping. Castle carried the satchel as the two officers left their vehicle. Manning preceded him slightly. The windows of Harry's car were so dirty that they couldn't tell if Murphy was inside, but Harry raised his left hand and jerked his thumb toward the rear. Manning stepped aside and guarded the door so Castle could deal with Murphy. Castle had one foot into the car when he realized that Murphy was not there. In that same instant, the back seat fell forward like a guillotine. There was Murphy crouched in the trunk pointing a .12 gauge sawed-off shotgun at Castle. At that range, a shot would tear him in half.

"Drop the money and run," Murphy said.

Castle dropped the satchel and stepped back. The supercharged motor of the Chevrolet roared and the car screamed away. Castle and Manning were left standing in a cloud of carbon monoxide and burnt rubber smoke. And Murphy had just added $100,000 to the Plymouth mail money.

The fun and games were over.

Every city cop, state policeman, FBI agent, and postal inspector who had touched on the Plymouth mail robbery investigation was looking for Murphy. Reno led the pack on the streets. He moved through the dingy dives and plush hangouts of the criminal elements of Boston like a rip-saw. "Where is Murphy?"

None of the answers suited him and he left a trail of bent noses and broken furniture. Everybody who had a hole crawled into it and prepared to remain there until the heat was off.

Castle concentrated on the scraps of information that could be picked up through the wire taps—and was attempting to compose a long and precisely detailed memorandum of how Murphy had gotten away with the $100,000. He was in serious jeopardy. But the entire community of crime seemed to have fallen silent. Nobody's phone was ringing; nobody was calling out. He was up against the wall.

Manning alerted the entire state police force to watch for any of the vehicles Murphy or Harry were known to use, particularly the souped-up Chevy. Privately, he let it be known that since Murphy was armed with a shotgun when last seen by reliable witnesses, it would not be regarded as untoward or over-zealous police action if Murphy happened to be wounded or even killed in the process of apprehension.

Humboldt was even more direct. Within two hours after Murphy's dash from the rendezvous with the reward, Humboldt, Clappin, and Leibowitz were banging at the door of Murphy's house. Murphy's wife let them in, although they had no warrant. They began an immediate search from cellar to attic while Mrs. Murphy screeched loud protests of innocence and ignorance about her husband's activities or whereabouts. When she attempted to block Humboldt's way from a midpoint landing to the second floor bedrooms, she was brushed aside and went rolling head over heels down the stairs to the first floor. In Murphy's second-floor bedroom, they found $290 on a shelf in his closet, and two bank money bags, which turned out to be from a branch of the Shawmut Trust, which may have been the only bank in Boston not to have been robbed in the last ten years. They confiscated both the money bags and currency as evidence and left the house without bothering to close the door behind them, or to see if Mrs. Murphy had sustained any injuries in her tumble down the stairs. She was only bruised.

It all failed. Murphy was gone. Reno decided it was time to put Murphy officially outside the law. He gathered up all of the information available on the Canal Street job, threw in a memorandum identifying Murphy as both planner and participant in the job and— unready for this step but desperate—turned to the U.S. Attorney's office. Within an hour, the Grand Jury was summoned for a special sitting, Dan Murphy was indicted on charges of armed robbery along with eight other men (most of whom he had never worked with, but who were viable as suspects), and a warrant was issued for Murphy's arrest. And while it is acceptable to avoid cops who want to ask you questions or punch you in the nose for playing expensive tricks on them, it is quite another to duck a warrant, which authorizes the police to hunt you down and perhaps shoot you if you resist the officers, or wear a tie they don't like. It's much safer to surrender. Murphy did just that under the protection of his lawyer, F. Lee Bailey.

On his way to jail, Murphy paused long enough to proclaim the occasion as a welcome opportunity to clear his name of this false accusation.

For all the bluster, Murphy was badly shaken by the arrest. It was Reno's monomania that frightened him. This was the frame-up he had feared. He had not pulled the Canal Street job, although he had planned it, and only the flu had forced him to the sidelines. To Murphy's way of thinking, it was not the same.

After spending the night in the Charles Street jail, Murphy was arraigned the following morning. He pleaded not guilty. No bail was set. Bailey protested that Murphy was a legitimate businessman who had not run afoul of the law for twenty years. The prosecution contended that Murphy was a dangerous and elusive bandit who could not be freed unless his possible flight would be a highly expensive adventure. Murphy said he was a poor man, and was returned to jail to await trial.

Within a few hours, Bailey filed a writ of habeas corpus demanding that bail be set for Murphy, or his client freed. He found a judge to grant the order, stipulating that bail be set within seventy-two hours or Murphy be released on a $50,000 bond. The prosecutor moved just as swiftly and, in an unprecedented move, the presiding justice of the Suffolk County Superior Court threw out the writ and set bail at $200,000 cash. And Murphy continued to pace the Charles Street jail. Shaken though he was by claustrophobia and paranoia, he also remained steadfast in his refusal to answer any questions.

For all of Murphy's strength among his confederates, they also knew well that he had certain weaknesses. They found it difficult to understand his paranoia because they did not share it. Most of them expected that at one time or another they would be arrested, perhaps even sent to jail, for crimes they had committed. It didn't make sense to them that Murphy was concerned about being put away for something in which he had not been involved since he had been involved in so very much.

Was there a threat to them in this circumstance? They weren't sure. Leaderless and worried, they decided to come together to discuss a course of action. Behind it all was the awareness that Murphy could put them all in prison with a few well-chosen reminiscences from his encyclopedic, photographic memory.

It was agreed that a meeting would be held in a small conference room of the Holiday Inn in Fall River on a June night. They were all there—Joey Marcetti, smiling, chewing gum, wisecracking; Frank D'Amato, grim and pugnacious, obviously concerned; Harry, looking blatantly innocent and, without Murphy, like a shadow that had lost its image and thus its purpose; Conrad, as nervous and jumpy as ever, never sitting in one chair for more than three or four minutes without jumping up and tugging at his belt; and Jerry Sternweiss, handsome and cool but touched with a frown of concern, an attack dog waiting in alert repose while its master is out of sight. There was only one order of business.

"Dan's got to get out of there," Conrad said. "It's going to drive him fucking nuts, locked up like that. He can't stand it."

"Ah, shit," D'Amato said. "You stand what you got to stand. He can put up the two hundred large and get out of there."

"How the hell can he do that, you idiot?" Marcetti asked. "He can't let anybody go anywhere near the money he's got."

"We have to put it up," Sternweiss said. "We have to get him out."

"Who's got two hundred thousand?" Harry wondered. "You? Me?"

"What if we don't come up with the two hundred thousand," Marcetti said. "And Dan goes bad . . ."

Marcetti continued to chew gum with snapping noises and his white teeth continued to flash. It was an evil thought, a shattering thought. They looked at each other in silence.

"Dan don't go bad," Harry said.

"Yeah, but if he does, we all hang," D'Amato said.

For a moment, each man looked into himself for stories that Murphy might tell about each of them.

"Maybe," D'Amato said, his glance going from one to another, "we can come up with one hundred of it between us. I know a baker in Roxbury we could go to for the other half. When you think about how much Dan knows . . . about him going bad . . . so we take him out of there and he goes away. Dan goes away. El gonzo. And he can't go bad anymore. We could maybe get the two hundred off Dan before he goes, or the baker goes away, too."

Simple expediency. Beg and borrow the $200,000 cash, free Murphy, make Murphy repay the money, then kill him. And kill the baker loan shark, too. Sternweiss got to his feet slowly and deliberately and leaned across the table. His hands and face were only a few inches from D'Amato's. And D'Amato was terrified, for all of his bluster.

"I don't want to hear anymore shit about Dan going away," he said. "For all this guy has done for us . . . if I have to, I'll go in that fuckin' Charles Street jail and take out anybody who gets in my way and bring Dan out of there. One way or another, he's coming out of there."

Sternweiss straightened, glanced around the table, turned, and left, adjourning the meeting.

"That guy's crazy enough to do it, too," Marcetti said. He was still smiling.

"Yeah, but you guys think about it," D'Amato said. "Just think about it. If Dan goes away, everybody here is all right."

It was the end of the discussion. They left and found their cars without suggestion of further association.

Ten minutes after the last car pulled out of the lot—which happened to belong to Harry, who had sat and thought in the darkness about what was happening—a lone figure walked from the parking lot into the motel and into the conference room, where the door had been left ajar. He locked the door behind him, crawled under the conference table, and turned off the small tape recorder that had been attached there. He removed it, slipped it into his pocket, and left.

Dan Murphy sat on the edge of his bunk in the Charles Street jail and glared at the small black tape recorder on the tiny fold-down table attached to the wall as the reels began to spin and the voices crackled out of it. They were easily identifiable, these gruff, crude members of his old gang, and they were talking about him. Talking about killing cops to get him out of jail. Talking about borrowing the bail money, making him pay it back after they got him out, and then killing *him.* The most cynical and ruthless of men, Murphy could hardly believe that his life and loyalty were weighed in such a manner. Where were the voices raised in protest or alarm? Only one. Where was the loyalty he had nurtured so carefully? Very little. Who spoke for Dan Murphy other than a professional killer who seemed to be spinning out of control?

Although he would remember each sound and syllable as he remembered everything, Murphy played the tape twice. He wanted to be absolutely, utterly certain of what he had heard, including the silences, the pauses, the emotions. When it was over he paced the cell for ten minutes.

"Tell them I want to talk," he said finally.

"Who?"

"The Feds. The Feebees. I can deal with them."

"What are you going to tell them?"

"Almost everything they want to know."

The shock that ran through the Boston underworld was beyond measure. Even to suggest that Dan Murphy had "gone bad" and started talking to the Federal Bureau of Investigation was unthinkable, unspeakable. But one of the guards at the Charles Street jail did say just that as soon as Castle led a team of FBI agents into the building and they sequestered themselves with Murphy. The agents could barely contain their jubilation. Murphy was spilling his guts, and what a collection of stories he had to tell.

More nervous than ever, more worried than he had ever been in his life, Conrad went to see Murphy. Why worry about guilt by association if Murphy was talking? That in itself was the peril to a thousand and one criminals across the country. It was once a boast that "the sonofabitch knows everything." Now it was an alarm. Conrad took Murphy several packages of digestive mints and asked after his health. Murphy knew why he was there.

"Don't worry. And you can tell Harry the same thing," he said.

"What about the others?"

"Marcetti and D'Amato are going away for lying to me about the apartment fire and wanting to kill me. The Actor, too. For other reasons."

"The Actor? He follows you around like a dog. He would do anything for you."

"That's the problem," Murphy said. "I created a monster and the monster is out of control. There's only one way to stop him. He has to be put away. It's our families we have to think about."

"Jesus Christ," Conrad said.

"Yeah," Murphy agreed.

Reno realized that Murphy had beaten him as soon as the Feds crowded into the Charles Street jail and the bargaining began. Their crimes, he knew, would be regarded as much more important than his crimes. And Murphy had them figured. Murphy would tell them a few things they wanted to know about the

big shots of organized crime they had so much difficulty reaching, and the Feds in turn would blow away
such minor incidentals as a payroll robbery here, a
bank job over there. What the hell difference did they
make, after all? A few million dollars down the drain,
nobody hurt except a few of the bastards in the same
business. Did anybody care about that? If they did, they
cared more about taking the dons of the Cosa Nostra
into court, humiliating them as much as possible,
tying them to murders and the larger business of commercial wickedness. That's what Murphy would give
them.

Reno felt momentarily sorry for himself, considering all the time and trouble he had spent chasing Murphy. But he felt even sorrier for Humboldt, because he
knew that the Plymouth mail robbery would never be
solved now. His only consolation came from the
thought that the events of the immediate future, and
the public exposure that Murphy would have to un-
dergo to make good his deals with the FBI and the
federal prosecutors, would put the bastard out of business. As good as Murphy was—no, Reno amended, as
great as Murphy was at his job—nobody would trust
him after this. More of them would go to jail because
of it. Their jobs would reflect poorer planning, shorter
vision, faulty preparation, ignorance in execution.
They would all miss Murphy.

Reno picked up the phone and called Humboldt.

"We've been fucked, sweetheart," he said. "Murphy
is talking to the FBI, and you might as well go back to
Portland."

Phil Kalis was among the first to know. He
suffered a spasm of anxiety so intense that it left him
staggering into a stall of the men's toilet at the Postal

Inspection Service, emptying his churning bile into the porcelain bowl. If Murphy was talking, was he talking about everybody—or was he being selective about the mortals that he plucked from the incredible data bank of his mind?

There was no one he could ask, because the Postals were a somber, sour collection of castoffs who were now getting their information from the FBI and not very much of that. He had no way of knowing that the one subject Murphy was *not* discussing was the Plymouth mail robbery. Kalis's rides on the commuter train became unbearable. Each roll of the wheels seemed to chant, "You're going to jail . . . you're going to jail . . . you're going to jail . . ." Sleep became virtually nonexistent for him. He began to imagine that every dark car on the street contained an FBI man sent to maintain a close watch on his whereabouts until Murphy's information could be presented to a Grand Jury for indictments. Then they would come crashing through his door. His career and his life would be over.

The gun in his hat had been driving him crazy for months, but it had been his only comfort. Kalis retraced his steps to the shop and bought two more pistols: one, a short barreled .38 of the sort police carry, which he wore in a shoulder holster; the second, a .32 caliber automatic, which he strapped in an ankle holster beneath his right trouser leg.

The hell of it was, they didn't make him feel any better, only heavier, as he staggered beneath the burdens of guilt and fear.

$ XV $

Judgment Day

The game, the game. Where does it begin? Where does it end?

Big Dan Murphy, fifty-five now, a caged lion who had successfully eluded capture for more than twenty years, had been the prime mover in more than fifty major crimes during that period. A staggering amount of money had come his way and been hidden away in bathroom walls or loan-sharking operations, a few legitimate businesses, and several real estate holdings.

But it was all over now. There he was, behind bars, pacing his cell, ready to talk. He was defeated.

So they thought.

Murphy's deal with the FBI was plea bargaining on a grand scale. He offered to tell them about planning a $25 million counting-house heist with the top mafia leader, the man reputed to be the foremost boss of New York. He offered to talk about assisting Actor Sternweiss in planning and preparing for the murder of two intruders into the Providence, Rhode Island, fiefdom. He offered to talk about the reported head of the organized crime operation in Boston, who participated in payroll robberies by "washing" loot into older, cleaner money. They were real prizes, these three top East Coast criminals, and Murphy said he could deliver them. That and much more—bits and pieces of background information about crimes and criminals. He agreed to go into court and testify, to name names, dates, times, and places about almost everything. The Plymouth mail robbery? No, he would not talk about that. His price seemed low. All he wanted was to walk out of jail after he had talked and resume his life. He would, of course, retire from robbery.

It seemed to be a fair bargain to the investigators. The deal was made. As Murphy talked and notes were taken, arrangements were made to take him before three Grand Juries, where he continued to deliver information against a number of minor and major criminals. He told the Suffolk County Grand Jury that he had planned the $68,000 Jamaica Plain payroll robbery but had been too busy planning other jobs to take part in it. That, he laid at the feet of some well-known Boston criminals who were promptly indicted along with the head of the local mafia family. They were eventually acquitted.

He told a federal Grand Jury about supplying Actor Sternweiss to set up the double gangland murder in Providence. Sternweiss and two other men were indicted for first degree murder, and the Mafia don was indicted for conspiracy. All were convicted. The don was given a jail term while Sternweiss was sent away for two consecutive life terms plus ten years. As he was being led from the courtroom, Sternweiss turned, glanced toward Murphy, and said, "Ask the motherfucker if he loves me now."

Murphy told another Grand Jury about planning the Canal Street robbery for six bandits including Marcetti and D'Amato, both of whom went to prison. Then he told another Grand Jury about planning payroll robberies for the top mafioso, who was arrested and questioned, but never brought to trial.

During the course of these Grand Jury appearances, and in his testimony at the trials that resulted, Murphy admitted to planning as many as twenty successful robberies and an equal number that were aborted for one reason or another. It took him about a year to complete his half of the deal. During that time, he had to repeat himself on many occasions and his testimony was precisely the same in each appearance. There was never a moment when either a prosecutor or a defense attorney could catch him in a mistake or a contradiction. By early 1971, it was all over and Murphy was free to go. The prosecutors kept their part of the bargain and no charges were brought against him.

It was Reno who realized about halfway through Murphy's courtroom odyssey what was happening, as he saw some men go to jail, others go free.

His awareness came with the conviction of Marcetti and D'Amato.

"Look what he's doing," Reno said to one of his men. "He's mixing up the cases and the crooks to suit his own purposes. He's taking people from one caper and putting them in another one with all the right times and places and even the money, but the wrong people, unless he wants to put them away. The others get off. The sonofabitch is serving as his own judge and jury."

The officer was incredulous. "Nobody could do that. All that stuff he's been involved in, nobody could remember all those details and do it over and over again."

"Murphy could," Reno said.